CW00542837

The Privileg

The Privileged Few

Clive Hamilton and Myra Hamilton

polity

Copyright © Clive Hamilton and Myra Hamilton 2024

The right of Clive Hamilton and Myra Hamilton to be identified as Author of this Work has been asserted in accordance with the UK Copyright, Designs and Patents Act 1988.

First published in 2024 by Polity Press

Polity Press
65 Bridge Street
Cambridge CB2 1UR, UK

Polity Press
111 River Street
Hoboken, NJ 07030, USA

All rights reserved. Except for the quotation of short passages for the purpose of criticism and review, no part of this publication may be reproduced, stored in a retrieval system or transmitted, in any form or by any means, electronic, mechanical, photocopying, recording or otherwise, without the prior permission of the publisher.

ISBN-13: 978-1-5095-5970-1
ISBN-13: 978-1-5095-5971-8 (pb)

A catalogue record for this book is available from the British Library.

Library of Congress Control Number: 2023948769

Typeset in 11.5 on 14 Adobe Garamond
by Fakenham Prepress Solutions, Fakenham, Norfolk NR21 8NL
Printed and bound in the UK by CPI Group (UK) Ltd, Croydon

The publisher has used its best endeavours to ensure that the URLs for external websites referred to in this book are correct and active at the time of going to press. However, the publisher has no responsibility for the websites and can make no guarantee that a site will remain live or that the content is or will remain appropriate.

Every effort has been made to trace all copyright holders, but if any have been overlooked the publisher will be pleased to include any necessary credits in any subsequent reprint or edition.

For further information on Polity, visit our website:
politybooks.com

Contents

Preface

The privileges enjoyed by some are an endlessly fascinating and at times infuriating topic of conversation. In private and online, people express feelings of injustice and exasperation. They dissect the ways power and privilege work. For them, reading this book may provoke all kinds of emotions. It might even work as a kind of therapy through the power of knowing. We hope, however, that it goes beyond therapy to initiate a serious and sustained debate that leads to social change.

In the game of privilege, we will argue, everyone is a player. So, if we are to write about privilege, we should declare our own. We have had many advantages in life. We are both white, well-educated and well-paid, and we hail from culturally, although not materially, rich families. One of us is male. We have therefore benefited from the many unfair advantages that white middle-class Australians enjoy. It should be mentioned that we were both educated at state schools.

Social scientists are nowadays asked to acknowledge their privilege because their privilege may get in the way of understanding the lives of those they write about. In our case, because we are studying people generally seen as well above us in the social hierarchy, our problem is not so much that we are privileged as that we are not privileged enough. If we had hailed from wealthy families and attended exclusive private schools, we would undoubtedly have deeper and more empathetic insights into the world of wealthy elites. The drawback, of course, is that we would be less likely to subject elite privilege to a critical gaze. We would see the world differently.

As we have not walked in the shoes of the privileged elites, even if we have occasionally borrowed their Havaianas, we utter the same gasps of dismay that pepper the dinner-table conversations of everyday citizens when they hear about a rich businessman or celebrity being granted an advantage denied to others. After the dinner-table conversations, we have been left wondering how this system of privilege works and why it elicits such strong reactions. It is our privilege as academic researchers to be in a position to take the time to find some answers.

Acknowledgements

We would like to express our thanks firstly to three experts – Jane Kenway, Elizabeth Cham and Ilan Wiesel – who read draft chapters relevant to their expertise and provided invaluable guidance and encouragement. Jane Kenway's extensive influence on our thinking will be apparent to readers.

Peter Saunders and Mark Evans gave generously of their time to read the entire manuscript and provide extensive comments that helped us improve the argument in a number of ways. We are grateful to them, as we are to two anonymous readers chosen by Polity to review the manuscript. Their expert observations led us to make extensive changes to the text, making it, we hope, more robust.

Peter Christoff and Christie Breakspear lent the project early support, for which we thank them. Peter Kanowski provided valuable data and background information.

As always, none of these scholars can be held responsible for any mistakes or misinterpretations that remain in the book. They all belong to us.

We are also grateful to the survey respondents and focus group participants who shared their time, perspectives and experiences in a way that deeply enriched our understanding of privilege.

Finally, we wish to thank John Thompson and the publication team at Polity for guiding this project from start to finish with professionalism and good grace.

Note: at the time of writing, US$100 = A$150 = £80, approximately

CHAPTER ONE

Introduction

It was the same during the Great Plague of London in 1665–6. As the Covid-19 virus spread in the early months of 2020, and London began to shut down, wealthy families fled the city for their sanctuaries in the country. Others took to their yachts or flew to Caribbean islands. Estate agents fielded inquiries from the super-rich for 'mansions with bunkers'.[1] Newspaper stories reporting the flight of the rich attracted a torrent of bitter and cynical comments from the public. The author Lynsey Hanley captured the mood.

> Our experiences of the lockdown are shaped by class. How can they not be, when the rich have escaped to second homes, when bus drivers and nurses are dying on their jobs, and when our ability to tolerate large amounts of time at home or to properly self-isolate is determined by how much space we have at our disposal?[2]

It was the same in the United States, with an exodus from New York's up-market districts to the Hamptons, the vacation playground of the rich and famous. One wealthy philanthropist who joined the migration from the city wondered whether, with the pandemic and Black Lives Matter protests, she and her friends would ever return.[3]

In July 2021, Sydney was in the grip of its worst outbreak of the pandemic and struggling to cope with its highest daily caseload on record. The whole city was in lockdown: workplaces and schools were closed to all but essential workers and movement around the city was strictly limited. The worst affected local government area was Fairfield, the city's most disadvantaged, with extensive poverty and high levels of low-paid work in essential services such as retail, care work and warehousing.[4] As it reeled from burgeoning case numbers, Fairfield also had among the lowest vaccination rates in the state, and not because of vaccine hesitancy. The New South Wales government imposed a much stricter lockdown on Fairfield and the surrounding local government areas than on the rest of Sydney and the state. Students in the area were being schooled at home, many in situations where both parents were working and education levels were low.[5] Home schooling was pushing many of them to breaking point.

It was a different story for children at Sydney's elite private schools. As experts worried that school students in Fairfield were falling further behind, students at Scots College, an exclusive private school, were permitted by the government, in an apparent exemption from the lockdown restrictions, to travel to the school's outdoor education campus in the picturesque Kangaroo Valley for a six-month camp. There, Year 9 students would undergo 'a rite of passage into manhood', according to the school's website, a place where they would be 'challenged physically, spiritually, emotionally, socially and academically', developing in a way that 'would set Scots boys apart'.[6]

Soon after, students at the elite private school Redlands (Sydney Church of England Coeducational Grammar School, where fees for senior students are A$42,000 per year) were permitted by the NSW government to travel to their Jindabyne campus, in the snowfields of the Snowy Mountains. Over their third term, at a cost of an additional A$17,000 each, students of Years 9 and 10 would combine intensive study with eleven hours a week of ski or snowboard training from qualified instructors and race coaches, opening doors for students interested in a career of competitive international snow sports.[7]

In July 2021, a surge in Delta strain case numbers prompted the Australian government to halve the number of Australians permitted to enter Australia from abroad each week. Thirty thousand citizens were stuck overseas on a waiting list to fly home to Australia.[8] Among them, stranded in India, were more than two hundred unaccompanied Australian children who had travelled to India with their grandparents before the border closures and had been unable to reunite with their parents since.[9]

At the same time, stories were emerging about wealthy individuals and celebrities experiencing no such barriers. Flying into Australia on private jets, they were granted exemptions from state-controlled quarantine in designated hotels and instead allowed to sequester themselves in luxury homes and estates.[10]

These incidents, widely reported and discussed in the community, soured the euphoric feeling of 'we are all in this together' that had marked the opening weeks of the pandemic restrictions. It seemed to many that the veil had been lifted, revealing the ways people with privilege can bend or sidestep rules that apply to the rest of the community. The public expressed dismay and anger at news stories about special treatment for wealthy businesspeople and celebrities. They resented it when children at elite private schools left the city for retreats while students at public schools in less affluent suburbs suffered at home, learning online in cramped conditions while their parents buckled under the strain of work and care. Social media and media comment sites lit up with aggravation. 'This surely is a joke.' 'One rule for them another for the rest of us.'

In short, the pandemic and lockdown experience suggested that a minority of people in privileged positions were granted special benefits and rights withheld from the rest. Watching this unfold prompted us to ask, 'How does that work?' 'What are its social impacts?' This book is our attempt to answer these questions.

§

When we stop to consider it, elite privilege is a richly complex object of study. Yet as a social phenomenon it is under-researched.[11] It's true that research *related* to elite privilege is extensive – including studies of inequality, the role of exclusive schools, luxury consumption practices and money in politics. But elite privilege as such has received little scholarly attention. The absence of critical attention serves to normalise it, to allow the practices and norms that sustain it to go unchallenged, and to disguise its social impacts.

Using evidence drawn mainly from contemporary Australia, our goal is to make visible the characteristics of elite privilege, the beliefs, attitudes and processes that underlie its reproduction, and its effects. What, in fact, is elite privilege? Is it coterminous with wealth or with influence or power? How, exactly, is elite privilege used to evade rules? How do elites signal that a benefit is to be granted to them and why do others respond by bestowing it on them? What are the ways by which social institutions and political structures sustain elite privilege? What are the emotional and practical effects of elite privilege on people at different levels of the socio-economic spectrum? What is the relationship between elite privilege, social exclusion and economic inequality?

While there are extensive bodies of literature on male privilege and white privilege, our focus is on elite privilege, the advantages and benefits conferred on the basis of having wealth or influence. Of course, elite privilege is interwoven with and amplified by male privilege and white privilege, giving rise to complex questions of 'intersectionality', which we consider later. Even so, we will argue that the distinctiveness of elite privilege is occluded when it is corralled with more common usages of 'privilege'. Nevertheless, we will see that recent work on male and white privilege can shed new light on the dynamics of elite privilege.

In the last decade or two, reflecting sharp increases in inequality, considerable scholarly attention has been directed to the super-rich or the 'one percent'. Thomas Piketty's work *Capital in the Twenty-First Century* (2014) supercharged the debate.[12] Piketty's historical data on the accumulation of greater wealth by elites led him to write of the emergence of a new 'patrimonial capitalism'.[13] The renewed interest is a return to questions of *distribution* after some decades in which social researchers had been preoccupied by questions of identity or *recognition*.[14] The surge of interest in the super-rich has concentrated on how they accumulate wealth and how they spend it, with some attention to the ways the wealthy shape policy and social arrangements to their own advantage.

Welcome as this new scholarship is, elite privilege is not the same as wealth. While often associated with wealth, elite privilege refers to the exclusive advantages and benefits that are *socially* conferred. These advantages are associated not just with wealth but with influence, two resources that are often but not always coupled. Two people with the same fortune can enjoy quite different levels of elite privilege, and some people with limited wealth enjoy many privileges. Elites in politics, media, the professions, academia and culture, where high status need not be linked to wealth, often enjoy extensive privileges. The cultural elite, for example, includes celebrities whose cultural influence may give them privileged status and access, irrespective of their wealth. An economic approach to studying elite privilege, therefore, limits our understanding. So, while our primary focus will be on wealthy elites, it is not their economic assets as such that are of most interest. And we keep in mind elites in other fields where forms of 'capital' other than wealth allow them to receive privileges denied to everyone else.

§

In this book, we argue that, to understand elite privilege, it is not so much who elites *are* or what elites *have* that is of most interest but the way privilege *works* – that is, the social practices and processes by which advantages and benefits are conferred on those with wealth and influence. It is these processes and practices that sustain, reproduce and legitimise elite privilege. Our focus, therefore, is on the social practice and social effects of elite privilege. Existing work on the composition of the privileged elite and what they possess (wealth and influence) is focused on the privileged elite themselves. The *practice* of privilege is less well understood. Where studies have examined the practice of privilege, in most cases the focus remains on the actions and activities of those at the top, such as their consumption behaviours. In contrast, we argue that the practice and reproduction of privilege is a process that spans social strata.

Our emphasis on the practices of privilege arises from the thought that privileges do not appear magically just because someone has money or power. Privileges are granted or bestowed by others every day. Elite privilege is sustained through broad social compliance with demands for privileged treatment and toleration of the institutions and norms essential for its reproduction. In other words, elite privilege should be regarded not as a mere by-product or perquisite of wealth and influence but as an organising principle in society, a set of social practices that sorts and reproduces social strata. The alchemy of these processes, how privilege is performed in interpersonal interactions and social relationships, is a central concern of this study. We take as our starting point the array of interpersonal, situational and institutional interactions and processes across the social strata through which privilege is 'done'.

Consequently, elite privilege is not just a private matter, something 'they', the elites, enjoy. Privilege is a social issue that involves and concerns everyone. First, everyone sustains the system of privilege by participating in the granting of privileges, whether that be in our daily interactions, our involvement in institutions that benefit elites, or our participation in broader social and political processes that underpin elite privilege. Secondly, in various ways, elite privilege causes harm. In the closing chapters, we identify three kinds of harm arising from elite privilege – psychic, economic and social harms – although the harms are implied throughout much of the analysis to follow.

§

In understanding how elite privilege operates as an organising principle, we sometimes use the analogy of a machine to draw attention to the social 'machinery' that sustains, reproduces and legitimises elite privilege. This *machinery of privilege* is comprised of the social practices and norms that confer exclusive advantages and benefits in patterned ways at the interpersonal and institutional levels to reproduce disparities of power, wealth, status and influence. Individuals, groups, organisations and institutions all play a role as 'cogs' or 'wheels' in this machine, but the parts most fundamental to its operation are institutions. We argue that most of a nation's important institutions, such as schools, the labour market, the legal system and a host of others are organised in ways that generate exclusive benefits and advantages to those who already have wealth and influence and deny those benefits to others.

This machinery of privilege prevents the ideals of meritocracy from being realised. Western societies proclaim their meritocratic ideals, and there is a broad consensus that we are working towards greater fairness and equality of opportunity for everyone, albeit with problems and setbacks along the way.[15] For gender and race, Western societies have indeed seen greater equality over the last five or six decades.[16] By law, and often in practice, women, people from culturally diverse backgrounds, and other minorities have more equal access to domains previously reserved for straight white men – domains including professions (from medicine and law to trades and professional sports), political office (from local mayors to national leaders), literature and the arts, universities, corporate executive positions, boardrooms, country clubs, and so on. However, we argue, the machinery of privilege has ensured that *nepotism and hereditary advantage* remain embedded in institutions, thwarting the aims of equality of opportunity and co-opting 'merit' to conceal the ways it strengthens and reproduces elite power.

Our objective is to make visible this machinery of privilege – to reveal how it is entrenched in institutions, the forms it takes, and its manifestation in a wide range of relationships and interpersonal interactions, all in ways that sustain hierarchical societies resistant to challenge. The more one looks, the more one sees that every member of society is a cog in the machine, helping to keep the engine turning over smoothly and generating its outputs – exclusive benefits for elites. The durability of the machinery of privilege explains why liberal democratic societies remain enduringly stratified and unfair and will continue to be so until sand is thrown into its gears.

§

A guide to the book's structure will help. In chapter 2 we explain what we mean by 'elites' and 'elite privilege', drawing on a combination of qualitative data on the perceptions and experiences of people from different socio-economic backgrounds and on the theoretical tools in the existing literature. Here, we rely on the ideas of Pierre Bourdieu, especially the distinctions between economic, social and cultural capital.

In chapter 3, we start our examination of the practice of privilege by exploring everyday interpersonal interactions, what we call the micropolitics of privilege. We explore the relational processes that underlie the conferral of privilege in everyday social interactions.

While the micropolitics are important, the components most fundamental to the operation of the machinery of privilege are institutions. Chapters 4 to 7 consider the role of certain sites where elite privilege is sustained, reproduced and legitimised. They explore the social practices and norms conferring special advantages that are embedded in each of the institutions and how they are oriented towards reproducing disparities in wealth and influence. The first site (in chapter 4) is elite suburbs and elites' relationship to space. Beyond simply localities where the rich live, these neighbourhoods are places where privilege is 'consecrated' and where forms of capital are actively accumulated. Chapter 5 investigates exclusive private schools, where elite privilege is passed on to the next generation. They are places where forms of capital are transubstantiated, facilitating greater accumulation of power and influence. In the machinery of privilege, exclusive private schools may be seen as the engine.[17] Chapter 6 reports the ways in which the privileged status absorbed through elite private schooling radiates out to other social institutions, such as the arts, sport, the honours system and the judiciary.

We show that the gains in gender and ethnic diversity in some of these institutions sit alongside declines in 'class diversity' over recent decades.

The final site for the cultivation of elite privilege, philanthropy, may seem surprising (chapter 7). However, on closer inspection, the fascinating world of elite philanthropy turns out to be a vital field for the consolidation of elite power and the extension of elite influence into society.

Across these sites, the role of social capital is essential to the operation and reproduction of elite privilege and power. Chapter 8 looks more closely at the networks formed and reformed by elites and the ways they serve to protect and advance their influence, both individually and collectively. It also considers more directly a phenomenon that has appeared periodically in the text – the relationship between elite privilege and other kinds of privilege.

While the operation of the machinery of privilege across many of society's institutions is detailed in the first half of the book, in practice that machinery is often veiled. In chapter 9, we analyse how elite privilege is concealed or justified as benign, such as by the spread of individualist ideology and narratives of deservingness.

Chapters 10 and 11 consider the second question raised early in this introduction, that of the social effects of elite privilege. They clarify the harms imposed by elite privilege on others and society – the psychological harms such as everyday slights and humiliations, the economic harms visited on others when elites exploit their advantages, and the corrosion of social cohesion and civic values when privilege is allowed to flourish. In the last chapter, we ask what might be done to curb elite privilege, offering several proposals that may be steps on the way to more just and harmonious societies.

§

'Researching up' provides practical and ethical challenges.[18] Firstly, elites are 'notoriously difficult' to gain access to, so the inner workings of elite groups are more difficult to study.[19] They are skilled at protecting themselves from unwelcome intrusions; after all, policing boundaries defines their status. If access is gained, the subjects can often 'set the terms for being studied, manipulate research results, and control dissemination.'[20] Ethnographic researchers need to be able to manage the interpersonal power relations and possess the right cultural characteristics to gain the trust of the rich. (In her study of super-yacht buyers, Emma Spence wrote that, 'in order to identify and engage with the superrich, I found that as a researcher I must possess, or develop, sufficient *cultural capital*').[21] In addition, wealthy elites have lawyers and PR experts at their disposal, and they know people in positions of power, such as newspaper editors, grant-makers and senior politicians. Nevertheless, a few elite researchers have penetrated the barriers and exposed to the rest of society how elements of the system of privilege work, and we draw on their research.

Even so, research has shown that one cannot rely on what elites say about their own privilege. As Shamus Khan and Colin Jerolmack write, 'the narratives that they construct in an interview are at odds with situated behavior.'[22] In their interviews with students at elite schools, they found that most students had a well-rehearsed narrative of achievement through hard work. Yet their observational research indicated that the students do not work hard 'and actually marginalize the few that do.' These students learn from an early age to rhetorically embrace meritocracy, and their schools, whose campuses are monuments to privilege, constantly reinforce the message. Posturing, suggest Khan and Jerolmack, 'is at times an exquisite art.'[23] It's also an acquired form of cultural capital. When the rich and powerful are interviewed for newspaper profiles, adopting a certain persona is the default disposition.

Adam Howard and Jane Kenway commented on the risks of alienating those one is studying – in the research process itself and by publishing discomforting papers and books.[24] Academic researchers who study elites may have a legitimate fear that those they study will use the law or their friendships with university executives, media editors and politicians to punish the researchers for writing critically of them. Still, as Gaztambide-Fernández writes, 'risk-taking is at the heart of what it means to be engaged in social justice efforts through research.'[25]

Finally, for some affluent, highly educated researchers, studying elite privilege may produce the 'personal cringe' that comes with recognising in themselves some of the discomforts and rationalisations that the elites sometimes display, a cringe that challenges objectivity and calls for a measure of 'dis-identification'.[26]

§

This book draws on a wide range of scholarly research bearing on elite privilege, augmented in the first instance with data gathered from government documents released under freedom of information laws, media stories of various kinds, and public reactions to manifestations of privilege across news and social media sites. Most of the evidence used to make our argument is drawn from Australia, although we often refer to studies from the United States, Britain and various European countries. We think that the contours of the argument we develop about elite privilege can be adapted, with allowances for national variations of history, economic structure and culture, to describe most developed countries. The rules of the game are broadly the same, whether they concern 'the micropolitics of privilege', the function of expensive suburbs, the role of elite schools, or the way the power of wealth is amplified through philanthropy.

For this study, new Australian evidence concerning perceptions of privilege and reactions to it has been generated by a specially commissioned public opinion survey of 1,229 adults. The details, including the interview schedule, are in Appendix 1. After collecting respondents' demographic data, including the type of high school they attended (public or private, high-fee or low-fee), the survey explored beliefs about wealthy people finding ways around rules, whether it's OK to use connections to get around the rules, and how they feel when wealthy people or celebrities are given special treatment. They were asked whether they have felt ashamed about where they live, the school they attended or their parents' occupation, and whether mention of the school they attended helped or harmed their chances of getting a job. They were also asked whether they believe the rules are applied fairly or whether there are different rules for the rich. Finally, they were asked how they see the role of elite private schools.

Deeper insights into public perceptions of privilege have been drawn from a series of discussions carried out for this study in eight focus groups. The details of focus group recruitment are in Appendix 2. The participants, recruited from Melbourne and Sydney residents, ranged over younger and older cohorts and were divided between those with average incomes and wealth and those with high incomes and wealth (referred to in the text as 'average income' and 'wealthier'). The 'wealthier' participants owned assets, excluding the residential home, worth at least

A$3 million, so few were among the very wealthy elite who are the focus of this study (the kind of person unlikely to join a focus group). We found, however, that, with jobs such as lawyer, tax consultant, doctor, finance manager and asset manager for philanthropists, our participants had had personal contact with the very rich and personal exposure to exclusive schools and were therefore able to offer insights into the world of elite privilege.

The focus groups explored understandings of the nature of privilege, beliefs about how fairly rules are applied, perceptions of unfair access to benefits and rights, attitudes towards elite schooling, and feelings of anger, shame and resentment at one's social position in a stratified society. The transcripts provide 250 pages of new data on this complex subject.

Summary

The differing experiences of the pandemic and lockdowns, in which privileged people seemed to be able to bend or sidestep the rules, caused widespread resentment. This book aims to make visible the practices, beliefs and attitudes that characterise elite privilege and allow its reproduction. Elite privilege, a richly complex subject, is under-researched. Our focus is on privilege associated with wealth and influence rather than with male and white privilege, although in practice elite privilege is entangled with male and white privilege.

We make two main arguments. First, we want to know how privilege *works* as a social phenomenon – the practices and processes by which it is sustained, reproduced and legitimised. Privileges should be regarded not as the by-product of wealth and power but as an organising principle in society. Secondly, elite privilege is not just a private matter but is a social issue. We all sustain the system of privilege by participating in the granting of privileges, directly or by involvement in systems that grant privileges. In addition, we are all harmed by elite privilege. The *experience* of privilege is therefore not confined to those at the top who have it; it is a force that conditions and influences all strata of society.

Finally, the system of privilege can be thought of as a machine that reproduces disparities of wealth and power. The *machinery of privilege*, or social practices and norms that confer exclusive advantages and benefits in patterned ways at the interpersonal and institutional levels, counteracts the ideals of meritocracy and is the means by which elites continue to use nepotism and hereditary advantage to remain at the top.

CHAPTER TWO

Understanding Elite Privilege

Who are the elites?

Any study of 'elite privilege' should begin by describing what we mean by 'elite' and 'privilege'. Defining the various elites may appear easy but is, in fact, troublesome, not least when attempting to establish boundaries between elite and non-elite groups.[1] Some clues might be provided by the membership of the Qantas Chairman's Lounge, described as the 'most secretive and exclusive club for the top echelon of business leaders, politicians, high court judges and triple-A gold-plated celebrities'.[2] Membership is said to be 'the ultimate status symbol, an acknowledgement of power and prestige'. Invitations, approved by the Qantas chairman, are highly prized because they are offered to a select few, those whom the airline's specialists assess as being the most influential in the country.

> Money alone won't get you in, nor will the lack of it stop you, and there is no membership fee. What it is about is that most desirable and intangible of all assets – influence. If you've got muscle – corporate, financial, political, sporting – you've got a chance.[3]

When members pass through the unmarked doors of the lounges they walk into a rarefied atmosphere – quiet, spacious, tastefully decorated and with discreet, professional customer service. 'When you arrive in the lounge', one member revealed, 'they ask if you would like a massage or a spa, or if you'd like to book a meal.'[4] Another described the lounge as 'a revolving door' of industry and government leaders. 'You'll go into the lounge and every time you will see someone you know. It's people in business very similar to you.'[5]

Arguably, the experts at Qantas who select those invited to join the club know more than anyone about identifying Australia's elites.

Although other airlines have invitation-only exclusive status cards – BA has Executive Club Premier, American Airlines has ConciergeKey and Emirates hand delivers a card to those chosen for its iO status – Qantas seems to explicitly target the nation's power elite.[6]

How Qantas identifies the most influential among the power elite is 'a tightly guarded secret'.[7] It's likely to involve more art than science and to be biased towards those who can contribute to the airline's commercial interests. In this book we will use a moveable definition of 'elite' depending on the context, albeit with an emphasis on the wealthiest.[8] Reflecting sharp increases in inequality in recent decades, attention has been drawn to the 'the one percent' of top wealth owners. Thomas Piketty's pioneering work points to the disproportionate growth in the wealth of the top centile (the 1 per cent) and the top tenth of the one percenters (the 0.1 per cent). Both, and even more so for the top 0.1 per cent, derive their income and wealth not from salaries but from returns to capital – dividends, interest and capital gains.[9] Below the 1 per cent, among the top 9 per cent of income earners we find 'doctors, lawyers, merchants, restauranteurs, and other self-employed entrepreneurs'.[10] But, as long as they depend mainly on their wage and salary incomes, they will not be elevated in the stratosphere of the 1 per cent and certainly not the 0.1 per cent. Earned income is not enough.

In studying elite privilege, elites other than the rich ought to be included (we discuss three in a later section). In the extensive literature on elites in sociology and political science, the emphasis is on the power they exert.[11] When the focus is on influence as well as power, to the wealthy elite must be added elites in the fields of business, politics, bureaucracy, media, academia and culture, those with enough status to gain exclusive access to resources or rights. Notice that the injustices of privilege are not delimited by inequalities of wealth and income, though they are often closely aligned with them.

Recognising privilege

Although there is an extensive literature on male and white privilege, the privilege of elites, although often mentioned, has received limited systematic attention. As a phenomenon it evades clear definition. Alison Bailey describes privilege as the unearned advantages of dominant groups, advantages systematically conferred by social institutions and beyond those available to marginalised citizens.[12] Bob Pease adopts a similar approach in his compendium of kinds of privilege.[13] The idea of its being unearned advantage is more helpful for describing privilege arising from differences in gender and race, categories that are more clear cut. For privilege due to differences in wealth and influence, the distinction between earned and unearned, like the distinction between deserving and undeserving, lies in a grey zone, both contestable and morally ambiguous. The public is divided over whether those with wealth are entitled to the advantages that go with it, with some – and not just the rich – believing that even great wealth can be earned – that is, justified – if it is obtained by hard work, thrift and virtuous behaviour, as we will see. We prefer the term 'exclusive benefits' to reflect the fact that the benefits, earned or unearned, are not available to people who lack sufficient status to be eligible to receive them.

When asked what privilege means, our focus group participants began with wealth and what it can buy. Privilege means 'not having to worry about money,' said one. They commented on the absence of obstacles and the opportunities open to the wealthy that are closed to others.

So when I think of privilege, I think of a lack of barriers, whether it's education, travel, jobs. It's a lack of barriers that you need to consider to do what you want and follow your dreams. (Ashley, average income, younger, Sydney)

Well, I suppose it means being able to go to the best schools, having private health cover, living in one of the more leafier suburbs. Just having more opportunities, I suppose, than some other people. (Farah, average income, older, Melbourne)

A second feature of privilege stressed in the literature is the set of qualities or psychological dispositions possessed by members of the elite. In their study of privilege in elite girls' schools in the United Kingdom, Claire Maxwell and Peter Aggleton write:

The term 'privilege' can be used to describe the set of self-understandings, dispositions and worldviews observed among young people and families, who largely see power as natural or unquestioned. Privilege is connected both to a person (as a set of attributes or as an identity) and to being embedded within a particular space – in this case a private/elite school – which 'shapes and interacts with subjects who cross or inhabit this terrain'.[14]

When asked how they recognise privileged people, focus group participants frequently stressed disposition and personal presentation. Many referred to their bearing or, as one put it, 'having a certain way about you'.

> I'm occasionally at a function and I can pretty much work out who the key players are relatively quickly, just in the way they carry themselves, the confidence they have. They certainly have an ability to speak with a level of confidence others potentially don't have. (Mark, wealthier, older, Melbourne)

> The way they present themselves or if they're describing themselves to you, sometimes they like to talk about themselves more than ask you questions. (Luca, average income, younger, Sydney)

> I think it's a mixture of like dress, job, where they live, but then also how they hold themselves. (Ashley, average income, younger, Sydney)

These members of the public recognise privilege as *embodied*. Patterns of socialisation are written into the body; the external is internalised through largely unconscious imitation. Embodiment includes posture, stride, mannerisms, facial expressions, accent, and manner of speaking, a kind of muscle memory of class. These patterns are also inscribed in our mental habits, our ways of classifying and valuing the world, aesthetic appreciations, feelings and so on. As we will see, these internalised lessons from the past have a powerful role in shaping our future life course, much more than we care to admit in a society supposed to be meritocratic.

Observing girls at elite schools, Maxwell and Aggleton were struck by their 'surety' – that is, the sense of uniqueness and 'confidence in their future educational and employment success'.[15] Our focus group participants commented on the surety of the privileged elites. Josh (wealthier, younger, Sydney) had attended an elite private school and regarded himself as privileged. He spoke of the unconscious 'assumptions that we build into ourselves, often granted to us by circumstance'. *What kind of circumstance?* 'Birth mostly.'

> ... they're usually confident I find and sure of themselves. (Farah, average income, older, Melbourne)

> The way they talk, how they conduct themselves ... a bit of a show off kind of a feel about them. (Phillip, average income, older, Melbourne)

Observations about how people hold themselves and exude confidence are akin to Pierre Bourdieu's idea of *habitus* – that is, one's preconscious disposition, bodily orientation, sense of self, tacit knowledge, cultural preferences and mastery of the subtle rules of the game.[16] Although some not born to it attempt to simulate the habitus of the wealthy elite, these sensibilities are learned or, rather, absorbed in the family home and childhood milieu, including elite schools. Josh, from a wealthy but not super-rich family, found himself becoming friendly with an 'extraordinarily wealthy' family that inhabited another world: 'I've had enough times by now with this family to build a rapport with them and to even get into some difficult political arguments with them. But you can never wipe away that smell of wealth' (Josh, wealthier, younger, Sydney).

The correspondence between wealth and certain ways of being in the world are strong enough to give rise to cognitive dissonance when they appear to conflict. The apparent oxymoron 'bogan billionaire' or 'boganaire'[17] was applied to Nathan Tinkler – a working-class man who through luck and entrepreneurial flair found himself in possession of a fortune.[18] Tinkler splashed out on racehorses, fast cars and McMansions, and when he lost his fortune, the media presented it as the tradie returning to his rightful place.

In addition to wealth and disposition, certain attitudes, beliefs and behaviours are often associated with privilege. It is the role of habitus, Riley notes, to translate different class positions into observable behaviour.[19] Although there is some stereotyping, there is enough recognisable evidence to justify the assumptions, at least, according to our focus group participants.

I have a colleague ... [and] when we were talking about saving for a house deposit, she was just saying, 'Oh, my parents gave me 500 grand. Doesn't everyone have that?' (Drew, average income, younger, Sydney)

On the other hand, a few participants stressed that wealth and privileged attitudes do not necessarily go together.

You can have a very privileged attitude, a very privileged personality type, but actually don't come from a privileged background in any way, shape or form. You know, one of the better expressions, you just might be an arrogant turd. (Ryan, average income, younger, Sydney)

And going the other way:

I work with a lot of philanthropists, a lot of people that have a lot of wealth and are giving it away. And they're very humble and want to learn. (Hana, wealthier, older, Melbourne)

I've got a mate who's a doctor, a specialist doctor. He definitely earns a hell of a lot more than I do. But he's pretty down to earth and friendly. ... But then I've met doctors in hospitals who are complete wankers as well. (Luke, average income, younger, Melbourne)

Some analysts focus on the *relational* nature of privilege. Alan France and others write of how it 'reflects not only an individual's wealth, but also access to institutional, social and intergenerational attributes of families within a specific field.'[20] In the literature, 'relational' is used in two distinct ways: one refers to the relationship between the privileged and those deemed the Other; the second refers to the relationship between the privileged and the system that confers advantages on them.[21] Our emphasis on the doing of privilege (explained in the next chapter) focuses on the relationship between members of elites that seek the award of privileges and those in a position to bestow privileges on them, whether the bestowers themselves are privileged or not.

Although the presence of 'the Other' was apparent in the focus group conversations, especially in the wealthier groups, boundaries between social strata are blurred, even at the very top of the wealth distribution, as the case of Nathan Tinkler indicates. In her study of American and French upper-middle classes, Michelle Lamont identifies three kinds of boundary between social strata, divisions that recurred repeatedly in our focus group conversations (as we'll see).[22] Socio-economic boundaries delineate social positions based on wealth, power and professional success. Cultural boundaries separate strata according to education, disposition, tastes and affinity to higher forms of culture. A moral boundary is drawn when superior moral qualities, such as honesty, reliability, trustworthiness and 'character', are expected of the wealthy elite. As we will see, we can map 'moral geographies' across cities, attributing value to people according to where they live.

Helpful concepts

As the membership of the Chairman's Lounge attests, wealth alone, although it goes a long way, is not a necessary marker of elite status. A purely economic approach ignores elites in politics, public administration, the professions, media, culture and academia, 'where the command of disproportionate resources is not always, or only, economic.'[23] There are two elements of this. The first is the existence of other elites who gain privileges less from their wealth and more from their positions of power and influence. The second is the way in which types of capital other than financial can amplify the privileges associated with wealth.[24]

Elites are aggregations of powerful individuals drawn together by social, professional or cultural links. Thinking of them in this way allows us to notice that there are various elites mobilising resources or 'types of capital' in different social spaces or fields, even if they sometimes overlap in membership. Pierre Bourdieu distinguishes four types of capital – financial, social, cultural and symbolic. They provide a conceptual framework for looking beyond wealth (financial capital) to capture the roles of personal connections and influence networks (social capital), the dispositions, knowledge and behaviours required to reproduce and enhance privilege, status and wealth (cultural capital) and the awards, credentials and prestigious positions that signal esteem (symbolic capital). These forms of capital are *fungible* – that is, they can be converted into one another – although some are more liquid than others. (Cultural capital, for example, requires a long time to build, while fortunes can be made quickly.) These concepts, considered in more detail in the next section, provide a valuable framework in the chapters that follow.

Bourdieu, whose focus was on social stratification through cultural differences, saw financial capital 'at the root of all the other types of capital', which were only transformed and disguised forms of wealth.[25] In our view, social and cultural capital have their own potency in particular fields, providing the leaders in those fields with access to privilege. Although they are rarely poor, some powerful elite figures are not necessarily wealthy. Political leaders, newspaper editors and certain kinds of academics and celebrities come to mind.

We use the notion of *field*, borrowed from Bourdieu, to refer to a social space of shared interests in which elites operate. Each field has its own culture, boundaries and rules of the game. The composition of capital owned by elites in differing fields varies. A newly minted billionaire may not have much cultural capital, but the director of the National Gallery would have a surfeit of it. As we will see, members of elites often mobilise their resources across several fields, competing and cooperating to improve their positions, accumulating more resources and privileges. An elite member influential in one field may have little influence in another. Elites in the law, politics, the civil service, media, culture and academia are likely to be awarded privileges in some settings, whereas in others their signalling of a status deserving of privileges may elicit little response. On the other hand, the cross-pollination and overlap among elites in different fields is at the centre of accumulating great power and influence. Although this conception may appear to be individualistic in its orientation, in fact it maintains that individuals exist within their collectivities of networks, conventions and rules.

Forms of capital

Among the most affluent, wealth is almost always paired with connections, influence and social esteem, assets essential to further accumulation of wealth. When asked how privilege works in practice, it is remarkable how often our focus group participants talked about 'connections' and 'networks'. Hana (wealthier, older, Melbourne) spoke of her work with a charity that secures university scholarship for kids from disadvantaged suburbs. They do very well in their studies, she said. 'But then to get the job, forget it, because they don't have the parent connections. Because they're South Sudanese, and to become a doctor or a lawyer they don't have the connections … because they didn't go to those schools.'

We will explore this networking among elites in our consideration of corporate boards and philanthropy. Bourdieu referred to these networks of personal relationships as *social capital*. The influence attached to wealth depends on the owner's social capital, which has a multiplier effect on their financial capital. 'The volume of social capital possessed by a given agent', he wrote, '… depends on the size of the network of connections that he can effectively mobilize.'[26] The purpose of certain exclusive clubs is to concentrate social capital and, in so doing, augment it. It's possible that the continued exclusion of women from certain gentlemen's clubs is motivated as much by a desire not to dilute the benefits of membership because women's networks are seen to be less valuable to the men. The concentrated social capital of successful people in Qantas's Chairman's Lounge explains its allure. 'It's private and you get to catch up with people that you know', confided one member, 'and it's a good opportunity to bump into people you may not have spoken to for a while.'[27]

Cultural capital refers to the elements of group identity that allow members to speak of 'people like us'. It encompasses familiarity with the tastes, modes of dress, bodily disposition, manners, and the material belongings associated with a social stratum or class. Bourdieu proposed three forms of cultural capital – embodied in 'long-lasting dispositions of the mind and body', objectified in cultural goods such as paintings, books and monuments, and institutionalised in forms such as educational qualifications.[28]

Embodied cultural capital is assimilated from birth and is typically acquired unconsciously, making it second nature to the bearer. It can be embodied in the form of one's bearing, cultivated gaze, poise and tastes.[29] Less obviously, embodiment takes the form of an air of knowingness, of being at ease in the world.[30] Ease, suggests Khan, is the 'signature emotion' of the privileged in an age of open access and meritocracy. It is similar to 'surety', a confidence absorbed at home and at school that one's future in the world is assured.[31] Maxwell and Aggleton found that surety is 'bestowed through self-understandings originating with the self, the family and the school[, and it is] strongly supportive of a hierarchical sense of personal and social "difference" from others.'[32] A girl attending an elite school in southern England made an unwittingly revealing comment about her parents: 'my parents have brought us up to have manners and things ... but they haven't tried to make us anyone that we're not, you know.'[33]

The distinction often made between old money and new money arises from the fact that 'the link between economic and cultural capital is established through the mediation of the time needed for acquisition.'[34] In other words, converting wealth into internal characteristics takes many years. As a rule, wealth brings more status and power than cultural capital, although each can amplify the effect of the other.[35]

A further resource of elites is sometimes referred to as *symbolic capital* – credentials or positions that do not in themselves confer power yet signal high esteem.[36] These signs of distinction can be mobilised to attract more privileges. Among business elites, chairing the board of a major cultural institution is a symbol of elevated civic responsibility, trust and esteem in the cultural field, a symbol whose power spills into the business world. As we will see, philanthropy can be a highly effective means of converting wealth into symbolic capital, the more so if it leads to the award of board positions, patron status or an official honour. The state is often instrumental in dispensing symbols of esteem, such as honours that provide official recognition of prestige and authority. The desirability of the latter form of symbolic capital is indicated by the fact that those who have received an official honour are usually eager to wear on their lapels the miniature gold badge that advertises it.

Among intellectual elites an honorary doctorate from a prestigious university may serve a similar purpose in their field. In the law, elevation to King's Counsel or Special Counsel carries esteem in the legal field as well as in the wider community. And it converts into financial capital because one can immediately charge twice as much for one's services.

While the self-interested and instrumental nature of economic capital is plain for all to see, cultural and symbolic capital are misrecognised as disinterested, as reflections of the pure character of the owner.[37] Symbolic capital allows possession of the three other kinds of capital (financial, social and cultural) to be seen as 'self-evident'. It takes on an ideological function, argued Bourdieu, because it conceals the arbitrary way capital is distributed in society by rendering legitimate the distinction (and privileges) that accompany wealth.

The other elites

Since privileges go with influence as well as wealth, we would like to identify three particular elites beyond those considered in the tradition of Bourdieu – the positional elite, the cultural elite and the intellectual elite.

The *positional elite* possesses what might be called positional capital – that is, the power and influence accrued by occupying a position of substance (rather than of symbolic significance). Possession of power arising from a position permits us to include political and administrative elites, some of whom enjoy enviable privileges without being wealthy. Strong networks are typically needed to attain the offices of prime minister or president, senior government minister, or chief of a powerful state agency. Even so, social, cultural and symbolic capital enhance the power and influence of the position rather than define it. The existence of political powerbrokers who have deep networks but hold no substantive positions tells us that the two do not necessarily go together.

Wealth and positional capital are in some degree interchangeable. Financial elites can enhance their power by acquiring positions, such as chairing a corporate or government board. On the other hand, the financial rewards of a career in business or a profession may be relinquished to pursue the influence of political office. Transience is a distinctive feature of the privileges of the positional elite; when office is relinquished, the privileges that go with it evaporate. However, some manage to parlay the experience and networks they acquired while in office into lucrative business careers, bringing new power and privileges. (The former Australian Treasurer Peter Costello, for example, now chairs a major media corporation and the nation's sovereign wealth fund.)

The *cultural elite* exercises influence in the field of culture, broadly defined. The cultural elite, which we distinguish from the intellectual elite, shapes the cultural ideas, norms, customs and social behaviour of a society. It includes influential members of the culture industries, artists, musicians, advertising creatives, authors, social media influencers, and so on, along with celebrities of various kinds, from high-brow to low-brow, who may be more or less wealthy but whose fame gives them cultural heft and access to privileges. Sporting stars form another group among the cultural elite. To pick a few among the most influential, Anna Wintour, Michael Jordan, Beyoncé, Joe Rogan and Salman Rushdie come to mind.

In recent years, conservative commentators have criticised 'left-wing cultural elites', by which they mean the intellectual and media elites, for wielding outsized influence and enjoying privileges they would deny others. The conservative commentators who make this accusation sometimes have better access to major media outlets and closer associations with powerful business and political elites than the 'left wing cultural elites' they have in their sights. The influence and privileges of cultural elites on the left tend to be confined to the cultural sphere, with some spillover into the political sphere. In part this is because left-wing cultural elites tend to be less comfortable 'consorting with the enemy' than conservative elites, for whom wealth and the power that goes with it are a natural part of liberal capitalism. In 2013, Nick Cater, the then opinion editor of News Corporation broadsheet *The Australian*, published a book denouncing the influence of the new 'ruling class' of cultural and intellectual elites.[38] Apparently unaware of the irony, the book carried on its cover an endorsement from his boss, Rupert Murdoch.

Where does the *intellectual elite* fit into the scheme? Intellectuals are sometimes bundled with cultural elites, but we think it makes sense to add 'knowledge capital' to the other types of capital – that is, the social power that comes with control over ideas.[39] It's true that, since the corporatisation of universities, the esteem in which professors were once held has waned. At the same time, university presidents and vice-chancellors, increasingly powerful as leaders of major corporations, enjoy considerable privileges. Although the influence of public intellectuals has been declining, universities still host prominent intellectuals whose ideas have changed public understanding and, at times, policy. In the West, Noam Chomsky, Paul Krugman, Mary Beard, Francis Fukuyama and Camille Paglia are conspicuous examples.

If public intellectuals are in decline, there are some outstanding academic researchers who are admired by their colleagues, smiled on by university administrators, and granted privileges denied to their less illustrious peers. These high achievers are mostly scientists. They might be showered with awards, grants and even government board positions. A Nobel Prize certainly opens doors.

Beyond the scientists, there is a small cohort of celebrity academics who have become stars, usually by writing topical books attracting extensive media exposure. The evolutionary biologist Richard Dawkins, the historian Niall Ferguson and the art historian Simon Sharma come to mind. Universities use the stardom of their celebrity academics to market their 'brand', attract fee-paying students and schmooze wealthy donors.[40] These A-list academics are often given inflated salaries in secret employment contracts. In other words, they enjoy privileges that the vast majority of academics can only dream of.

It's worth noting that, in our focus group conversations concerning elites and their privileges, participants drew on examples from the fields of business and finance, politics, sport, philanthropy and the media. Universities came up often, but as places to cultivate elite privilege in other fields. No one mentioned privileged academics, although Ashley (average income, younger, Sydney), who works at a university, recounted an incident she read as indicative of privilege among university executives. 'I was once in a committee meeting where three quite senior managers of the university, just for no reason whatsoever, turned around, looked around the room and said, "Oh, we have the Holy Trinity here."' They were referring, she said, to 'Scots, Joeys and Kings,' exclusive Presbyterian, Catholic and Anglican schools.

Doing privilege

We see privilege as having three elements or phases – *as a state and disposition, as a form of practice, and as a set of outcomes*. In the literature on *elite* privilege, in contrast to studies of white and male privilege, little attention has been paid to the middle phase, the doing of privilege. In this book, we aim to emphasise the multitude of daily practices, sometimes small and hidden, available to the wealthy, powerful and influential that ease or facilitate their efforts to obtain what they desire. These practices always involve two parties, the elite member seeking a privilege and the person (usually on behalf of an institution) in a position to grant the privilege. Privilege is not something owned by those at the top but is granted daily by others who may be among elites themselves or just as likely in positions below them but able to bestow exclusive benefits on them – cogs in the machine. Privilege is something that is ceded and achieved.

Our emphasis on doing elite privilege is stimulated by the well-known paper by Candace West and Don Zimmerman on 'doing gender'.

They recast gender as a 'new understanding of gender as a routine accomplishment embedded in everyday interactions'. For them, gender 'involves a complex of socially guided perceptual, interactional, and micropolitical activities.'[41] These activities are habitually presented as expressions of the natural social order or, if not taken as natural, accepted as immutable. They are just 'how the world is.' This way of thinking about gender and male privilege can be adapted to thinking about the micropolitics of elite privilege.

Most of the literature on elite privilege emphasises the first or the third elements, as a state or set of outcomes. As we've seen, the public usually begins by thinking of what wealth can buy. Analysts usually focus on the preconditions for a privilege to be granted – wealth itself and elite disposition.[42] In our view, privilege ought not be confined to the size of a fortune, a psychological disposition or a social position. It entails *action* resulting in an actual benefit.

In our three-phase conception of privilege as being, doing and having, focusing on the doing of privilege draws attention to the relationships that enable it. This way of thinking helps avoid the pitfalls of structures wholly displacing agency, which risks characterising people as puppets controlled by outside forces.[43] In popular and academic discussion, the default conception of the social structure is typically a pyramid with the elite at the top wielding power and influence, the benighted masses in the bottom layers, and various intermediate classes and sub-elites in between, usually serving the interests of the elite.

While it reflects a real hierarchy, a drawback of this kind of model is that it tends to fix and naturalise the position of elites at the top of the pyramid, as if that's just how the world is. And such a model, taken too rigidly, does not easily allow investigation of reciprocal relationships among elites or the ways elites and those below them interact to establish and reinforce their privileged status. Webs of relationships are always in flux, becoming more or less effective over time and across contexts. In studying elite privilege, therefore, it is helpful to supplement a pyramid model of social stratification with an understanding of elites as constantly re-created in webs of relationships within and outside their own strata.

In this book, we argue that, in modern societies, elite privilege is not simply a by-product of wealth but an organising principle guiding behaviours that secure exclusive benefits for elites. Allocation of privileges to elites is therefore essential to the reproduction of unequal and unfair societies. It operates through a signalling system indicating that the privileged person is to be granted an exclusive benefit. Social and institutional languages have evolved so that gradations of privilege can be signalled, recognised and rewarded. This interactionist perspective on elite privilege reminds us that privileges do not just happen; they are negotiated daily, often in ambiguous situations where subtle signals are sent and understood by another, so that a consensus is reached that the bestowing of a benefit is appropriate. Moreover, the transaction must often be made under the mutually agreed fiction that the benefit is being granted because of merit rather than of power and appears to be morally legitimate. Clearly, the navigation of these situations requires subtle skills of interpretation and deception in both parties.[44] (For an illustration, see Kerry Stokes's doctor's certificate in the next chapter.) These routinised interpersonal norms and practices are the bearings that keep the machinery of privilege ticking over.

Having said all this, the exercise of privilege is not limited to daily interactions in which an exclusive benefit is sought and awarded. Privilege is a product of social dominance, which in turn is used collectively by elites to build and protect the institutions that put them in privileged positions. It is in this extended sense that privilege is a form of power, the power to shape practices and institutions to benefit oneself and one's group even in the face of resistance.

Classes, elites and hierarchies

Although we occasionally use the word 'class' for convenience, in this study we find it more helpful and less befuddling to think in terms of social hierarchy, one defined by social and cultural factors as well as economic ones. The traditional Marxist conception of class based on relationships with the means of production has lost much of its explanatory power because of shifts in the economic structure from a manufacturing to a services economy. Business ownership has been separated from operation, with highly paid salaried executives in charge, joining professions in the finance industries as the most highly paid.[45] Moreover, some 'working-class' households own significant amounts of wealth invested in the share market through pension schemes or in property. (Today, some traditional working-class trades do much better financially than many white-collar workers.) On the other hand, exploitation of labour has in some ways worsened in recent times, reflected in the spread of the gig economy and the rise of the precariat.[46] Exploitation is seen no longer as a general problem associated with wage labour but as arising from certain employment circumstances – casualisation, zero-hours contracts, wage theft, migrant workers, gig work, and so on.

It's difficult to define class in an operationally useful way, other than by identifying classes with socio-economic groupings. So, Mairi Maclean and her co-authors pick out an 'upper class' drawn from those whose parents had high wealth or occupied 'a leading position in society', an 'upper middle class' drawn from top professionals, a 'lower middle class' drawn from white-collar occupations of lower status, and a 'lower class' drawn from occupations such as 'workers', miners and van drivers.[47]

Attribution of class membership has traditionally carried with it expectations of certain kinds of political behaviour and cultural practice. It is a commonplace now to point to the rupturing of political behaviour and class position. Voting for one's cultural and social concerns is as strong a motive as voting for one's economic interests.[48] The decline of labour politics and the rise of phenomena such as 'Howard's battlers' (working-class voters in Australia who abandoned the Labor Party in favour of conservatives) have strengthened the perception that class is dead. Yet, as Diane Reay has written, this depends on a particular understanding of class – that is, class consciousness seen 'narrowly in terms of a *politicized* understanding of class location'.[49]

All of this receives some confirmation from the conflicting ways members of the public classify themselves when asked in opinion surveys which class they belong to. Over 90 per cent of Australians identify as middle class.[50] An 'objective' division of class will not, on the evidence, show much correspondence with self-descriptions.[51] The confusion is multiplied, but also partly explained, when we compare self-classifications in Australia with those in Britain and the United States, where 'working class' and 'middle class' are understood quite differently. Most 'objectively' middle-class Britons describe themselves as working class. For Americans, Markovits uses 'middle class' to describe 'working people without formal degrees or professions'.[52]

In some respects, the recent focus on the very rich is a return to the sociological study of elites in vogue in the 1950s and 1960s. We agree with the argument of Mike Savage that sociology needs to escape the 'problematic of the proletariat' and focus on wealthy elites.[53] It's a shift away from the preoccupation with 'looking down' while remembering that the privileges enjoyed by the wealthy elite are part of the same system that creates disadvantage and underprivilege. As Savage observes: 'Over the last thirty years, there seems to have been a radical remaking of the highest levels of the class hierarchy.'[54] Our concern is with the way wealthy elites use their power and influence to secure privileges that buttress the unequal distribution of wealth, income and opportunity.

Although the public struggles to speak coherently about post-industrial societies in terms of classes, they have no difficulty understanding them in terms of social hierarchy. When our focus group participants were asked whether 'there is a social hierarchy in Australia, with some people at the top and some people at the bottom', the unanimous, and at times vehement, answer was in the affirmative.

> Absolutely. Everywhere. Where would you like me to start? (Tony, wealthier, older, Sydney)

> I think Australia has a hierarchy wherever you go. Even if you go to the shops, even the way you dress, where you go, where you live ... where you holiday ... what you buy. (Maria, average income, older, Melbourne)

Ashley has worked in the law and universities.

> I've seen social stratification. I've seen how it works and the privileged attitudes that people take from their families and their backgrounds. And I think it just reproduces itself in ways that we maybe don't recognise too much. ... in Australia wealth absolutely begets wealth and it filters down through generations. (Ashley, average income, younger, Sydney)

Summary

This chapter begins to describe the components of the machine of privilege. Defining elites is not straightforward, and we adopt a flexible approach. Although our attention is centred mainly on the wealthy elite, influential figures in politics, bureaucracy, media, culture and academia also enjoy privileges. In addition to financial capital, elites build social capital (networks of relationships), cultural capital (mental and bodily dispositions and knowledge) and symbolic capital (markers of distinction such as awards). There is a correspondence between wealth and a way of being in the world. In addition to the ability to buy what one wants, the public understands privilege as a certain disposition, the way some people 'carry themselves'.

These forms of capital are convertible, one into another, and can be used to multiply financial capital. Elites operate in fields with their own cultures and rules. Great power and influence come from building each form of capital and operating across fields.

Privilege has three phases – being (a state or disposition), doing (the practice of securing a privilege) and having (the outcome of securing a privilege). The middle phase, doing privilege, involves two parties, the elite member seeking a privilege and another in a position to bestow it. This interactionist perspective reminds us that privileges do not just happen but are negotiated daily, often requiring subtle skills, including strategic deployment of influence so that the machinery of privilege operates smoothly.

'Class' is a conceptually confusing category. Studying elites rather than classes allows us to illustrate better how privilege works. And it reflects how the public thinks about hierarchy in their societies.

CHAPTER THREE

The Micropolitics of Elite Privilege

Signalling

To understand how we are all cogs in the machine of privilege, we begin by studying the micropolitics of elite privilege. The idea of 'doing privilege' suggests that privilege is interactional, an 'emergent feature of social situations'.[1] The bestowal of privilege relies on processes in which an expectation of privileged treatment is conveyed, recognised and responded to by others. These processes take place in myriad ways, large and small, every day. The bestowers may be among the elites themselves or they may occupy positions in lower strata. Unless they have already established their status in previous interactions, a member of the elite seeking a privilege must send a signal, or display their status, to the person in a position to bestow it. The elite member may need to negotiate their way through a system, sending signals along the way. The system that must be negotiated is typically a set of rules, practices and norms laid down by state, commercial and civic organisations, rules that ostensibly apply equally to all. Rules may be applied flexibly or be set aside, such as when an elite member is put at the front of a queue or fast-tracked through an administrative process.

There is no 'book of privileges' setting out the benefits due to each person according to their wealth, influence or status. In fact, the bestowing of some kinds of privileges must be shrouded in secrecy. In some contexts, privileged treatment is officially frowned upon and must be covered over with ready excuses, of which the most frequently used is the insistence, if questioned, that the benefit was granted based on merit. From this vantage point, government often entails managing the tension between rules that may favour elites and maintaining the semblance of fairness. The tension must be managed even in autocratic societies because widespread resentment over the injustice of elite privilege can destabilise regimes.

Signalling that a privilege should be granted does not need to be conscious, nor does the person who grants the privilege need to follow a process of deliberation. The process can become automatic. Children from wealthy families grow up absorbing a cultural unconscious, a 'set of basic, deeply interiorized master patterns',[2] which may be embodied as a disposition or comportment that conveys superior status. As we saw, our focus group participants often said they can recognise a privileged person by their bearing.

> It's generally how people carry themselves. It's not definitive, but it gives you a good general idea because of the confidence and the way people will carry themselves in a room. (Mark, wealthier, older, Melbourne)

> ... their body posture is a huge one. I'm generalizing here, but the way they walk, and the sense of entitlement people have because they're used to a certain way of life that is already privileged. ... So the way they carry themselves mostly. You can spot it a mile away. (Leah, wealthier, younger, Sydney)

Unless the signalling of elite status is only to establish social dominance (requiring deference), perceiving the signal calls for a response, the bestowal of an exclusive benefit. While the reflexive response of our focus group participants was to say they do not treat wealthy people any differently, as discussion progressed more candid assessments were offered. One conceded that, if they knew someone 'has money', then 'I probably would pay them more attention and give them more of a hearing' (Lydia, wealthier, older, Melbourne). Another admitted that she provides special treatment to wealthy arts patrons.

> I've worked at a few arts festivals, and I know that if we have interactions with donors who are very, very privileged [then] we take extra care when dealing with [them] because they're pretty much funding the arts ... So, in that situation, I'm going above and beyond for that reason, which is kind of a shit thing to say, but it's just the way it is in the arts. (Nicole, average income, younger, Melbourne)

The language of status

The system of privilege is sustained only through broad social compliance – that is, deferring to the exercise of privilege and the institutions and norms essential for its reproduction. Status symbols or signs of distinction are used as cues so that others can correctly identify a person's place in the hierarchy, or at least identify them with the status rank they want to convey.[3] A status symbol becomes a signal that the bestowal of a privilege is expected.

In his classic article 'Symbols of class status' (1951), Erving Goffman observed that a harmonious society requires that people of diverse social statuses both perceive correctly and behave in ways that are consistent with their status and with how others perceive that status.[4] The harmonious matching of perceptions and behaviours requires effective communication of one's true status.

In a privileged society, 'harmony' requires that elite status is not only perceived correctly by subordinates but responded to in the expected way. This vision of harmony is a little too easy; the system of privilege may be working as intended yet each interaction may leave a legacy of resentment. On the other hand, if a signal is not correctly received, or received and not responded to, then the elite member is liable to react indignantly, perhaps declaring 'Don't you know who I am?', as an intoxicated MP infamously did when asked by restaurant staff to leave.[5] An elite member may accept a rebuff with a feeling of resentment or decide to mobilise more resources, such as calling on a powerful person to impress upon the recalcitrant subordinate the need to reconsider – the strategy of the billionaire Kerry Stokes as described in the next section.

The expressive value of a sign of distinction depends on where it locates the bearer in the social hierarchy, including the distribution of wealth and positional power. The system of signs is often subtle. In fact, as our focus group participants' reactions suggested, it's often hard to say what exactly it is about a person that makes an impression on us; it emerges from their overall presentation and manner. Most of the acts communicating elite (or other) status, wrote Goffman, are 'performed unthinkingly under the invisible guide of familiarity and habit.'[6] Often, if acting out status is done in a deliberate way, it appears inauthentic. Signs of distinction can be used fraudulently, and they usually embody devices for restricting their misrepresentation.[7] Collectors of fine art, for example, can separate the authentic connoisseur from the cashed-up pretender by whether the latter possesses that ineffable thing called 'taste'.

Moreover, systems of signs are always shifting. Symbols standing for high status can be debased by excessive supply or by 'cultural inversion', whereby 'practices which originate in one class [are] adopted by the members of a higher one'[8] or the reverse, as has been the case with the 'democratization of luxury' – that is, when luxury goods consumed by the rich are made available to the masses so that the discerning rich look to replace the 'contaminated' symbols with new symbols of distinction. So identifying another's position on the social gradient can be perplexing, and misrecognition is common.

Once the other's place has been identified and the expected privilege has been bestowed, both sides (and observers) will make judgements about their feelings and the justice or otherwise of the interaction. Granting a privilege may be appropriate to the situation but unfair. It might violate the rules or be within the letter of the rules but against their spirit. Just as in the context of gender, both parties' actions 'are often designed with an eye to their *accountability*, that is, how they might look and how they might be characterized' if called to account later.[9] Civil servants granting favours to elites must be careful about what they put in writing.

As acquisition of cultural and symbolic capital can take time, there can often be a mismatch between actual status as conferred by wealth and the cultural and symbolic markers that typically go with it. For someone rising on the wealth scale, cultural and symbolic deficits can retard their progress, causing frustration. If they are falling, then a 'surplus' of cultural and symbolic capital can slow the decline in social eminence; the loss of a fortune may leave one living in 'genteel poverty'. There can also be a mismatch and tension between the dispositions of members of a class and the field in which they operate. It is not only students from working-class backgrounds who feel out of place at university; academics from working-class families do too.[10]

Bourdieu argued that people internalise the objective circumstances they face; they learn to 'read' the future and choose 'the fate that is also statistically the most likely for them.'[11] In other words, and despite the rise of the meritocratic society, the subjective expectations they form tend to match the objective probabilities they face. At both the upper and the lower end, we are taught our rightful place in the world. It's distressing to have one's ambitions repeatedly thwarted or, for those at the top, to fail to live up to social expectations.

The rules of the game

Attaining and maintaining privileges requires effort, even for those well-endowed with capital. In fact, elites are constantly striving to gain an advantage. Success depends not only on how much capital of various kinds they bring to the contest but also on how well they understand the *rules of the game* in a particular field – that is, how to deploy their capital most effectively.[12] This game works against the principles and practice of meritocracy. The analogy is less with a game of football, where the rules are clear and a referee adjudicates, and more with game theory, developed to help understand the kinds of strategies people adopt when competing for limited rewards. David Swartz puts it well: 'Actors are not rule followers or norm obeyers but strategic improvisers who respond dispositionally to the opportunities and constraints offered by various situations.'[13] Game theory allows for actors to cooperate if doing so is the best way to optimise returns, a strategy that elites often use when, for example, lobbying for or against a change in a policy or a law.

Across their lives, most people negotiate their ways through a maze of opportunities and obstacles to secure benefits they would not otherwise receive, even if they are entitled to them. Underprivileged people are often required to play by different sets of rules in other spheres, such as negotiating pathways through the social security system. With different levels of 'resource system capital'[14] (the understanding and skills required to navigate the social security system), some are better than others at securing what they are entitled to. It hardly needs saying that the game of ensuring a fortnightly welfare payment, while high stakes for those who must play it, is not the kind of game that brings great benefits, such as avoiding tax through tax havens or jumping a queue for life-saving medical treatment.

The elites are, almost by definition, those more skilled at strategising and negotiating in the games with higher rewards. In addition to having more capital at their disposal, their habitus gives elites a 'feel for the game'. It becomes second nature. Building on these insights, Karl Maton developed what he called legitimation code theory.[15] He studied how areas of social life are revealed by the rules of the game, rules that are often tacit so that only people from privileged social backgrounds understand fully how they work. People learn the 'legitimation code' to operate successfully in those areas of social life, what they can aim for and get away with.

This practical mastery of subtle and unwritten norms and rules – which allows one to negotiate a path through them – is absorbed in childhood as an internalised understanding of how the system works, the sense that 'people like us' naturally use that knowledge to make the machinery of privilege work in their favour, as a form of institutionalised nepotism. Drawing on personal experience, a focus group participant explained how it begins in childhood.

> I think it's also about the training you receive, whether that's informal, sort of being in the room at the time. The conversations happen among people of privilege. And you pick up that language. Often it might be a bar mitzvah you go to, a restaurant, or the Sunday school that you attend and the people you are around. It could be the speech days or other school events. The point is, you are able to be in those rooms to pick up those lessons, which are then unconsciously brought into you. And then, as you grow older that's constantly reinforced, you're conditioned to continue to establish that and execute that privilege. (Josh, wealthier, younger, Sydney)

The elites' confidence that they know the rules and can manipulate them was on display during the pandemic lockdowns. In 2021, an Australian billionaire wanted to gain an exemption from the strict overseas travel ban so he could fly in his private jet to an Asian nation to pursue business deals. He spoke with the ambassador of that nation in Canberra who made phone calls securing the exemption documents needed to allow him to enter the country. The billionaire exited and re-entered Australia several times.[16]

In 2021, most Sydneysiders were enduring a strict and extended stay-at-home order under which they were allowed to leave their places of residence only for a limited set of reasons (essential work, care or health care). Holidays and travel more than 5 kilometres from home were strictly banned. However, it emerged that wealthy Sydneysiders with second residences elsewhere in New South Wales were moving freely between their homes and holiday homes. After complaints from local residents in regional areas that wealthy Sydneysiders were seeding Covid outbreaks in their towns, the crisis cabinet explicitly prohibited travel to holiday homes except to carry out necessary maintenance.[17] Reports began filtering through that wealthy Sydneysiders were travelling to their holiday homes to mow the lawns.

It was a similar story in Victoria. In August 2021, during one of Melbourne's strict lockdowns, a focus group participant, Gail (wealthier, older, Melbourne), was a data collector for the national census in a wealthy district. When members of her team returned from knocking on doors they asked: 'Where are all the people?' Many residents of the district had escaped the tight travel restrictions of the city for their holiday mansions in Portsea and Lorne, seaside retreats for the city's rich.

This is how privilege is practised on a daily basis. The elites bring more resources or forms of capital to the game and have a practical mastery of it. Using a football analogy, exceptional players have a deeper understanding of the flow of play in a wide range of situations. They can 'read' the game, seeing possibilities invisible to others. They know the rules, but they also know the rules are open to interpretation by those charged with enforcing them. So they understand how to game the rules and manipulate the referee. In the sphere of public administration, the rules typically have various conditions and exceptions and so are open to interpretation. In other words, there are paths through the rules for those who know how to find them or who know someone who knows the ways through. But knowledge is not enough; once they find the gatekeepers, they need to have ample influence for the gates to be opened.

Again during Sydney's hard lockdown in 2021, all school excursions were banned and students at public schools were ordered to stay at home and learn remotely. In fact, under the public health order, Sydney residents could not 'leave their residence unless they have a reasonable excuse.' The elite Sydney Anglican school Redlands wanted to send sixty-four of its students for a term at its High Country Campus for 'a residential program combining academic study with snow sports training'. The campus is near Jindabyne in the Snowy Mountains,

450 kilometres to the city's southwest. Redlands wrote to the Ministry of Health seeking permission, arguing that it would not be a school excursion but a normal part of school activities.[18] To prepare, the school consulted with the public health liaison officer for the snowfields and instructed its own risk and compliance manager and head of outdoor education to develop a sophisticated risk assessment plan to accompany its request. It also worked closely with the Jindabyne community and liaised with police who would make sure the school's buses stopped only at the authorised places. The school nurse would be on site, and a pathology service stood ready to swab the children. Redlands also made sure it had the active backing of the Association of Independent Schools, a powerful lobby group.

Correspondence between Redlands and the Ministry of Health shows that Redlands' request for the bestowal of a privilege engaged the attention of at least a dozen civil servants (and several public relations specialists), as well as the chief health officer, surely the busiest and most pressured person in the state at the time, along with her staff. She agreed that the proposed travel was not technically an excursion and was within the rules. She approved the plan. The CEO of the Association of Independent Schools emailed the public health liaison officer for the snowfields: 'I appreciate all your work in supporting and advising the schools.' The public servant had provided advice on improving the school's risk plan, inspected and approved its campus, and offered onsite testing for students and staff.

The school marshalled its extensive resources and specialist staff members in the middle of the state's most serious public health emergency in decades in order to find a way through the strict regulations so that a group of privileged children could spend a school term at the snowfields. Redlands knew the rules and their loopholes; they knew the details of what they had to put in place and had the specialist resources to do it; they knew whom to approach and whom to call on for support. In short, the elite school understood how to guide its request for special treatment through a complex bureaucracy in times of a state emergency. One of our focus group participants, reflecting on the networks emanating from elite schools into the top echelons of society, commented: 'Even if you have the capability to solve the problem, unless you speak to the right person at the right time, in the right circles, you know you're never going to get anywhere. Privilege enables that' (Ryan, average income, younger, Sydney).

The strategizing of elite schools is matched by the strategizing of the parents who send their children to them. When placing their children in the 'best' schools is essential for wealthy families, success in this highly competitive game requires elaborate strategizing (although spaces will always be found for children of powerful old boys, billionaires and state premiers).[19] For those outside that world, it's surprising to discover just how obsessed parents can become. The process begins with the entry of the baby's name on waiting lists for several elite schools and paying the substantial fees. It's a race that can be taken to comical lengths. The admissions office of Scotch College in Melbourne (annual fee A$38,280 for year 12) measures the prospective parents' commitment to the school by how quickly they place their child's name on the pre-waiting list.[20] Savvy parents are known to phone the school from the birthing room to add the still-red infant's name to the pre-waiting list, as if the umbilical cord, detached from the mother, is reconnected to a 'privilege machine' that will provide sustenance throughout life.[21] The same process occurs in Britain.[22]

The infant graduates to Scotch College's actual waiting list when the parent sends a copy of the birth certificate to prove they were not lying about the time of birth. At that point they pay a non-refundable holding fee of A$5,000.[23] Entry onto a waiting list is only the first step on the path to securing a place at an elite school. Over the next years, parents pursue a range of training and tutoring strategies to give their child an edge in the tests and interviews for admission, including building children's 'credentials' in music or debating or the sports that are favoured by particular schools. Some exclusive high schools give credit to applicants who have shown precocious leadership qualities, so parents are known to encourage their children to work hard at becoming captain of their primary schools.[24]

Of course, the game does not stop with acceptance; it shifts to another phase of preparation for admission to prestigious courses at prestigious universities, where elite advantage is given the imprimatur of merit. In the education game, affluent, experienced and well-connected parents enjoy an enormous advantage over parents from poorer backgrounds who do not know the rules of the game. As participants in the process, students at exclusive schools acquire a deep understanding of the rules of the game played by their parents to secure entry into the school.

A case study: public administration

No civil servant likes to hear the words 'I was speaking with the minister about a problem I have, and he suggested I contact you.' Name dropping is a technique for establishing a power relation, a means of making an impression resulting in a benefit being given, or perhaps simply establishing social dominance over another by indicating the powerful circles in which one moves.[25] Beyond name dropping, powerful people seeking bestowal of a privilege can mobilise other powerful people to intervene on their behalf.

Documents obtained by the authors under freedom of information laws, along with news stories broken by the journalist Hamish Hastie, provide a fascinating insight into how the powerful exercise their privilege by manipulating the rules of the game.[26] In this case, the billionaire media and mining mogul Kerry Stokes wanted to return home with his wife in his private jet from their ski lodge in Beaver Creek, Colorado. However, on 15 March 2020, as Covid-19 spread like wildfire around the world, the premier of Western Australia, Mark McGowan, declared a state of emergency. Nine days later the state's borders were closed; only West Australians outside the state were allowed in, but they had to quarantine for fourteen days in designated hotels. On 1 April, border restrictions were imposed between regions within the state, limiting travel to emergency services only. Movement was restricted even more tightly within the Kimberley region, which included the coastal town of Broome, to protect vulnerable Indigenous communities.

Stokes had a problem. He did not want to return to Perth and hotel quarantine; he wanted to fly to Broome and quarantine at his luxury compound near Cable Beach, famed for its pristine stretches of white sand. He needed an exemption from the rules. Yet it was a time of barely disguised panic, with his home state adopting the harshest rules in the country. McGowan declared there would be no exemptions; the rules would be applied 'to all Australians coming home from overseas'. Even heart-rending appeals for exemptions, such as the man in hotel quarantine desperate to visit his wife dying of Covid, were refused.

Stokes's doctor wrote a letter supporting his exemption from hotel quarantine on the grounds of a recent medical procedure. The letter was sent to the state's director-general of health, Dr David Russell-Weitz. It is a sign of Stokes's clout that the director-general immediately contacted the office of Premier Mark McGowan.

Stokes, who owns WA's only major newspaper, the *West Australian*, along with Australia's highest-rating television network, Channel 7, is the most powerful man in Western Australia (also the home state of the country's two richest people, mining barons Gina Rinehart and Andrew Forrest).[27] Stokes's media monopoly allows him to set the agenda, so he is not a man to be crossed by any politician. As one media insider put it: 'there is a slavish devotion to the *West* [the *West Australian* newspaper] from all sides of politics.'[28] In its turn, the *West Australian* had consistently praised McGowan for his performance. McGowan and Stokes are close. Private messages revealed in a court case show 'Mark' and 'Kerry' texting each other to massage the other's ego.[29] When McGowan banned all exports of natural gas from the state, he exempted one project, Stokes's joint venture.

Now Stokes wanted a favour, a big one. Standing in the way was the chief health officer, Dr Andrew Robertson, on whose advice the commissioner of police, Chris Dawson, also the state emergency coordinator, would decide on the exemption request. Robertson was no pushover. He had been in the navy, rising to the rank of commodore, with duties including three tours in Iraq as a UN biological weapons inspector. He'd been on the ground in response to the Indian Ocean tsunami, the Bali bombings and the Fukushima nuclear disaster.[30] He played by the book. His advice was that, due to his medical condition, Stokes and his wife could self-quarantine at home in Perth but not in Broome. Following this formal health advice, the police commissioner notified Stokes that he would be exempted from hotel quarantine but had to isolate in Perth.

Stokes was unhappy, so he contacted his friend the premier, everyone's boss. In an email marked of 'high' importance, Premier McGowan's chief of staff, Guy Houston, raised the pressure on Andrew Robertson. He included a 'revised itinerary' for Stokes, purporting to show his travel would be less risky. But the chief health officer was unmoved.

Thwarted, Stokes decided to wheel out a bigger gun. He phoned Canberra and spoke with his great friend Mathias Cormann, the federal minister for finance, also a senator from Western Australia. In Canberra, the atmosphere was feverish as the federal government grappled with the unfolding crisis, trying to work out how to respond to the pandemic, including the deeply uncertain impacts of lockdowns and the implications of a likely global recession on the nation's finances. Still, the finance minister was able to find time to intervene on behalf of the billionaire.

Stokes and Cormann went back some way, with Cormann keen to please. Cormann was a regular at Stokes's marquee charity event in Perth, the Telethon Ball, promoted as 'the premium entertainment and fundraising event of the year', where Channel 7 personalities and WA's business and corporate leaders gathered to help raise funds for children's health. In 2019, as the telethon coverage approached its Sunday night finale, the minister for finance phoned in with some good news. 'I'm pleased to report I have been able to find another $1 million [from federal coffers], so we will be adding another $2.3 million today to the $2.5 million the Prime Minister committed yesterday.'[31]

When Stokes called for his help, Cormann emailed McGowan's chief of staff, Guy Houston, about the situation, telling him he had 'been discussing this with the premier' and attaching the physician's letter. The finance minister piled on the pressure: 'I hope this helps secure the necessary … authorisation for arrival and self-isolation at their residence in Broome.' Houston reacted quickly, contacting the chief health officer with the new information. Stokes's people emailed Cormann: 'Dear Minister, Thank you for all your help.'

So now, amid a national health emergency in which unprecedented lockdown measures were being developed and implemented on the run, Kerry Stokes's application for an exemption from the rules had mobilised the state premier, his chief of staff, the chief medical officer, the director-general of WA Health, the police commissioner and state emergency commissioner, and the federal minister of finance, along with numerous underlings.

Chief Health Officer Andrew Robertson was now under enormous political pressure to accede to the billionaire's wishes. As anyone who has worked in a bureaucracy knows, reasons can always be found to bend the rules as necessary. But for the ex-commodore rules are rules, and he replied that his advice was unchanged; Stokes must return to Perth and not Broome. The freedom of information documents do not reveal how Stokes reacted to the foiling of his will, but he and his wife were forced to endure fourteen days in their Perth waterfront mansion.

At the time of writing three years later, Andrew Robertson was still the chief health officer. Police Commissioner Chris Dawson had been appointed state governor. Mark McGowan stepped down as premier in June 2023, citing exhaustion, and now advises mining corporations. The premier's chief of staff Guy Houston now works for Kerry Stokes. And in 2021, Mathias Cormann moved to Paris to take up his new position as secretary-general of the OECD.

A few lessons can be drawn from this episode. Activating the privileges of wealth often relies on political networks. If this seems obvious, we see here just how brazen the exploitation of political connections can be when the super-rich want something done. The enthusiasm of political leaders to accommodate powerful friends crosses party lines – McGowan is Labor and Cormann Conservative. The second lesson is that, in a democracy at least, civil servants in positions of power can resist pressure to give preferment, even from the most powerful. However, it comes with serious risks and takes personal courage, a quality that, in truth, is rare. Few senior bureaucrats are willing to stand on principle; justifications for giving way can always be found.

The third lesson is that no one could admit that Stokes was being given special treatment because he is wealthy and powerful, which points to the role of the doctor's certificate. The certificate, although kept secret, was the device by which a resolution based on power was converted into a resolution based on merit. (A medical emergency was not enough for the man whose wife was dying.) A final observation is that, given the risks of leaks and FOI requests, everyone couches written communications to ensure deniability. When McGowan and Cormann were asked by journalists if they had applied pressure on behalf of Stokes, they were evasive: 'I get constituent inquiries,' 'I do not publicly comment on the private details of individuals,' 'the decision was made by the relevant authority.' Everyone knows how it works, but what can you do in the face of this stonewalling? The world moves on and the power of elite privilege remains undiminished.

In our view, to claim that the primary function of the state and its three arms – political institutions, public administration and the law

– is to protect and reproduce elite power and privilege is too crude. It is undeniable, however, that these arms of the state are prominent sites where privilege is exercised with a view to protecting and enhancing the position of elites, as the Stokes case illustrates. When elites succeed in protecting and advancing their interests by engaging with an arm of the state, the state serves to validate and entrench privilege.

Unconspicuous consumption

Elite consumption behaviour is a form of display where one signals status or asserts dominance over others without any other goal. There is an extensive academic and popular literature on the spectacle of conspicuous consumption and brazen displays of opulence by the rich, and we comment on the meaning of some of the more suggestive ones in later chapters. Although the gulf between vulgar and tasteful forms of consumption is a common theme, the display of privilege and wealth is often a more subtle business. In one of our focus groups, Hana (wealthier, older, Melbourne), who works with very wealthy people, said: 'It depends on your definition of privilege. Like, if someone's wealthy they usually don't show it.'

A waiter at an expensive fine-dining establishment spoke of how a very wealthy customer would arrive dressed casually in well-worn jeans.[32] But there were other signs. He was clearly at ease in hatted (or Michelin starred) restaurants and paid with an Amex black card, so he was shown to the best table. The same phenomenon was commented on by one of Ilan Wiesel's informants: 'I see extraordinarily wealthy guys walking around Mosman on a weekend in daggy old shirts, and a pair of sandals.'[33] Displays of indifference by the super-rich may in truth be ways of 'loftily affirming their social supremacy by declining to compete',[34] as if to say, 'I don't need to engage in symbolic display and I'm quite happy for you to know it.'

These instances of 'the conspicuous absence of conspicuousness' defy the usual homology between social position and material symbols of distinction. The obvious signals are (apparently) abandoned because the bearer feels so comfortable in his or her position in society. This kind of symbolic inversion, Bourdieu noticed, brings 'a sort of semantic fuzziness which does not facilitate the direct deciphering of social signs.'[35]

Understatement and concealment do not always go together – at least, at first glance. Josh (wealthier, younger, Sydney), who had a privileged background and had mixed with very wealthy people, observed:

> Often those who are privileged may not feel that they need to display their privilege, whereas people who come from less privileged backgrounds can sometimes want to be gaudy in their privilege and displaying their status. So I think privilege can be displayed through wealth, but often it's a wealth that is not so obvious at first glance.

In his study of how social status is expressed through various symbolic forms, Jean-Pascal Daloz draws a distinction between conspicuous forms and 'unconspicuous' forms of consumption. He uses the neologism 'unconspicuous' rather than the usual 'inconspicuous' because it 'better suggests a direct negation of conspicuousness …'.[36] To be inconspicuous is to go unnoticed, which is a drawback for elites who desire privileged treatment. In some contexts, conspicuous displays of symbols of wealth are considered appropriate, while in others conspicuous displays may be read as brash and insensitive to in-group norms. In these contexts, understatement by deploying discreet symbols is a better way to establish one's distinction.[37]

Daloz's analysis assumes that the purpose of displaying one's assets is simply to be recognised for one's distinction. He argues that conspicuous and unconspicuous symbols of standing are used primarily within groups at the top of the social hierarchy because 'domination over the lower strata … is largely taken for granted.' However, when it comes to securing privileges (the best seats at the theatre, exemption from a government regulation), the right signals often need to be sent to people lower down the social hierarchy, perhaps a booking clerk or a mid-level bureaucrat. As misrecognition is common, unconspicuous display may not be picked up.

So, understatement instead of ostentation may be a sophisticated way of establishing social distinction. One of our focus group partici-pants spoke of the 'humility' of the ultra-wealthy philanthropists she works with. Yet she and everyone in that field are very conscious of the distinctions among the philanthropists based on their 'generosity' and the pecking order within the philanthropic community. Among the super-rich, there are those who engage in 'vulgar' displays (buying the longest super-yacht) and those with 'more refined' sensibilities who prefer to spend their money on avant-garde pictures and good works. Wiesel documents the ways in which established residents of 'glamour zones' dismiss the suburb's parvenus for their vulgar displays (knocking down historical houses and driving around in super-cars), which can be understood as a way of reinforcing the boundaries and keeping the newcomers out of the networks that allow them certain privileges that 'money can't buy'.

The wealthy may feel obliged to engage in elaborate shows of hospitality, requiring grand houses suitable for impressing clients or foreign guests who may misinterpret understated lifestyles. Daloz refers to the story of a corporate chief who invited his peers to dinner at his home. While the others arrived dressed formally, the host appeared in casual clothes, 'thereby instantly setting himself apart.'[38] It was a power play, an expression of superior distinction. The cultures of some countries, notably Scandinavian ones, include an expectation of 'conspicuous modesty', while Australia boasts a culture of 'shared ordinariness' that veils elite privilege.[39] The risk of conscious modesty is that one's social status, and the privileges that go with it, may be underestimated by relevant others.[40]

Boundary riders

A young person interviewed by Holmqvist for his study of an exclusive community in Sweden explained that he grew up around business executives and 'high-up people' who came to dinner at his home. They became just normal people, and 'you quickly lose your fear of them.' So he didn't grow up feeling he should know his place, or, rather, he knew where his place was. 'It doesn't worry me in the least to go for some dinner where the CEO of our company is also present.' Holmqvist's study led him to conclude that such children learn that they are privileged and therefore *better*. Instead of dwelling on the enormous advantages they receive, they believe they are smarter, work harder and 'are generally just "better" than other people.'[41]

The disposition of elite membership inevitably carries with it an internalised understanding of a hierarchical world. This habitus 'conveys a sense of place and out-of-place in a stratified social world.'[42] Sometimes the boundaries between social strata, or the privileged and the under-privileged, are clear and uncrossable. In the words of a focus group participant: 'There's definitely levels of society and social spaces that people are locked out of due to their income, their location, their job, their status, whatever it may be, their class' (Luke, average income, younger, Melbourne).

Classes gaze across social boundaries, often with a mixture of incom-prehension and derision. In a revealing ethnographic study of two organisations ostensibly based on principles of equality and fairness, where social status should not count, Lidia Manzo demonstrated how elites cannot help but find ways of asserting dominance.[43] Her case studies were of a karate *dojo* and a food co-op, both in a rapidly gentri-fying district of Brooklyn.

In the *dojo*, the external self is supposed to be left outside. Everyone dresses in the same uniform except for the colour of the belt, which estab-lishes a clear hierarchy of esteem based on merit – that is, skill at karate. As it happened, most of the advanced students, with higher level black belts, were older residents of the area from lower socio-economic groups, with jobs such as construction worker, driver and nanny, while the weaker students were newer arrivals from elites moving into the gentri-fying area. The status and power hierarchy was the reverse of the one out on the street. The ethos of the *dojo* required beginning students to show deference to more advanced ones. Upper-class practitioners struggled with the dominance over them of lower-class but more advanced students. Manzo noticed that the students from privileged backgrounds were 'less willing to take lessons from advanced practitioners of lower socio-economic status,' so those with brown or lower-level black belts found ways to avoid 'the swift indignity of being treated as weak.'[44] They chose to train with the intermediate class because in the advanced classes low-status practitioners would have power over them, while in the intermediate class they would be among the 'head students', both more skilled at karate and entrusted with carrying out the class rituals.

At the food co-op, where all members must do voluntary work, the volunteers tended to be affluent white elites, while the employed workers were people of colour from low socio-economic strata. Manzo found that the elites chafed against any assignment down the pecking order where employed staff were in charge. And she noticed that workers of colour, who in the outside world experience the slights and humiliations visited on them daily by elites, were not averse to getting some of their own back when in a position to do so. So the affluent elites preferred to volunteer for positions with more responsibility, such as group coordinator.

Manzo concluded that, when the exterior markers of higher status are absent, upper-class performances allowed the 'hidden, deeply-rooted signs of elite distinction' to emerge.[45] The elites found ways to re-establish the symbolic boundaries within which they could comfortably operate.

When boundaries are crossed, the 'interloper' feels out of place. A focus group participant told of the time she had enough loyalty points to fly business class on a holiday.

> We are not wealthy, but it was just strange to interact with the people that always fly business class … like, okay, I don't belong here. Really strange. … It's quite nice [but] I don't belong in here. These people, they travel all the time, and they just feel a bit better than us. (Brooke, average income, younger, Melbourne)[46]

When social boundaries are actively policed, most quickly adjust their subjective expectations to their objective circumstances. This process was at work in an incident related by a focus group participant concerning a man he knew who sent his children to Barker College, 'a pretty upmarket school'.

> He met some parents over dinner one day. And it's chit chat, you know. 'Tell us a bit about yourself, your background. What you do for a living?' He said, 'Well, I'm a self-employed tradesman, fridge mechanic.' They said, 'What? You're not a doctor, you're not an accountant, a lawyer? And what sort of car do you drive?' He said he drove a Ford Falcon. 'What? You don't drive a Mercedes or an Audi or BMW?' And he just said 'enough's enough.' He just walked out. He said, 'bugger you … you're all a pack of arrogant snobs' and walked out. (Trevor, average income, older, Sydney)

Another focus group participant told of a subtler way of being graded, this time in the Qantas Chairman's Lounge.

I've been fortunate enough a couple of times to be a guest in [the Chairman's Lounge] ... and it's a totally different flying experience. It's just completely different. And you simply wish you could be there, but you never could be because you're not in that particular grade. (Mark, wealthier, older, Melbourne)

Contrary to the narrative of a classless society, these Australians are saying that they understand their 'rightful place in the world'.

Tastes and class

Bourdieu's 1979 masterwork *Distinction: A Social Critique of the Judgement of Taste* is largely devoted to how differences between social classes are expressed through dispositions, behaviours and attitudes; through these, we communicate our status in ways that others recognise and respond to.[47] The marketing industry is now deeply implicated in these processes, and it is nigh impossible to step outside of the system of social types and status. Even when we go to the supermarket, the items we place in our baskets speak to our cultural dispositions and place in the social hierarchy. As Rob Moore observes: 'There is an internal relation between the items in the basket, the structuring principles of consciousness in the head of the shopper and in social relations – in the principle of social order and difference.'[48]

The logic of hierarchical social difference is stark when we find ourselves comparing the basket of goods coming from an Aldi supermarket and one being taken from a farmer's market. Or when we look surreptitiously into the basket of the shopper ahead of us in the queue, we make judgements about their cultural and social position, and do so from our own assumed position in the hierarchy. If, as Bourdieu once noted, how we classify the world classifies ourselves, when we judge the contents of another's shopping basket, then glance up to check that the other shopper looks like the image we have just formed of them from the contents of their basket, we are placing ourselves just as firmly on the social scale.[49]

The cultivation and expressions of tastes is of continuing concern within and between social strata. Bourdieu commented on the distinction between avant-garde theatre, which is more cerebral and astringent, and conventional 'bourgeois' theatre, characterised by social display and enjoyment.[50] Analysing Parisian high culture in the 1970s, he argued: 'Of all the [capital] conversion techniques designed to create and accumulate symbolic capital, the purchase of works of art, objectified evidence of "personal taste", is the one which is closest to the most irreproachable and inimitable form of accumulation ...'[51]

Nowadays, works of art play a less potent role as a sign of distinction for the wealthy elite, not least because of the vulgarisation of the international art market since the 1980s – 'vulgar, Eurotrashy and masturbatory', in the words of one memorable put-down.[52] When Russian oligarchs and oil sheiks begin to outbid all for old masters, it's time for the discerning collector to move on. Even so, the art world's symbolic force should not be underestimated, a topic we explore in the chapter on philanthropy.

In their study of elite cultural preferences in 1990s America, Peterson and Kern analysed the shift away from a refined, high-brow cultural diet to a more eclectic style, even an 'omnivorous' one.[53] A new elite generation began to consume a broader variety of popular culture as well as high culture, suggesting a shift from 'snobbish exclusion to omnivorous appropriation' as a marker of elite status. This broadening in elite taste was a sign of significant changes in power relationships. Peterson and Kern suggest the shift may reflect five factors: greater class mobility making exclusion by culture more difficult; value changes concerning gender, race and religion helping to dissolve cultural boundaries; the breakdown of the high art division between sophistication and vulgarity (think Andy Warhol or Damien Hirst); generational shifts, with young people of all classes consuming popular music genres such as hip-hop; and the fact that cultural omnivorousness provides advantages for elites in a globalised world.[54]

The rise of the cultural omnivore should not be interpreted as the washing out of cultural differences between classes. It is better seen as cultural appropriation by elites, with popular culture often consumed in an ironic way or instrumentally to facilitate dealings with a wider range of people. Elite consecration is as strong as ever, and elite privilege continues to rely on cultural differences as a means of establishing social boundaries that work to exclude outsiders from entering the hallowed grounds. In Australia, highly cultivated tastes are more often a signifier for intellectual and cultural elites than for wealthy and political ones.

Even so, as we will see, the wealthy make sustained efforts to convert financial capital into 'high-brow' cultural capital.

In his study of a small city in Norway, Vegard Jarness interviewed the elites with high cultural capital – artists, academics, cultural producers, and so on – and those with high financial capital.[55] The latter were *nouveau riche*, who had become rich because of a booming oil industry. Jarness classifies the artists, academics, and so on, as those 'located in the cultural fraction of the upper regions of the social space'. He reports them as 'feeling marginalised in an environment perceived as inhabited and dominated by people conspicuously displaying lifestyles, tastes and values alien to their own.' To describe the *nouveau riche*, the cultural elite used words such as 'flashy', 'tacky', 'vulgar', 'indiscreet' and 'loud', words interpreted by Jarness as a 'striking entanglement of moral and aesthetic evaluative criteria'. The rich return the contempt. The cultural elite are 'snobs' and 'elitist', and their strange preferences 'are pretentious expressions of dubious striving to be special' merely 'for the sake of standing out from the crowd'.

Mismatches between cultural capital and financial capital are a staple of comedy. The premise of the television serial *The Beverly Hillbillies* is the awkward cultural misunderstandings and hostilities when a poor family that has struck it rich buys a house among the privileged. In Australia, *Upper Middle Bogan*, whose title also contains the incongruity, works the other way when a middle-class doctor, Bess, who lives in a leafy suburb with architect husband Danny and children Oscar and Edwina, learns she was adopted. When she decides to track down her birth parents, they turn out to be Wayne and Julie, a working-class couple in the outer western suburbs. Bess is disconcerted to find she has three siblings, Amber, Kayne and Brianna, and the family's passion is drag racing. Laughs follow at her expense. Contrary to real life, these programmes always 'punch up', although the English comedian Rob Beckett, a 'chav' whose girlfriend is posh, makes jokes about his own *faux pas* as well as ridiculing his in-laws.[56]

Summary

Special treatment does not just happen. Gaining an exclusive benefit often requires sending a signal that one is being sought, although elites prefer to set the rules of the game so that privileges are built into the system and accountability is easier.

Elites are skilled players of the game of privilege; through early family experience and at elite schools they acquire a 'feel for the game'. The game often requires putting resources into the process of gaining a privilege, especially if the privilege requires negotiating one's way through a complex system involving a variety of actors. The negotiation is often made easier by the orientation of social norms towards the granting of advantages to the elites, norms that are important components in the machinery of privilege.

Where the granting of a privilege is likely to generate blow-back (public outrage, for example), those granting it may use devices to convert an exercise in power into a situation of merit. Even so, if a decision-maker is willing to take the risk, elites seeking privileges may not get their way.

When embodied as a disposition, a signal may be unconscious. Whether explicit or implicit, the privilege seeker and the bestower may need subtle skills to interpret the situation, not least because each may need to account to others for the 'transaction'.

Taste continues to be a powerful means of classification, especially among elites. Elite consumption behaviour is a complex system of signalling status. The very rich often conceal their wealth or display it in ways recognised only by the relevant few. Understatement can be a superior way of expressing dominance. Even so, an unceasing process of classification takes place in hierarchical societies. Boundaries between social strata, even in societies that pretend to be egalitarian, tend to be clear and policed in both subtle and direct ways. In a stratified society, people 'know their place' and adjust their subjective expectations to their objective circumstances.

CHAPTER FOUR

The Geography of Privilege

Privileging space

It's about the space they move in as well. I find that people who are privileged are less comfortable in spaces where they have to jostle, they're less comfortable with crowds. (Josh, wealthier, younger, Sydney)

This comment, from a focus group participant who has worked with the super-rich, was a theme developed by Mike Donaldson and Scott Poynting in their study of 'ruling class men'.

In this atmosphere, the children of the very rich quickly become habituated to large amounts of personal space and remain that way ... Feeling crowded is largely absent from these men's understanding – so much so that they find the infrequent sharing of space discomforting.[1]

Elites create spatial boundaries, the separation confirming their distinction. Elites with access to private suites at the Melbourne Cricket Ground 'enjoy the comfort of exclusive viewing behind sliding glass windows.'[2] At the Qatar World Cup, beyond the spacious VIP enclosure at the main stadium, a special enclave allowed 'VVIPs' to avoid altogether any interaction with the crowd.[3]

Spaciousness is not only a marker of elite status in itself; the elite's discomfort at mixing with others outside their own class is allayed when they control the space and therefore control others who enter it. And easy mobility between exclusive spaces is highly valued by elites. At the upper end, all of these come into play when we try to understand the powerful appeal of super-yachts. It's true that these boats are expected to attract awe when docked in glamour ports such as Monaco (nothing signals 'super rich' better than a super-yacht); but there is more to their psychology than flagrant display.

In the *New Yorker*, Evan Osnos writes that the 'yachts extend a tradition of seclusion as the ultimate luxury.'[4] Said one owner of a mega-yacht: 'If you're on your boat and you don't like your neighbor, you tell the captain, "Let's go to a different place."'[5] Like private islands, an expanse of ocean between oneself and the rest of the world creates a unique sense of seclusion unattainable on land. An experienced super-yacht captain noticed that, once owners and guests relax on board, 'you've got all this extra space, both mental and physical.'[6] The gigayacht owned by the casino magnate James Packer – at more than 100 metres in length it's said to be one of the most impressive in existence – was built by Benetti to incorporate everything one could want for luxe getaways to the world's 'most remote and iconic spots'.[7]

One of our focus group participants had for a time moved in the orbit of a younger group of yacht owners. She explained how they would rendezvous far from land.

> Actually the younger group that were coming up into this industry that were related either by blood, or they were alumni of each other's schools, they actually had this social connection where they would send each other their GPS coordinates, meet somewhere in the middle of the sea on their yachts. I'm not kidding. They would form a group where they all attached their yachts together, spend some time out of the spotlight, and they would exchange details with each other. This is how they socialise. So very, very influential people with a very, very strong sense of this boys' club. (Lilla, average income, older, Sydney)

Perhaps it is not fanciful to suggest that the ultimate dream of owning one's own space – escaping the crowds and the petty intrusions and irritations of social living – is Elon Musk's missions to Mars.

Back on land, in 2004 Beaverstock and others noted that geographers have rarely 'questioned the immense claim that the super-rich make on the landscapes of contemporary cities'.[8] The wealthy elite occupies a vast amount of space, whether it be palatial homes on large blocks in suburbs with wide streets, penthouses covering an entire floor, rural retreats, private art galleries, private islands, capacious offices, or the rolling lawns of the private schools they attend. Space is demanded even after death; it's said that the Packer family vault is the largest in Sydney's South Head Cemetery.[9]

It's not just the amount of space but the quality of it. With a dozen of the city's most expensive suburbs surrounding it, Sydney Harbour is, in effect, owned by the super-rich. For the global super-rich, say real-estate agents, those suburbs have become 'the new mecca'.[10] In this glamour zone, elite private schools, already occupying some of the most expensive real estate in Australia, have been spending millions buying up adjoining properties to provide more space for their pupils.[11]

The super-rich also use a disproportionate volume of natural resources to satisfy their consumption appetites. While a great deal of research has exposed the differing impacts of rich and poor countries on the natural environment, little attention has been devoted to the differential environmental impact of rich lifestyles in affluent nations.[12] Yet the gap is vast because higher consumption spending, and therefore higher resource use and waste, closely tracks higher incomes.

Data are scarce, but a study of how elites are responsible for urban water crises found that the rich in Cape Town, South Africa, used fifty times more water than the poorest.[13] More agricultural land is used to feed each very rich person and supply the wines they drink; they use more fresh water for their lawns and swimming pools. More mining is required to make the various cars and houses they own. And the super-rich have an immense claim on the atmosphere because of their higher consumption levels; at the extreme end, a billionaire is responsible for a million times more carbon emissions than the average person. Their personal jets and yachts account for much greater emissions than their several dwellings.[14]

Consecrating elite suburbs

A city's exclusive suburbs have functions well beyond providing luxury living and signalling status; they also function as sites for the concentrated exercise and cultivation of privilege. Buying into an elite neighbourhood is one of the principal means of converting financial capital into symbolic capital and, over time, cultural capital. Symbolically, residence in an elite suburb signals elite status and the expectation of special treatment. Elite suburbs facilitate the formation of powerful networks that are of benefit to the residents individually and collectively when they need to come together to resist threats. They are also places, as we will see, where the transubstantiation of financial capital into other forms of capital, and back again, is self-reinforcing. They are hothouses for privilege where advantages are passed on to the next generation.

London has been the focus of most scholarly work on the way the super-rich shape and inhabit cities. Atkinson and others have studied the effect of 'the global "über-wealthy" on the local social, economic and political geography of London'.[15] London, however, is a special case, because ultra-rich transnational elites have flocked to its glamour zones of Mayfair and Kensington to establish safe-haven residences and to park money, often ill-gotten, in the City's virtual vaults.[16]

The transubstantiation thesis has been developed in a pioneering study by Ilan Wiesel examining how the privileges of elites are 'supported by the structures, dynamics, and everyday lives of the cities and neighbourhoods in which they reside.'[17] Wiesel carried out an ethnographic study of residents of three of Australia's most affluent and 'glamorous' suburbs – Mosman in Sydney, Toorak in Melbourne and Cottesloe in Perth. These are places for the 1 per cent and even the 0.1 per cent to reside. Mosman is not quite the most expensive suburb in Sydney, but, as Wiesel notes, it is occupied by very affluent professionals, with high concentrations of lawyers, senior managers and doctors.[18] It occupies a unique place in the constellation of values, images and symbols that define Sydney's urban geography. Cottesloe occupies a similar position in Perth.

Exclusivity is not only maintained by the high costs of entry to elite neighbourhoods; through grand houses, acres of lawns, high walls, sleek vehicles, surveillance cameras, and quiet, leafy streets, they also manage to create an atmosphere of wonderment and unapproachability, making outsiders feel out of place. Beyond the cost of a residence, these neighbourhoods project an aura of distinction and rank; they occupy an outsized space in the urban imaginary of the city's residents.[19] A rich person enhances their status when they occupy a residence in a glamour neighbourhood because, no matter how undistinguished they may be, they soak up the collective aura of the neighbourhood. A property ownership deed in an elite suburb, notes Wiesel, 'can be understood as an institutional guarantee of status ....'[20] Farah (average income, older, Melbourne), who had lived in Toorak before her marriage dissolved, spoke of how, when she told people where she lived, they were 'in awe'. She added, 'It's like you were from another planet.'

The famous and 'people of substance' congregate in elite suburbs – from owners of corporations, high-powered barristers, and political leaders to film stars and media personalities. Sydney's Vaucluse, for instance, counts among its residents the powerful Packer family, celebrated developer Harry Triguboff, former cricket captain Michael Clarke, popular media personality Hamish Blake, high-profile hotelier Justin Hemmes, and former chair of the Australian Competition and Consumer Commission, Rod Simms. They are well known for their frequent appearances in the media. The society pages rarely forget to mention the suburb in which the featured person resides. Houses are often known for who lives in them, or once did so. Tour groups pay to gaze at them.

In his ethnographic study of Djursholm, an enclave of privilege outside Stockholm, Mikael Holmqvist noticed that the presence of famous and powerful personages stamps the suburb as one for leaders and those of significance in society, conferring on other residents, who speak proudly of their prominent neighbours, a sense of importance; they assume a certain stature simply by living there.[21] The suburb is *consecrated*, and may therefore be desecrated when the wrong type buys in. This is not to say they always identify themselves with the suburb's public image; some like to give the impression that they are not really of it and present themselves as slightly amused observers of the suburb in which they have chosen to reside. Ilan Wiesel suggests the reluctance of some to identify with their rich neighbourhood may be a peculiarly Australian phenomenon.[22]

The language used to sell houses in glamour suburbs is pitched to appeal to buyers confident of the high esteem in which they are held and their worthiness to occupy a residence of distinction. In advertisements for houses in Toorak, we are told that the property (or 'estate') provides a 'rare opportunity' to own a residence occupying a 'commanding' position. Created by a 'renowned architect' and situated in a 'tightly held precinct' close to 'elite schools', it is a 'celebration of refined elegance'. 'The grandeur of the external aesthetics' creates 'a stunning introduction' to the 'unforgettable' interior spaces.[23] The price is available only 'on application.' For potential buyers judged genuine, there will be no jostling with others to inspect the property; a 'private viewing' will be arranged.

The tone of exclusion is unmistakeable. 'Perfectly private behind its high walled security entry, a powerful facade of concrete, iron and glass precedes equally impressive interiors.' The advertisements are not so gauche as to declare that these homes are suitable only for people of high distinction and quality, but the message is clear enough. Unless a buyer considers themselves to belong to that discerning class, they will feel that living in Toorak is not their place. For those who feel they do belong there, it's implied, it is because of their refinement, their elevated qualities as a person, and their position in society rather than their money. It is for this reason that *nouveaux riches* who buy into the suburb only to flaunt their wealth in flashy displays are so unwelcome – they expose an uncomfortable truth.

Elite suburbs evolve to signal to the rest of the world that only certain kinds of people reside there – those who know how to behave and present themselves, people who are comfortable with the awe that an imposing residence in Toorak or Vaucluse attracts. Others with the ability to buy know it's not a place for them. They feel intimidated by the atmosphere and alienated by the smugness of the in-groups. Hana (wealthier, older, Melbourne) chooses to live in a middling suburb even though she owns a property in expensive East Malvern. She said she does not feel comfortable in the city's leafy elite suburbs. She is unwilling to do the work required to make herself acceptable. Others do not want their children growing up in a rarefied environment remote from the normal world, a place where they might absorb the attitudes of privilege and entitlement.[24]

Elite suburbs as sites for accumulation

Through interviews with residents of elite neighbourhoods, Wiesel showed how residing in and soaking up the reputation of a neighbourhood from which the great majority are excluded brings a quiet pride and feeling of self-satisfaction while also presenting opportunities to build social and cultural capital. Holmqvist reported that the symbolic value of an address in Djursholm, the exclusive enclave on the edge of Stockholm, has material value. As one of his interviewees said: 'A home address in Djursholm is quite clearly useful in your professional life.'[25]

Elite neighbourhoods are places where the cost of entry provides the opportunity to build valuable social capital. Many residents report having high-powered friends, such as CEOs, business owners, judges and MPs. Even the very rich invest money, time and effort in local facilities, including serving on boards and even cleaning up the park. Some Cottesloe residents mentioned Andrew Forrest, mining mogul and Australia's second richest person, 'donating extensively to the school his children attended.'[26] In Mosman, with a concentration of finance professionals and lawyers, those who work in the Sydney's central business district across the harbour are known to socialise on the morning ferry. 'When you're on that ferry it is actually a powerful place,' a resident told Wiesel. 'These people are like scarily high up in various businesses ...'[27]

Wiesel showed how these friendships are often built through the organisations of the elite suburb, such as schools, residents' associations and sporting clubs. Tennis, rugby, cricket and swimming clubs are seen by some as influential institutions so that board membership can be a powerful status symbol and 'an entry point into elite social networks'.[28] Schools are viewed as an opportunity for children to build networks that will be beneficial in later life. It's similar in Sweden, where Holmqvist wrote of residents in Djursholm frankly admitting they adopt an instrumental approach to building social networks through their children's schools, both for their children and for themselves.[29] The parents take an active interest in who shares a class with their children, pressuring the schools to place their children in classes that allow them to make the 'right' friends and cultivate the best networks to serve them in the future. As one teacher put it: 'Parents here think in a highly strategic manner about their children and their school. ... Moving to Djursholm is a social investment for many; there's a hope that you can get something out of it professionally, and not least something also for your children.'[30]

While these networks are personally advantageous, they also improve the cohesion of neighbourhood elites. From their suburbs, elites can reach into centres of power via well-connected and influential individuals to respond to threats to the amenity, ambience and distinction of the suburb. Most obviously, if influential political figures live locally, friendships can blur 'the boundary between socialising and lobbying'. One of Wiesel's interviewees told him: 'if you whisper in the right ear, you can get results.'[31] A high concentration of residents who understand how the system works – indeed, who work in the system – is a fast track to privileged treatment.[32] On planning issues, street protests are 'unbefitting'. However, as one Toorak resident explained it to Wiesel: 'Generally it's just having a quiet word to people and pressing the right buttons. ... Everything's possible in a democracy. Well there are so many Queen's Counsel living in Toorak and so many incredibly important businessmen, there's no way the council's going to ignore them.'[33] They may, however, be pitted against other powerful interests, such as developers with deep pockets and political connections.

Being among the elite demands a mastery of social classification, both to function successfully and to defend one's own place in the hierarchy. Each elite suburb has its place within a city's hierarchy of distinction, and within elite suburbs there are fine gradations of status – a generally shared understanding of which streets are more prestigious and which parts of certain streets have greater distinction.[34] Of course, there is always rivalry, generally good-humoured but occasionally breaking into argument. Wiesel recounts the attempt by residents of more prestigious areas of Mosman (those with harbour views) to have the suburb divided into five suburbs, with residents of the most up-market area 'seeking to differentiate themselves from less prestigious parts of Mosman.' Residents of the other areas opposed the plan.

Toorak is generally regarded as Melbourne's most prestigious suburb. It is sometimes compared with Sydney's Bellevue Hill, although the competition at the top for Sydney's smartest suburb is lively.[35] The rivalry extends from elite suburbs to elite schools, with a few competing for the appellation of best school.

The most prestigious suburbs face the threat of 'contamination' should the wrong sort of people move in.[36] The *nouveau riche* provide perhaps the most serious and persistent danger because they do not have the cultural capital to fit in. Wiesel noted that globalisation has brought greater ethnic diversity to the wealthy elites. He recorded anxiety expressed by his participants about wealthy Chinese people moving in, but he also noted the potential for shared class identity and conservative-capitalist values overriding ethnic difference.[37]

Moral geography

Holmqvist writes that today a rich person is assumed to be not only talented but also 'a *good* person in a moral sense', certainly by other wealthy people.[38] The observation goes back at least to Shakespeare, who wrote of gold in *Timon of Athens*:

> Thus much of this will make black white, foul fair
> Wrong right, base noble, old young, coward valiant.

Or, in Marx's pithier version, 'Money is the supreme good, therefore its possessor is good.' Places where money concentrates take on the aura of wealth.

While pointing to a general truth, the homology between wealth and good character is more complicated on the ground. While most who live in elite suburbs enjoy or even bask in the distinction it confers, for some it carries a stigma. It is not only residents of low-status suburbs who, when asked where they live, dissimulate. In our focus group conversations, Jessica (wealthier, younger) admitted she hides the fact she lives in Dover Heights, an expensive suburb in Sydney's east. 'There's many times I'd say that I'm not from the suburb I am in, just to avoid that discussion.' When Holly (wealthier, younger) from Vaucluse was asked about her suburb, she shut down the conversation with: 'I don't really talk about my suburb.'

Wiesel suggests that the burden of being known to reside in an elite suburb is felt mainly by women and young people.[39] Wealth is not admired everywhere and can attract derision – accusations of snobbishness or being a 'silvertail'. Wiesel notes the assumption made by some that, while men are assumed to have 'earned it', women and young people are 'sponging' off a wealthy family.

People carry in their heads a 'moral map' of the city in which we live (and those we get to know) as if each suburb is shaded with its own moral qualities. A few suburbs are the colour of prestige, distinction and power, although some may be overlaid with the tint of snobbishness and self-satisfaction. Other suburbs are coloured trustworthy and reliable, some are dull and law-abiding, while at the disreputable end of the colour code are those shaded unsavoury. As a rule, moral judgements about the people who live in a suburb are masked by words that describe the area itself.

These moral maps include nuanced variations both between similar suburbs and within suburbs, often street by street. Real-estate agents have a sixth sense for these differences.

In his interviews with residents of affluent suburbs, Wiesel uncovered 'the complex discourses of classification and stratification of neighbourhoods within and across cities'.[40] Toorak, for example, is seen by its residents as 'the place for people of distinction'. In the business world, being recognised as a Mosman resident meant being perceived as of good background, reliable and 'good for your word'.[41] Mosman residency is seen as a kind of 'gold star', one said. It is a privilege simply to be able to buy into an elite suburb and cloak oneself in the moral qualities projected onto it.

When the focus groups were asked whether mentioning the suburb in which they live opens or closes doors or changes the way people view them, the stories they told came easily.

> It's just, it's the face. ... I just take it that they look down on me because I live in Altona. (Hana, wealthier, older, Melbourne)

> I'd say 'out west' and say the suburb, and you'd actually see people cringe and, you know, say stupid comments. ... I definitely have said it [his suburb's name] to people and seen them cringe. (Luca, average income, younger, Sydney)

As an expression of revulsion, the cringe is a highly functional gesture in maintaining urban stratification.[42] The cold silence works the same way. Patricia (average, older, Sydney) told a revealing story about working at a private bank. The very wealthy clients accepted her readily after it became known she lived in an up-market suburb.

> I worked with another woman who lived in Mount Druitt, so a very different suburb. Polar opposites ... There was a noticeable difference in the way that some of our clients would interact with me. They would ask a lot more personal questions and be interested in me and be very friendly. I mean, they'd give you gifts at the end of the year and what have you, whereas there was potentially ... well, I used to feel that, for whatever reason, there was not as much interaction with the other woman who worked in the same sort of role as I did. ... I felt really self-conscious about that ... [but] you can't call anyone out on that sort of thing.

Asked if her colleague noticed it, Patricia replied:

> Absolutely. And she felt quite excluded by some of the ways that people would talk to me, right in front of her, mind you. There was a sort of inherent closeness for some reason that people felt they could relate to me almost instantaneously, as opposed to this individual.

Within a city's middling or average suburbs there are widely understood gradations that influence perceptions of residents. Phillip (average income, older, Melbourne) referred to differences among the northern suburbs of Melbourne: '... in the northern suburbs where I come from ... [there is] a bit of a separation, differential, like for example, if you were from Coburg or Essendon [or] Moonee Ponds, it's different than if you were in Bundoora or Epping Park or Thomastown.' He later put it in a colourful way: 'If I see a guy driving the Lamborghini up in Coburg or Craigieburn I think, yeah, he's definitely a drug dealing boss. If I see one in Toorak, he's a lawyer or a billionaire.'

In 2022, a conservative MP and former housing minister in Victoria, Wendy Lovell, said the unsayable in parliament.

> There is no point putting a very low income, probably welfare-dependent family in the best street in [up-market] Brighton where the children cannot mix with others or go to the school with other children, or where they do not have the same ability to have the latest in sneakers and iPhones. ... We have got to make sure that people can actually fit into a neighbourhood, that they have a good life, and that people are not stigmatising them because of their circumstances.[43]

Although Lovell framed her argument against social mixing in elite suburbs as one of concern for poor children, her desire to impose boundaries with 'the other' is common among wealthy elites.[44] She was lambasted for perpetuating 'misguided stereotypes' about the poor. One of the 'most respected' comments beneath the newspaper story revealed the moral geography behind Lovell's opinion: 'There are many, many people requiring public housing whose *values and personal qualities* are the equivalent of and often exceed those found in wealthier suburbs. Regrettably, this privileged politician does not have the wit to realize this.'[45]

On not having to wait

If elites have a distinctive relationship with space, the same may be said of their relationship with time. It's a truth that becomes apparent when we consider waiting. Jumping or avoiding queues is an obvious manifestation of privilege, one commented on by our focus group participants. Drew (average income, younger, Sydney), reflecting on 'the community of privileged people', told of obtaining special tickets from a friend who works for the agency that manages major sporting venues. 'I have never had to ever queue up when going to the footy or whatever and going to get food or drink at the football.' Josh (wealthier, younger, Sydney) spoke of how the very rich not only jump queues but often move in spheres where there are no queues, worlds without queues that those without privilege are not aware of.

The relationship between waiting and privilege goes beyond the ability to use power and influence to save time. Waiting and, even more so, being made to wait is a way of experiencing the power of others over you, creating a feeling of weakness and vulnerability, a sense that 'one is not fully in command of one's life'.[46] Anyone who has had the misfortune of spending hours in a hospital emergency ward knows that the medical system is 'one of the sites par excellence of anxious, powerless waiting'.[47] In a seminal study, Barry Schwartz came to a blunt conclusion: 'the distribution of waiting time coincides with the distribution of power.'[48]

> The relative immunity from waiting which the powerful enjoy is guaranteed because they have the resources to refuse to wait …. The privileged also wait less because they are least likely to tolerate its costs; they are more inclined to renege from as well as balk at entering congested waiting channels.[49]

The theme was taken up by Bourdieu. Making people wait, he wrote, is essential to the work of domination.[50] The state and its bureaucracies 'impose temporalities' – that is, impose certain relationships with time as an expression of state power. Citizens are compelled to wait with little control over the outcome, so these temporalities shape the citizen–state relationship.[51] Unlike everyday citizens, elites do not view the state as a mysterious and alien force. They understand the processes of bureaucracy and where the points of discretion lie. They know people and how to use their resources (networks, status, power) to remove blockages. If they are unfamiliar with a system, they know someone who can advise and guide them.

For members of the elite, accustomed to being granted the privilege of special access, when the tables are turned and they must wait, it becomes intolerable. At the extreme end, a close observer of owners of super-yachts wrote that the most consistent way to upset them is to make them wait. Everything must happen to their schedule.[52] The distress is magnified if they are also forced to rub shoulders with the crowd. Waiting makes them feel dependent, subordinate and disrespected, so they find ways to avoid it. Sometimes simply paying more does not work, because doing so may be illegal, violate a rule of fairness or expose a decision-maker to rebuke.

During the harsh and exceptional conditions of the pandemic, elites were required to submit to state power by waiting. This imposed immobility was intolerable for some. However, our examination of documents released under freedom of information laws, notably those bearing on Kerry Stokes, confirm that, for the powerful citizen, the state can respond with deference and urgency to a request to bypass normal channels or gain exemptions.

Elites responded in several ways to the new temporalities imposed by the state. A few did not have to wait for restrictions to be eased before resuming travel interstate or overseas. They were permitted to take private jets or they found loopholes to allow them to move around on their yachts. Some required to quarantine found ways of waiting it out in comfort at home or in secondary residences. As we will see in chapter 5, students at an elite school did not have to wait for lockdowns to be lifted before enjoying their winter term in the snow. And some did not have to wait until they qualified to receive a vaccination.

These ways of avoiding waiting, at a time of great social stress, allowed elites to regain control over their lives, to move through the world as they chose to rather than to put their lives in the hands of others. Uninhibited mobility is one of the privileges demanded by elites.

Summary

Elites make their own spaces, separating themselves from others and avoiding crowds, which they find discomforting. The privileges of elites are sustained by the image and dynamics of their suburbs, a subject explored by Ilan Wiesel. The presence of famous and powerful residents stamps these suburbs as places for leaders of society and people of distinction. Their atmosphere of wonderment and aura of exclusiveness consecrates them.

Exclusive suburbs are hothouses for capital accumulation. Buying into an elite neighbourhood allows financial capital to be converted into social and cultural capital. Networks can be built with influential neighbours, not least through sports clubs and schools, networks that reach into power centres. Along with shared culture and the symbolic value of an exclusive address, these networks can be converted back into financial capital.

Each elite neighbourhood has its own place in a city's hierarchy of distinction. Rich people are often attributed with a good moral character, so that buying into an elite suburb allows one to assume its moral attributes. Carrying around a 'moral map' of our cities, we all participate in this. When residents of low-status suburbs reveal where they live, they can be shamed and excluded. In certain social environments, residents of exclusive suburbs may be embarrassed to say where they live and are known to dissemble.

Elites have a distinctive relationship to time as well as space. Controlling others' time, such as by imposing 'anxious, powerless waiting', is a means of exercising dominance. The privileged do not tolerate having to wait and use their networks, status and understanding of the system to avoid it, methods that became more visible during the pandemic when the state imposed queuing and restrictions on mobility. The state showed how it permits powerful citizens to regain control over their time and mobility.

CHAPTER FIVE

Replicating Privilege: Elite Schools

'Educational apartheid'

In the machinery of privilege, elite private schools are the engine.[1] Our focus group participants often began speaking unprompted about elite schools when discussing privilege in society. The public holds strong opinions about private schools. Our survey results show that 45 per cent of Australians believe that expensive private schools 'entrench inequality in society'. Thirty-one per cent say that a better reflection of their opinion is that expensive private schools 'improve educational choice' (24 per cent can't say). Not unexpectedly, compared to those who attended public schools, those who attended high-fee private schools are twice as likely to say they improve educational choice (57 per cent versus 28 per cent for those from public schools), although almost a third of those who attended expensive schools agree that they entrench inequality.

We will suggest that, when Bourdieu writes that each group sets up the means of its own perpetuation 'beyond the finite individuals in whom it is incarnated', this applies par excellence to the creation of exclusive schools by wealthy elites.[2] In his ethnographic study of Djursholm, the enclave of privilege outside Stockholm, Mikael Holmqvist reached a similar conclusion; it is the schools that 'guarantee that the children have a shining, as opposed to a mediocre, future.'[3]

Most Western countries have schools for the exclusive education of the sons and daughters of the wealthy elite. In Britain, only 7 per cent of children attend private schools, with high fees ensuring that most are from very affluent families.[4] In *Engines of Privilege*, a book about Britain's private schools, Francis Green and David Kynaston describe them as powering an 'enduring cycle of privilege' that creates an 'educational apartheid'.[5] On average, the annual fee to attend a private day school in England is £15,000. The average for the ten 'best' schools (by GCSE results) is closer to £24,000.[6] A few of the most exclusive, such as Winchester College, Harrow and Charterhouse, charge more than £40,000 annually for the last two years of schooling.[7]

In the United States, close to 10 per cent of students attend private schools, most of which are church affiliated.[8] Most elite schools are private and charge well over US$50,000 per year. They have access to other scarce resources. 'Those resources', wrote Shamus Rahman Khan in his influential study, 'included academic capital, social ties to elite families and other institutions of power, the capacity to guide and transfer culture, economic capacity, and human resources.'[9]

Wealth brings its own rewards and often does so through the intercedence of exclusive private schools. A novel US study published in 2023 found that, after accounting for SAT/ACT college admission scores, children from the wealthiest 1 per cent of families are twice as likely as those from middle-class families to be admitted to the most prestigious colleges, the 'Ivy-Plus' (the eight Ivy League colleges plus Stanford, MIT, Duke and Chicago).[10] This advantage of wealth is explained by three factors: preference for the children of alumni (often wealthy donors), non-academic credentials, and the recruitment of athletes.[11] The authors note that student athletes are more likely to come from affluent families than poor ones. And non-academic credentials are actively cultivated at elite high schools. By preferring students from very rich families, the authors conclude, elite colleges 'perpetuate privilege across generations'. The Ivy-Plus colleges supply a quarter of US senators, half of all Rhodes scholars and three-quarters of Supreme Court justices. Graduates are more likely to enter the 1 per cent, attend elite graduate schools and be recruited to prestigious firms.

In Australia, private secondary schools educate a much higher proportion, around 40 per cent of students.[12] They can be divided between a small number of expensive schools (with annual fees of A$30,000 to A$45,000) catering to around 5 per cent of students, and mostly associated with Protestant churches, and a large number of low to middling-fee schools (with annual fees of A$4,000 to A$10,000) that are a mix of Catholic, Protestant, other religious and secular private schools. Lower-fee private schools rely on extensive support from state and federal governments, while elite private schools raise millions annually in fees, tax-deductible donations and investment revenues. They also receive government subsidies.

A few public school students are lucky enough to attend academically selective high schools. It might be thought that, by providing high-quality free education to clever kids from poorer families, selective public high schools help even up the advantage held by expensive private schools. In practice, selective public schools are overwhelmingly populated by children from affluent families, illustrating the enormous advantages conferred on children by the socio-economic status of their parents.[13] Spared six years of high fees, affluent parents whose children are accepted to these schools feel like they have won the lottery, except that it is not really a matter of luck. Winning a prized place at a selective school is usually the result of a carefully devised plan executed over several years by motivated parents with access to inside knowledge and resources for private tutoring.

Exclusiveness and distinction

In Australia, it is often said by elite school spokespersons that fees had to be raised because their expenses had increased. In fact, it's the reverse. The most expensive schools set their fees to send a signal of exclusivity to the market. Enrolment at an elite school is a 'positional good' – that is, ownership by a select few conveys something special about them: high social status. In Australia, elite schools have very large assets. Sydney Church of England Grammar School ('Shore'), for example, was estimated in 2019 to own assets totalling A$590 million, while Scotch College in Melbourne owned A$314 million.[14] Money pouring in from higher fees, donations and investment returns needs to find a use. There is always a new concert hall or state of the art gym to be built. In Britain, education finance expert Rebecca Boden noted the same phenomenon. 'By increasing the price they deliberately and consciously price out less wealthy families and end up with a lot of money which they put into ever-more luxurious facilities. This helps cement class power and privilege.'[15]

If Eton College were to halve its fees while otherwise remaining the same, the rich and powerful would soon begin sending their sons to Harrow and Winchester. Susan Ostrander reported an American mother of children at an elite school saying: 'You don't go to private school just for your education. You go there to be separated from ordinary people.'[16] The comment was made in 1984, yet it remains as true today. In Australia, there is evidence that parents in elite suburbs fear that sending their children to public schools would damage their social standing.[17]

Ostrander concluded that attending expensive schools is a way for the elite to 'create and maintain the exclusivity of their way of life and their social interactions.'[18] The women she interviewed recognised the class functions of private schools and 'fully supported them as necessary for their children's well-being.'

In an innovative research programme, Jane Kenway and her colleagues studied several elite private schools around the world to understand 'how class is choreographed and how choreographies of class … work to artic-ulate, disarticulate and rearticulate certain formations of dominance.'[19] Among many insights, they found that, in an era of rapidly worsening wealth distribution, elite schools are exacerbating the 'distances between the rich and the rest around the globe'.[20]

Kenway's selected schools relentlessly cultivate the sense of a tightly bound community of school, teachers, students and parents, like a special club. Occasionally, the exclusion of others and the perpetuation of privilege and power are publicly acknowledged by principals and parents. According to Timothy Hawkes, the former principal of the King's School in Sydney, 'The reality is that schools like King's produce a disproportionate number of people who are likely to be leaders in society and I don't think there is much to be gained from being coy about that.'[21] As Hawkes saw it, the boys at King's were being schooled to rule. Daily life surrounded by extraordinarily lavish facilities and beautified school grounds adds to the sense of their own eliteness.[22]

The same attitude pervades the top tier of private schools in Britain (known confusingly as 'public schools'). As one graduate observed: 'I joined Westminster School [in London] for sixth form. On my first day we were given a talk by the headmaster, who told us: "You are the crème de la crème of this country. Sitting around you are future leaders. Don't you forget it."'[23] Elite private schools, therefore, perform a function like that attributed to 'leader communities' by Mikael Holmqvist in his study of an exclusive suburb of Stockholm. In addition to the socialisation of a student into the culture and practices of elites, these schools aim at 'imbuing him or her with certain higher moral and spiritual qualities'.[24] (We later consider whether the students do, in fact, have higher moral qualities.) This process of elevation is referred to as *consecration*, the sanctification of students as beyond the ordinary. They are moulded into 'objects of authority, power and influence, with the result that others learn that "they are not just anyone, but "elite"'.

The process of consecration occurs through the continued re-creation of an aura arising from 'the culture, history, traditions, ceremonies, rituals, and institutions' of the school. The schools become, in the words of Kenway and others, 'spaces of elective affinity, imbuing students with the sense of wonder and specialness of the school worlds that they are initiated into and that they inhabit',[25] which explains why so many ex-students never leave their schools behind them. Green and Kynaston make a similar argument about Britain's expensive schools, with their sumptuous surroundings cultivating in their students 'the sensibilities of a privileged class, the feeling of being special'.[26] At the schools, students 'move with ease in affluent and august settings', imbuing them with the dispositions appropriate to the world of privilege. In Sydney, a student debater from a state school spoke of the 'aura of confidence' surrounding her opponents from the elite schools.[27]

In her study of elite schooling in Australia, Sue Saltmarsh found that the status of an expensive private school depends not only on its exclusive practices and high fees but also on whether it has been 'consecrated' as among the elite.[28] A school's age and history matter. A new school, even if it were to set the highest fees, could not be considered elite. Saltmarsh argues that elite status can be recognised by practices that discursively, through both its rhetoric and visual icons and images, consecrate certain types of schools 'as sites of power, privilege, and educational, social and moral superiority'. Websites, prospectuses and school histories, grand openings of new buildings with attendant dignitaries, and the daily affirmation of specialness within the school community are forms of symbolic power aimed at conferring entitlement.

Making symbolic capital

In the 1950s, Erving Goffman described Britain's private schools as 'a machine for systematically re-creating middle-class people in the image of the aristocracy',[29] which helps explain why Australia's most exclusive schools, particularly the boys' schools, work so hard to simulate the ethos and feel of the fabled English public schools such as Eton and Harrow. They are reconstructing the symbols of power and distinction.

Elite schools, write Kenway and others, marshal their heritage, iconographies, rituals and alumni to signal prestige and success and use them in 'hyper-celebratory, highly ornamental ways.'[30] They put their 'extraordinary historical archives and cultural patrimony to work' as a way of marketing and reinforcing their eliteness, constantly fortifying the view that those who attend are exceptional and confirming to parents that their money has been well spent. Under 'Our heritage and faith', the website of Sydney's Scots College displays old photos of boys playing bagpipes as if marching off to war – 'true examples of "Brave Hearts Bold Minds"' – and speaks of students being inspired by 'generations of Old Boys who walked the halls before them including eminent community leaders, Rhodes Scholars and world class sportsmen.'[31] Some maintain cadet corps to train boys and girls in military discipline and leadership.

The ceaseless celebration of famous and accomplished alumni serves several functions. Their esteem burnishes the reputation of the school and signals to parents and the wider community that the school has succeeded in its mission to create leaders. It also strengthens the school's networking with powerful people, helping to protect it from threats and providing current students with a leg-up in the world, not least when successful alumni serve as mentors.[32] And of course it has a financial payoff in donations.

Twice a year, Geelong Grammar (Australia's most expensive school and celebrated for hosting the young Prince Charles for a year) combs through the list of Australian honours recipients to identify alumni and congratulates them conspicuously. Similarly, the former King's School principal (Timothy Hawkes) wrote in one of his annual reports that 'it was a pleasure to note how many Old Boys and friends of the School were recognised in the Australia Day Honours List and the Queen's Birthday Honours List this year.'[33] One of Geelong Grammar's favourite sons is Tim Fairfax AC (Companion of the Order of Australia, the highest award, equivalent to a knighthood in Britain). Fairfax is a scion of the Fairfax family that made its fortune from newspapers and is prominent for giving away his inherited wealth to good causes. In an impressive ceremony in 2022, his alma mater awarded him the Geelong Grammar School Medal for Service to Society, the school's 'highest honour'.[34]

Elite schools mobilise their histories, duly airbrushed, to legitimize their existence. A glossy insert in the *Sydney Morning Herald* advertising the wares of the city's most expensive schools displays a number of patterns in the carefully curated text, layout and images selected by the marketing experts.[35] The students featured in the images displayed are notable for their neat, pressed, well-fitted uniforms. The more traditional schools proudly feature old-fashioned military-like garb and faux-Eton boaters. Several schools begin their pitches with statements such as 'For more than 138 years ...', 'Established in 1884 ...' and 'Founded in 1889 ...'.

In their marketing, elite schools deploy juxtapositional rhetoric, as Allan and Charles call it, to capture both the traditional ethos of the school and its commitment to innovation.[36] In the glossy insert, text and imagery meld the solidity of tradition with the excitement of the contemporary, perfectly captured by the photo used by Newington College of a hyper-modern glass building in which is reflected an old sandstone edifice reminiscent of the chapel at Rugby School. Stressing the opulence of its facilities, the school boasts to prospective parents: 'We are fortunate [although luck plays little role] to have beautiful and expansive grounds that include four ovals, tennis courts, historic sandstone buildings and wonderful modern facilities, including a purpose-built drama theatre, pool and gym.'

In their volume *Class Choreographies*, Kenway and her co-authors comment on elite schools' systematic investment in symbolic capital, noting 'the hegemonic work of anthems, honour boards, plaques, titles, regalia, costumes, uniforms, emblems and standards ...'.[37] This elaborate panoply of ornamentation is vital for legitimising the schools' specialness both at home and abroad, attracting foreign students whose parents carry around an imaginary of the great English public school, with its quirky traditions, ancient halls, supreme networks and (apparent) commitment to quality of education, all of which contribute to 'the shimmering elevation of the elite school over all comers'.[38]

Making social capital

Elite schools operate as sites for the transubstantiation of capital, where wealth can be converted into the higher forms of social and cultural capital. For the *nouveau riche*, in particular, sending one's children to expensive private schools is part of 'the timeless quest to make new money old',[39] where 'old money' is understood to be not merely money that has been in the family for a long time but money that has acquired the smell of wealth rather than of cash. For old money families, the years their children spend at an exclusive school are an indispensable condition for the intergenerational transfer of elite status.[40]

In 2001, the novelist Shane Maloney scandalised the assembled students and staff of Melbourne's elite Scotch College when he described their school as 'a machine for the transmission of inherited privilege'.

> It is not your fault, after all, that your families decided to institutionalise you. It is not your fault that your mothers and fathers elected to place you in the emotionally distorting and educationally deficient environment of an all-boys school ... Right now you are the victims. Later, of course, society will be your victim, and will suffer from the attitudes with which you are indoctrinated here.[41]

Networks are seen as vital at a very practical level; parents enrol their children at prestigious schools to give them social networks they can exploit later in life. The 22,000 alumni of Wesley College keep in touch with an app, promoted as the best way to open doors and maximise the benefits of the old school network.[42]

Our focus group participants were clear on this question. Tony (wealthier, older, Sydney), who works in the finance industry, said that, if a 'high-flying career job' comes up, 'the private school privileged child has some sort of immunity against the public school child.' Peter, a GP from the same group, observed: '... from an educational point of view, they [expensive private schools] don't necessarily turn out brilliant people. But there is again the privilege because of this Old Boys network and who you know and connections, which I think are much stronger than in public schools.' Gail (wealthier, older, Melbourne) spoke of how her brother used his attendance at an elite school to get jobs and to establish superiority in social situations, adding: 'Being a girl, it's not so important. So I was quite surprised when this man, who was the CEO, asked me, "What school did you go to?" And I could reel off some nice schools ... and he was "Oh"' [approvingly surprised]. The association of elite schools with powerful networks was shared across the focus groups. 'They're wealthy families who are putting their kids through them. That's the top schools. And so it's wealthy connecting with wealthy. It's a very privileged kind of network, you know what I mean?' (Paul, average income, older, Sydney). The heavy emphasis on school status seems to be more prevalent in Sydney and Melbourne than elsewhere in Australia. One focus group participant schooled in Adelaide noted that it is not such a big thing there compared to Melbourne.

In his ethnographic study of elite suburbs in Melbourne, Sydney and Perth, Ilan Wiesel confirmed the essential role of elite networking from childhood. One of his interviewees from Toorak was blunt: 'I think networks are really important and we all like to give our children the advantages we can.'[43] One explained how the powerful and prominent had all been at school together because they lived in the same elite suburbs, and if they come into the orbit of a powerful businessman or politician then 'it's quite likely that they've been to one of the three or four main schools, the Scots or Riverview and those ones.'

The same phenomenon prevails in Britain. In 2019, a Marlborough College old boy, Mark Tidmarsh, told *The Times*: 'Parents now expect that what they pay for is not just five years of teaching but lifetime membership to a special club. It's the reason people decide to send their kids to public schools [i.e. elite private schools] and not to the local academy, where they may very well perform better academically.'[44]

In sum, beyond families and suburbs, Australia's elite schools are the foremost unifying institution of the ruling elite, instilling in them a shared identity as the natural leaders of the nation. This helps to explain why even some of the busiest and most high-powered parents take time out to participate in the activities of their children's school community,[45] including taking a place on the school council, from where they can activate their powerful networks and managerial skills to advance the interests of the schools.

Making cultural capital

Among the elements of cultural capital are certain psychological dispositions, not the least of which is the way elite schools systematically instil in their charges the expectation of success, as measured by money, status and power. In its rendering of the neoliberal creed of personal success, Sydney Church of England Girls' Grammar School (Year 12 fee A$37,000) declares that 'We can choose to be in control of our destiny, or we can have it determined by others' (as if the girls' destinies were not already shaped by their birth into affluent families and enrolment at an exclusive school). The disposition towards success enhances their ability to navigate the fields of power. One of our focus group participants captured it this way.

> I think they give the students confidence. ... all of the kids just get confidence. It's like inbred, that we're all going to do well and we're all intelligent. ... Both of my sons went to Melbourne Grammar ... I certainly saw that. I think it's in the water there. (Lydia, wealthier, older, Melbourne)

It is remarkable how consistently exclusive schools tell students and parents that they are there to learn how to be leaders. Scots College declares: 'Leadership, Character, Spirit – as a College our challenge is to ensure that these intrinsic elements resonate richly in the hearts and minds of every Scots boy.'[46] In a colonialist echo, the deputy head of the King's School writes that 'Kingsmen' are trained to be thought leaders who 'assume a sense of responsibility for the global community'.[47] That the students will become leaders in business, the professions or politics is taken for granted, and it does not take long before the boys begin to exude that sense of themselves. Almost all these schools are owned by religious organisations, mainly Protestant churches with a few Catholic ones and Jewish organisations, and they teach a kind of 'success theology' more resonant with an MBA prospectus than the Sermon on the Mount.

The arrogance of assumed superiority that sometimes lies just below the surface of these schools was cruelly parodied by Chris Lilley playing private school girl Ja'mie in the mockumentary *We Can Be Heroes*.[48] In fact, judging by the evidence collected by Kenway, Langmead and Epstein, Ja'mie may be truer to type than the parody suggests, because the determination to create global leaders is just as characteristic of elite girls' schools as it is of elite boys' schools.[49] However, they argue that cocooning the girls at elite schools from the variety of social life leaves them poorly equipped to achieve positions of global leadership, and the neoliberal 'faux' feminism taught by the schools leaves them unprepared to confront and deal with the misogyny that lies deep in the world of elite employment.

The expectation that graduates will be successful and assume dominant social positions is not merely a disposition but becomes embodied in the postures, grooming, mannerisms and ways of speaking imparted by the schools. This embodiment is unmistakable to others; in South Africa, a black student from a poor township who was educated at an elite girls' school told of how, when she returns home, the people there say, 'Oh you're a coconut.'[50] As we saw, our focus group participants said they recognise a privileged person by 'how they hold themselves' and how they naturally dominate a conversation. Most conspicuously, the students are almost always slender and well-groomed. If they deviate from the norm then the other students may bring them into line. Allan and Charles report an instance of a girl judged 'a bit on the plump side' by her peers at an elite girls' school. Other students made it clear she was letting the side down and helped her lose weight.[51] Consideration of bodies naturally raises questions about the experience of girls at elite schools as distinct from that of boys. In their study of elite girls' schools, Kenway, Langmead and Epstein suggest that intense pressure to excel spills out in disorders such as anorexia – what they describe as 'thin and worried girls' concealed by the schools' 'façade of the blithely brilliant'.[52]

Holly (wealthier, younger, Sydney) told of how, after joining the workforce, she realised that she had unconsciously learned to speak in a certain way at her exclusive eastern suburbs school.

> I remember having a senior director come up to me and say, 'I recognize your accent.' I don't have an accent because I was born in Australia. And she told me, 'You need to go visit this partner [of the firm] in this room; you've got the same accent.' I went to visit them, and we went to the same school ten years apart. So after that, work became a little bit easier, just to have a role model who took time with me.

Habituated to the trappings of privilege, most children enrolled at elite private schools accumulate cultural capital unawares. However, for those not already familiar with it, learning how to carry oneself, to project ease and self-confidence, requires work. For students from less advantaged backgrounds and from overseas, accumulating the cultural capital offered by an elite school is liable to be a more conscious and onerous task, as Jane Kenway has pointed out.[53] For some, though, acquiring cultural capital takes second place behind strong academic results.[54] A focus group participant put forward her observation that parents from Asian countries seem less interested in a school's traditions.

> They don't value that old school tie. They value more, for example, [academically selective] Melbourne High School or Balwyn High School, where they're known for their high ATAR scores, so they would rather send their kids there than to one of those private schools where perhaps, you know, they've got the long history. (Farah, average income, older, Melbourne)

It is for this reason that elite schools, while chasing overseas students for the revenue, limit the number they admit to maintain the ethnic and cultural homogeneity that is necessary to sustain a close community. One elite school sets an informal limit of 10 per cent to maintain its 'whiteness'.[55] In publicity material, some schools feature the faces of their students from China and other countries in Asia while other schools show only white faces.

Moral distinction

Exclusive schools claim to imbue their students with higher moral qualities. Prospectuses and websites promise to impart to their charges exemplary character, and this spills into broader public perceptions. How deeply this presumption runs is suggested by a 2022 newspaper report concerning a graduate of an elite school jailed for a string of drug importation offences. The *Sydney Morning Herald* story emphasised that it was a 'long fall' from 'one of the most prestigious schools to prison', suggesting that those who graduate from elite private schools, in this case Sydney Grammar School, are of higher moral calibre, so that getting mixed up in criminality is a sad deviation from the expected.[56] The media would not characterise the path from suburban public school to prison as a 'long fall'.

As far as we are aware, there has been no scholarly study comparing the ethical standards of elite private school graduates with those of public school graduates. High-profile anecdotes – such as the disciplining of twenty students from the exclusive Knox Grammar for using a chat room to 'share racist and homophobic videos, messages and rantings on violent misogyny' – seem to occur with disconcerting frequency.[57] A more notorious incident in 2020 suggests something rotten beneath the appearance of moral distinction within the culture of these schools.

By way of background to what follows, a group of boys from Sydney Church of England Grammar School, the wealthiest school in Australia and known as 'Shore', were asked on a TikTok video to name Sydney's 'worst suburbs'. Dressed in their well-cut uniforms and boaters, they all replied 'Bankstown' or 'Mount Druitt', poorer suburbs 'out west' – the mysterious place in the upper-middle-class imagination where the unknown Other resides.[58] Asked why, they said that those suburbs are full of 'druggos' and 'eshays', referring to a youth street subculture of lads, similar to 'chavs', who wear sportswear and sneakers, speak pig Latin ('eshay' is pig Latin for 'sesh', or a drug session) and are said to be prone to crime.[59] It's apparent from the video that the Shore boys have learned that those from these suburbs are morally degenerate.[60] It followed another video in which Shore boys gloated about having superior facilities than their rivals at another elite school – a recovery pool as well as an Olympic pool, a library with views across the harbour and a gym that cost A$50 million.[61]

In the same year, senior students at Shore circulated a secret list of 'muck-up day' dares, each of which would earn points in a 'Triwizard Shorenament' competition.[62] In addition to various drug-related dares – 'drop a cap', 'snort a line', 'rip a cone', suggesting Bankstown and Mount Druitt are not the only suburbs full of 'druggos' – the challenges included humiliating or injuring vulnerable people. Students were dared to 'spit on a homeless man', have sex with a girl under fifteen or with a woman weighing more than 80 kilos, and whack a stranger in the testicles. Further points would be awarded to anyone who'd 'shit on a train' or rip the head off a pigeon.[63]

High-profile scandals such as this one disrupt the elite school discourse of moral superiority, places where the character of tomorrow's leaders is shaped.[64] They raise suspicions or reinforce beliefs that the schools cultivate a sense of entitlement that creates the conditions for this kind of behaviour.[65] The executive editor of the popular podcast and website *Mamamia*, Jessie Stephens, wrote: 'That list screams entitlement and privilege and not even in a covert way. In a cruel way. In a way that says I want to use my power to hurt and humiliate.'[66] Arguably, events such as these that spoil the carefully curated image of elite schooling are not aberrations but express the real pathology of them. That is the view of Jane Kenway, who asks why unsavoury events such as the 'Shorenament' keep happening at elite schools.[67] She argues that the 'dominant and dominating cultures' of these schools is a more plausible explanation than the well-worn 'bad apples' excuse. In particular, racist and misogynistic behaviour is worse among boys at expensive private schools because it is written into their class and ethnic positions. 'The "Triwizard Shorenament" is shot through with a sense of class superiority and class contempt for people who are "not us" ...'.

When these boys are surrounded by extraordinary opulence and told repeatedly they are the crème de la crème and destined to be society's leaders, what can one expect? They are powerful, and they know it, which is why they can envision committing serious assaults and other criminal acts, safe in the knowledge that they are immune from severe penalty. Inclusion of a dare to get arrested and handcuffed, implying little fear of the law-enforcement system, seems to confirm Kenway's first rule of entitlement fostered at these schools: 'You are entitled to have a privileged relationship with the rules and the law.'[68] After his ethno-graphic study of an elite community, Holmqvist commented on how the leaders see themselves as above the law. In the words of a municipal official: 'The law is fine as long as it backs up your own interests.'[69]

Shore school characterised the muck-up day list as aberrant behaviour that went against the ethos of the school and worked to ensure that the blame fell on the individuals involved rather than the institution. Yet a former student told a newspaper that the school actively encourages elitist beliefs, including a sense of superiority over residents of less privileged parts of the city.[70] Judging by the online comments reacting to stories such as the ones above, residents in the suburbs where these schools are located are well aware of the aura of untouchability assumed by the schools and their students. 'I live close to that school', one popular comment began, 'and they're a bunch of entitled brats ... who then evolve into bigger brats!'[71] Perceptions of entitlement at Shore were not helped by an earlier incident in which a dozen graduating students were photographed giving Nazi salutes and holding a large flag bearing a swastika. The school's deputy principal was featured in the photo with the boys. The headmaster dismissed the event as just a prank.[72]

It may be that the same kind of behaviour is present in public schools; but the elite private schools present themselves as imparting a superior moral code to their students, turning out boys with 'character', society's leaders. An analysis of the hierarchical power relations at elite schools also came from an unexpected source, the 2017 report of the Royal Commission into Child Sexual Abuse, in its comments on another scandal. Several boys from the Sydney Anglican boys' school Trinity Grammar were charged with offences arising from an extended campaign of sexual assaults against two boys at the school. Wooden implements were used to violate the boys, including a dildo made in a school woodworking class, while other students looked on cheering and laughing. Staff at the school were aware of the rape of one student for a month before they took any action.[73] Following the cover-up 'play-book' used by elite schools, Trinity Grammar first hired a PR consultant to spin the rapes as mere 'bullying'.[74] In court, the offenders, represented by top lawyers, eventually pleaded guilty to lesser charges and were placed on good behaviour bonds, with no convictions being recorded.[75] The Royal Commission noted the disproportionately high share of abuse taking place in private schools (both Catholic and Protestant), attributing it, *inter alia*, to 'hyper-masculine or hierarchical cultures' and 'a sense of being part of a superior and privileged institution'.[76]

The academic veneer

It's widely believed that children who attend elite private schools have more academic success than those who attend public schools. Certainly, the schools themselves never miss an opportunity to tell the world how well their students perform in competitive examinations. The evidence, however, does not support this belief. While 'hothousing' can push up university entry marks at high-fee private schools, evidence from England, Australia and the United States shows that students who graduate from public schools perform better at university than graduates from elite private schools with the same entrance marks.[77] Moreover, in Australia students from low-fee private schools do better than those from high-fee private schools. Most tellingly, students at public schools perform as well in state-wide tests as those from private schools once socio-economic differences are taken into account. It's the same across OECD countries, where reading scores are higher in public schools for students of similar socio-economic background.[78]

In addition to hothousing students by way of highly focused and well-resourced exam preparation, within elite schools other stratagems are pursued to make sure results live up to parents' expectations and to maintain the public impression that they are academically superior. Holmqvist observed that children trained to assert themselves pressure teachers to award higher marks, a tactic more effective if the parent is a powerful person in society. One teacher remarked that she had come across parents who emailed her from work so that she could see they were lawyers. 'Many of our parents have professions that are all about influencing their surroundings according to their own interests. They are made for this.'[79] One father admitted, 'We're used to calling the shots', and teachers are seen to be of a lower social rank. One teacher told Holmqvist: 'Parents and students have a psychological advantage over the teachers.'

Surprisingly, a diagnosis of dyslexia is another strategy used to gain advantage in Djursholm.[80] Making an allowance for their dyslexia, the upper secondary school admits otherwise underachieving students. Once there, those students are given extra support. As a result, reports Holmqvist, ambitious parents whose children are underperforming may have them diagnosed. Rather than being a stigma, in Djursholm dyslexia is generally seen as 'associated with creativity, engagement, and leadership'.

It is not difficult to make the leap from Holmqvist's conclusion that 'dyslexia offers a medicalized solution to a person's shortcomings' to reports in 2021 that students at Australia's most expensive schools were claiming the highest rates of disability provision, allowing them special measures when sitting for their final exams. This is despite that fact that private schools winnow out students with disabilities. So government schools have much higher proportions of students eligible for special provisions yet receive much less support.[81] The anomaly was explained by the ability of wealthy schools to hire staff to help 'navigate' a complicated and time-consuming system. For many among the public, the manifest unfairness of the situation is galling. The 'most respected' comment under the *Sydney Morning Herald* story read: 'Well, isn't that a surprise? NOT! The rich start gaming the system, sorry, I meant "navigating the system", from an early age. Who would have thought? Inequality starts in the cradle.'

A long-term special needs teacher in public schools wrote that their special provision applications for hearing and vision impaired students were nearly always refused. She remarked bitterly: 'Private schools have been able to get approval for the most minor of disability whereas public school students have been denied having support such as scribes and readers.'

Working the system to benefit privileged students at elite schools has also been reported in Britain. Elite schools devote more resources to identifying students who may qualify as dyslexic or other 'special needs', thereby securing 25 per cent more exam time for them.[82] An analysis by the BBC in 2017 indicated that 20 per cent of private school exam candidates received extra time compared with 12 per cent of state school students.[83] With budgets far in excess of state schools, elite schools also mount many more exam mark challenges, giving them a chance of higher marks, to the disadvantage of state school students. One private school head said: 'We are also fortunate to have proper resourcing and specialist departments [for identifying special needs students], which can be lacking in state-maintained schools.'[84]

The International Baccalaureate appears to be another way of gaming the system to give private school students an unfair advantage. Elite private schools offer the IB diploma as an alternative path to university. In Australia, some have 30 or 40 per cent of senior students taking it. IB students do not sit for the standardised state-wide tests but are assessed by IB teachers, opening the process to grade inflation. It was reported in 2022 that fewer than 600 students in New South Wales, all from private schools, took the IB, yet forty-one of them attained the highest possible mark (converting to a university admission score of 99.95).[85] Of the 55,000 students who sat for the Higher School Certificate, only forty-eight achieved the top mark. In other words, IB students were seventy times more likely to be awarded the top mark than HSC students. (It's worth noting too that students of the diploma diagnosed with a disability are given more generous allowances in assessments compared to students sitting state-wide exams.)[86] In short, private school IB graduates with inflated grades are taking places in prestigious university courses such as law and medicine instead of talented public school students.[87]

However, the fact remains that, despite the various ways in which elite schools game the system for university entrance, they still do not outshine students from public schools once socio-economic differences are taken into account. This raises a question: if parents are paying heavily to send their children to elite schools that do not outperform public schools, what are they paying for? We suggest that the apparent academic achievement promoted by elite private schools camouflages their true *raison d'être*, the transmission to the students of social, cultural and symbolic capital. The networks, friendships, cultural practices, system-knowledge, disposition and status will serve them well in life beyond school and university, securing them the career breaks and financial success to which they aspire. This is what exclusive private schools do; they consolidate and reproduce the advantages children have by being born into elite families. When elite schools, showcasing their famous alumni, promise to build character, expose students to a 'unique social environment' and turn them into future leaders, these are oblique ways of promising parents that their sons and daughters will receive invaluable, and invisible, assets that public schools cannot promise and cannot deliver.

Making global citizens

In a globalized world, ruling elites have had to acquire new skills and orientations in order to thrive. Future leaders must be 'global citizens' or at least have a cosmopolitan orientation towards the world. In their study of six elite schools from a range of countries, Adam Howard and Claire Maxwell explored how the schools produced 'cosmopolitan subjects through global citizenship education'. They found that, in some schools, including their Australian one, global leadership was interpreted as a 'means of advancing individual power and prestige' rather than leadership for the benefit of others.[88] In the glossy brochure advertising Sydney's elite schools, the creation of 'global citizens' is a prominent theme. Kincoppel-Rose Bay, for example, aims to empower its students 'to embrace global citizenship as a way of life', building their 'global competencies' so that they are competitive in the labour market and can 'drive innovative change for the betterment of the world'. Scotch College in Perth claims that it 'weaves longstanding traditions with contemporary education to foster global citizens.'[89]

To facilitate a global outlook, and as part of their 'commitment to social justice', most elite schools encourage students to engage in 'service' programmes at home and overseas. These trips to poor countries are seen as part of their leadership development and the responsibility to 'look after those less fortunate'.[90] Melbourne's Scotch College, for instance, has partnerships with the Indigenous Tiwi College on Melville Island and Chitulika High School in Zambia.[91] 'Africa', declared a school travel organiser, 'offers a plethora of engaging educational travel experiences to help students grow into global citizens.'[92] Pupils at Methodist Ladies College in Kew (annual Year 12 fees A\$34,200) have since 2010 regularly travelled to Tanzania to help raise funds for the School of St Jude, 'which provides poverty stricken children with free education.' The MLC girls 'participate in a community based learning experience.'[93] Students return from these kinds of trips speaking of the 'amazing' and 'eye-opening' experiences they have had in Tanzania or Nepal or Thailand, adding it to their list of accomplishments.

In their study of two elite girls' schools, one in Melbourne and one in the south of England, Allan and Charles write of how the students are encouraged to create a 'portfolio self', so that every activity, and especially extra-curricular ones, builds towards a successful future, not least by trips to poor countries to perform 'service'.[94] (Elite girls' schools appear to place more emphasis than boys' schools on learning empathy and care.)[95] Poor communities in the global South, they argue, serve as sites where privileged students enhance their travel experiences, hone their competence as future leaders and burnish their CVs. In a similar vein, Windle and Stratton observed in their study that the ways elite schools market their commitment to social justice are 'compatible with socially exclusive enrolments'.[96]

Kenway noticed the continuing presence of the colonial legacy at the elite Melbourne school she worked with – preserved from its foundation in 1866 in the ideology, routines, buildings and curriculum. A teacher at the school conceded that the 'colonial heritage ... is still very strongly a part of the school',[97] so it's hard not to interpret the school's modern outreach in these terms. As Allan and Charles read it, 'Assisting the non-white "good" others becomes a way of resourcing the middle-class self.' These good works in the global South 'work to maintain a hierarchical distinction between the normative elite schoolgirl, and the "other" in need of assistance.'[98]

Elite school overseas service programmes are similar to what is known as 'volunteer tourism', popular among students on gap years and often framed as 'an altruistic form of tourism by which tourists can "give back" to host communities' while at the same time having an authentic travel experience.[99] Scholars have pointed to how this kind of tourism romanticises poverty in communities seen as outside modernity and so more 'authentic'. The tourist gaze sees people who 'don't have much but they're happy', skating over the misery of impoverishment. Reviewing the ethnographic studies, Jane Godfrey and others note criticisms of volunteer tourism for 'perpetuating neo-colonialist discourses' and reinforcing power differences by stressing the 'neediness' of the host communities. One self-aware student conceded that they are taught they should want to help people, but their education makes them 'unable to really empathize with other people'.[100]

Allan and Charles write of how affluent families construct images of 'good' others and 'bad' others, a division that helps explain why elite schools typically send their students to engage in service activities in poor regions of the global South rather than in disadvantaged communities closer to home more likely to house the 'bad' others, such as the 'eshays' and 'druggos' of the western suburbs scorned by Shore boys.[101] The good others live in distant and exotic places, 'helpless' people grateful for aid. Unlike boat people, for example, they are 'fixed in place' so cannot contaminate the living spaces of the affluent.

The contours of elites change over time and across cultures, so elite schools have had to accommodate the globalisation of wealth and power. Future business and other leaders need to be able to negotiate their way through a variety of political systems and cultural styles. Their desire to generate 'global citizens' for the rapidly changing world must be balanced against their immersion in tradition (hence the juxtapositional rhetorics referred to above). With an eye fixed on the lucrative market for international students, moves to eliminate perceptions of racial exclusion were an early sign. Expensive Christian schools have become flexible in their faith so that wealthy parents, locally and from feeder countries, especially China, are not deterred. Wesley College in Melbourne reassures parents of its 'spirituality – embracing Christianity and other faiths'.[102] At Geelong Grammar, founded by five Anglican priests, admission is open to all faiths, asking non-Christian parents only to 'encourage their child to approach Christian teaching and Christian precepts receptively and openly.'[103] Sydney Church of England Girls Grammar School (SCEGGS) affirms its Christian faith but says the girls 'have the freedom and support to explore their own spirituality and to come up with their own answers.'[104]

The idea of a global citizen is a contested concept. Analysis by Kenway and others indicates that global citizenship is presented by elite schools in two ways. One is the cultivation of a moral and political being who learns the 'responsibility we all have for our fellow citizens around the world.' The other is the preparation of students for success in global labour markets and as businesspeople who know how to prosper in a globalised world.[105] More broadly, 'the discourses of global citizenship ... offer their children a patina of cosmopolitan sophistication.'[106]

Among other vehicles used by elite schools to make global citizens are the International Baccalaureate and the opportunities for international collaboration through membership of Round Square. We take each in turn.

With an emphasis on 'international mindedness' and transnational mobility rather than national concerns, the IB diploma positions itself as making 'global citizens'.[107] More than a mobile credential for university entrance, the IB was developed in the 1960s as a cosmopolitan dream to give students 'global competencies'.[108] With the local curriculum presented as limiting, students who take the diploma imagine 'transnational futures' for themselves. The IB is a central element of schools' presentation as globally linked up and outward looking, as well as providing an admissions path to top universities around the world that may have trouble deciphering national examination results.[109] At MLC, Sydney, the IB aims 'to develop internationally minded people who, recognising their common humanity and shared guardianship of the common planet, help to create a better and more peaceful world.'[110]

Established in 1967 at a meeting held at Gordonstoun, the exclusive private school favoured by the British royals, Round Square is an organisation of elite schools around the world. Its glamour is due in part to its links with royalty. In 2011, Queen Elizabeth opened its conference in Berkshire and, among civilian 'royalty', Nelson Mandela was a patron. Among the 200 global members are Gordonstoun School and Cobham Hall in Britain, Ivanhoe Grammar and Scotch College in Australia, and Holy Innocents' Episcopal School and the Hotchkiss School in the United States. Initially intended as a means by which wealthy schools could collaborate to help the needy, its principles include internationalism, leadership, service, environmentalism, democracy and adventure. It is now described as 'the illustrious, trans-national educational organ-ization'.[111] The transnational character and activities of Round Square can be seen as a means of transcending the stuffy nationalism of traditional elite schools to help mould an emerging global elite.[112] For Kenway and others, organisations such as Round Square 'are sites for anticipating possible futures, for constructing shared, trans-national, dominant-class imaginaries in ways that also encompass diversity according to nation, culture and religion but decidedly not class.'[113]

Round Square's promotional video features a dozen or so senior students (almost all girls) excited about the cultural enrichment they gained from their overseas exchanges and the leadership skills they acquired.[114] In fact, the organisation describes itself as 'a platform for courageous and compassionate leaders' and boasts of its 'world class approach to character education'. Although Round Square expects its member schools to promote 'equality, fairness [and] justice', state school students are excluded from it.[115] Instead, the cultural diversity to which students are exposed is enacted in exotic locations of the global South.

Illustrating what Petter Sandgren calls its 'balancing act between conservatism and progressivism', Round Square's website includes an image of happy students in their uniforms holding signs reproducing slogans commonly seen at youth climate protests – 'There is no planet B', 'Raise your voice not the sea-level'. Absent are angry signs challenging the system – 'System change, not climate change', 'The wrong Amazon is burning', 'Why should we go to school if you won't listen to the educated?'[116] The superficial networks built among elite young people contrast with the deeper and more authentic global networking among young climate activists built on the fellow-feeling and passion of the movement.[117]

Legitimation strategies

In democratic societies espousing social justice, fairness and success built on merit, the existence of exclusive private schools that serve to perpetuate the power and wealth of the nation's elite creates a problem of legitimacy, one all the more acute in an era of sharply rising inequality and declining resources for public schools. How do they justify themselves?

Kenway and her fellow authors describe the legitimation strategies used by elite schools to vindicate their existence.[118] One is to disavow the extent of their privilege. When criticism is directed at their public funding, a stock response is to claim that not everyone who attends comes from a rich family. 'We are open to everyone,' it is said. 'Some parents have to work two jobs' to send their child to the school (despite official data proving that a very large majority are from the wealthiest households). In Sydney, the headmaster of Newington College (Year 12 fee A\$39,000) admitted that all their boys are 'privileged'. However, they are privileged because they were born into 'families that value education and make big sacrifices' (as if low-income families don't).[119] This rhetoric morphs into another strategy that Kenway and others call the 'discourse of rich victimhood'. Tropes such as 'we pay taxes too' and 'some parents have to make sacrifices, you know', are intoned every time the privilege of elite schools is publicly challenged.[120]

Another tactic used by elite schools in Australia is to conceal themselves among the broad swathe of private schools, many of which cater for families of modest means.[121] Their lobby group, the Association of Independent Schools, consistently speaks as if all private schools are the same, using buzzwords such as 'diversity' and reporting state funding using averages, as if the wealth hierarchy on which elite schools rely did not exist.[122] As a result, schools charging A\$4,000 a year provide political cover for schools charging A\$40,000 a year. Put another way, private schools catering to poor families in the derided western suburbs are used to legitimise the most elitist schools in Vaucluse and Toorak.

Scholarships for Indigenous students have become a well-practised means of disavowing privilege by demonstrating commitment to diversity and social justice. Schools with a few Indigenous students can then hold themselves out as paragons of social justice, their generosity vital to the 'rescue' of some from the most abject group in Australia.

However, enacting a commitment to social justice is not always the driving motive. One Indigenous student spoke of a three-year battle with the principal of an elite Melbourne boarding school who refused the student's request to fly the Aboriginal flag on campus.[123] Apparently oblivious to the unique place of Aboriginal people in Australia's history, the principal said other students would then want to raise 'their flags'. The former student, Corey Atkinson, said he felt 'not valued' at the school.

For her pioneering doctoral thesis, Marnie O'Bryan interviewed many Indigenous students who had been admitted to private schools on scholarships, along with teachers and others involved in the programmes.[124] She reported that a number of those involved felt that the schools were more interested in publicising the presence of their Indigenous students than in developing 'well-articulated organizing principles' for their education. A former scholarship holder, completing a law degree at a prestigious university, told her: 'The people who laid the foundation for what I have been able to achieve came from my community and family, not the fancy white school I attended. To them I was a footballer, to my community I was a leader.' O'Brien wrote:

> … many young people described an expectation that they should be 'grateful' for the opportunities afforded them and respond accordingly. … A teacher participant recalled how [an Indigenous] student who did not want to be involved in a particular activity was told to remember that he was 'on a $60,000 a year scholarship' and that his contribution to a marketing video was not therefore optional.[125]

The pressure on Indigenous students to engage in promotional activity 'often continued for many years after they had left.' When one former Indigenous student was asked if he still had connections with the school, he told O'Bryan, 'No, because he was neither a famous footballer nor an artist, [so] he was of no use to them.' While initially excited at the publicity they receive at the school, Indigenous students soon become cynical about how they are being used. As one said, to begin with it was 'Wow! I'm on the front page of *The Australian*. … Wow, I got to ask the Prime Minister the first question on Q&A', but he outgrew his naivety.

He noticed that 'the blackest kids were often the ones who were on show', and they too became cynical.

> A number of participants (both teachers and alumni) reflected on how students were used as cannon fodder for the school or scholarship provider's PR machine, with seemingly little regard for the young person's own wellbeing. One recounted how, at a dinner attended by '500–600 people', a young man was asked to speak about how he understood the value of education in light of his mother's suicide.[126]

O'Bryan informs us that the former student who told her this story later committed suicide himself. In a pungent concluding remark, O'Bryan observed: 'Elite schools in Australia have roots reaching deep into the colonial era. In this social field are forces, almost force fields, which operate like the laws of physics; they bend and shape the space in which they function.'[127]

A less exploitative form of 'privileged benefaction' is to promise to share the benefits with others.[128] SCEGGS, for example, shares its splendid facilities with local organisations, not the local homeless shelter but organisations such as the Sydney Chamber Choir and the Sydney Youth Orchestra.[129] In 2022, Cranbrook School in Sydney's ritzy Bellevue Hill (median house price in 2022 of A$8.5 million) celebrated the opening of a A$125 million complex that included a new aquatic centre, a double-height orchestra room, a 267-seat theatre and an underground carpark.[130] Waxing lyrical about the new complex, the president of the school council, Jon North (who had personally donated a tax-deductible A$25 million to the project), said the Cranbrook boys find the new building 'really inspirational', adding: 'We had a 25-metre pool that wasn't very good for water polo. So we decided to build a proper pool and learn-to-swim school.' Perhaps intuiting how this tone-deaf bragging might be perceived beyond the harbourside postcodes, a school spokes-person wanted it known that the new facilities would be open to the 'broader community'. Services might be held in the memorial chapel or orchestral ensembles might perform in the theatre.[131]

Ideological work is a further legitimation strategy. Perhaps foremost is the appeal to 'choice'. Parents should be free to choose the kind of school to which they send their children, it is said. Of course, the great majority of parents cannot choose to send their children to schools with fees of A$35,000 a year, just as they cannot choose to purchase the kind of luxury vehicles lining up outside the elite schools twice a day. 'Choice' is a much more powerful slogan after the neoliberal revolution, with its emphasis on personal responsibility, self-advancement and entrepreneurship.[132] Community-minded arguments for public schooling – equal access to a good education and the social benefits of mixing across the social hierarchy – have much less purchase now than they did in the 1970s.

Still, the problem of social justice must be dealt with. In her US study of an unusual elite school that actively teaches its privileged students about social justice, Katy Swalwell found that teachers hoping to disrupt the reproduction of privilege found it difficult to overcome 'the deeply rooted, hegemonic nature of elite common sense', even with students apparently willing to confront their own privilege.[133] Acts of good citizenship were confined to 'individual, idiosyncratic acts of kindness', helpful for the CV but encouraging docility in the face of demands for social change.

Kenway and others found that adolescents across the variety of elite schools they studied gave 'polite, pat responses' to questions about social justice and inequality, as if rehearsed and 'calculated to create an impression of themselves and the schools as enlightened.' In other words, they enacted a kind of 'psychic blindness, an abnegation of the very privilege' in which they are immersed.[134] They, 'literally, did not have the language to talk about issues of poverty as a relational matter.' In this they are only conforming with the neoliberal narrative that displaced that of social democracy in the 1980s and 1990s, that poverty and disadvantage are not the result of social structures but arise from the failures and pathologies of individuals and their families.

Lastly, we comment on those not among the privileged but who enable the system to endure. Erving Goffman described the role of 'curator groups' in conferring symbols of class, referring to those from classes lower down the social hierarchy who are recruited to work for elites. Although not schooled from birth in the symbols of prestige, they are required to manipulate them in the interests of those with higher status.[135] Among curator groups we might include teachers at elite schools, who are further down the hierarchy than those they teach and their parents.[136] Holmqvist quoted teachers in Djursholm reflecting ruefully on their subordinate status.

The money might be good, if well short of the parents of their charges, and the working conditions easier than in a public school, but why do private school teachers appear to embrace their schools and proselytise for them? Kenway suggests they enjoy the higher status of working at an elite school and participate in its 'success' along with the rest of the school community.[137] And since their own children can be enrolled for free, or at a much reduced fee, perhaps their children will be elevated into the wealthy elites they serve.

Even so, in his study of teachers at elite private schools in Australia, George Variyan found that many recruited from the public system experience ethical misgivings.[138] To allay their discomfort they find rationalisations and soon adopt the same discourse as their students. They explain their own positions at elite schools as good fortune, a discourse that 'effaces their agency' in perpetuating a system of privilege. Even for those who cannot shake off their uneasiness with the injustice these schools embody, they become trapped or seduced by the benefits that the schools' wealth allows them. In the end, Variyan writes, 'teachers accommodate institutional life and thrive in spite of questions of guilt, morality and ethics.'[139]

Summary

As the prime mover of the machinery of privilege, exclusive private schools are the enemy of meritocracy. They induct their charges into a special club where they are 'consecrated' in the sense of being taught that they possess higher spiritual and moral qualities. The schools mobilise their histories, opulence, ornamentations, rituals, alumni and rhetoric to reinforce the symbolic power of being educated there. As a result, those who attend the most elite schools are regarded with a certain awe, even by cynical outsiders.

In practice, elite schools are sites for the transubstantiation of financial capital into social, cultural and symbolic capital. Social capital is built through the formation of networks, which help unify the ruling elite as well as providing graduates with access to privileges through life. The cultural capital acquired by students can be embodied in subtle forms of understanding, in postures and dispositions, and in a sense of ease and confidence in future success. Although elite schools project an image of superior moral quality, in practice they give rise to a sense of entitlement and specialness among their students that sees many of them believing they are above society's norms and rules.

Elite schools today place great emphasis on making 'global citizens'. Programmes encouraging 'service', such as good works in the global South, are in practice more a form of self-advancement than a way of imbuing students with a sense of social justice. Scholarship programmes for lower-income students are used to conceal the inherent unfairness of their elitism. Indigenous scholarship students are exploited for their public relations value.

To defend themselves against accusations that they serve as the foremost vehicles for perpetuating inequality and privilege, elite schools adopt legitimation strategies, including disavowal of their privilege and a discourse of victimhood. To obscure the advantages of class behind certificates of merit, they work hard to enhance their reputation for strong academic performance, co-opting the symbols of merit as they undermine meritocracy. In practice, their academic performance is no better than that of public schools, despite their extravagant resources and gaming of the system.

CHAPTER SIX

Sites of Privilege

The growing power of elite privilege has occurred at a time when many of the barriers to gender and racial equality have been removed, even if there is still a long way to go.[1] As we will see, our data for some domains suggest that, while gender and ethnic diversity have improved significantly, there has been no progress in 'class diversity'.

To explore this phenomenon, in this chapter we report some data about certain advantages enjoyed by the children of elites (and implicitly the harms to other children) arising from enrolment at exclusive private schools. The privileges afforded by the exclusive private school system radiate out across society, making them felt in domains that might be surprising – more so because the influence of elite privilege is masked in the popular mind by conspicuous advances in gender and racial diversity, giving the impression that the old ways are on the way out.

Elite colonisation of the arts and sport

We hypothesise that careers and professions that were often considered beneath the aspirations of the children of the affluent, such as professional sports and popular music, have become more attractive because of the wealth and fame that success in these careers can now attract. Sport is now awash with money, and thick networks link players to corporations, the marketing industry, billionaire owners and the media.[2] Media saturation and celebrity culture promise lucrative opportunities after retirement.

In Britain, the acting profession and the music industry are increasingly the preserve of the privately educated. James Bloodworth reported that 60 per cent of acts on the UK music charts in 2011 were privately educated or graduates of exclusive stage schools, a sharp increase over the previous two decades.[3] In the acting profession, 42 per cent of BAFTA winners were graduates of private schools. No equivalent studies appear to have been done for Oscar winners in the United States. In Australia, although no systematic data are available, it is striking how many of the country's most successful actors are products of private schools, many from the most elite ones. Cate Blanchett, Hugh Jackman, Heath Ledger, Rebel Wilson, Eric Bana, Hugo Weaving, Joel Edgerton and Simon Baker all attended private schools (Geoffrey Rush, Rose Byrne and Nicole Kidman attended state schools).[4]

In 2021, the coach of the Perth-based West Coast Eagles Australian rules football team said that recruits who attended public schools and came from single-parent families are too costly to manage off-field and the club might be better off concentrating on private school boys from stable families.[5] His comments came a year after a parliamentary inquiry found that elite private schools had provided 30 to 40 per cent of the state's AFL draftees in the previous three years, even though they accounted for only seven of the state's 300 secondary schools.[6] The committee was alarmed that state government funding for football development was going disproportionately to the elite schools, giving boys from those schools an 'unfair advantage'. The great Indigenous player Dale Kickett observed that football is one of the few careers in which the gap between Indigenous and non-Indigenous kids was narrowing. If the opportunity to play at the top level were taken away, the competition would become just 'a bunch of rich kids playing each other'.[7] Others pointed out that the West Coast Eagles' two most infamous players, plagued with drug problems, were educated at private schools.

Elite domination of sport is not confined to Australian football. The encroachment of privilege into sport is particularly evident in the sports that have a higher social status – rugby (but not rugby league), rowing, tennis, sailing, equestrian and cricket. In England, private schools accounting for 7 per cent of high school students supplied 40 per cent of England's test match batters born between 1986 and 1999. In an echo of the traditional division between upper-class batsmen and working-class bowlers, the private schools supplied 'only' 31 per cent of test match bowlers.[8] Both of these percentages had risen sharply compared to what had happened in the previous two decades.[9]

These figures, calculated by the authors of *Crickonomics*, Stefan Szymanski and Tim Wigmore, suggest that the privilege of an expensive private education extends to sporting success. Top coaches believe that the secret to becoming a world-class batter is high-quality coaching as a teenager and the opportunity to play often on good pitches – precisely what elite schools provide. Cricket coaches employed by exclusive schools, often former top-class batters, are also connected into the sport's top-level networks, so their pupils are more likely to come to the attention of academy selectors.

The private school advantage is not confined to cricket. Over the last two decades or so, elite schools have been pouring millions into providing world-class sporting facilities for their students. Harrow, for instance, brags of its Olympic-standard running track and own golf course.[10] 'Surrounded by acres of sports fields' and 'under the guidance of some of the country's leading coaches', its website crows, 'our elite sportsmen have an impressive record of achievement at the highest levels internationally.'[11] Reflecting the shift from high-culture tastes to cultural omnivorousness among the very rich (see chapter 3), sporting achievement enhances the prestige of elite schools, with famous sporting alumni used to burnish the brand. These schools increasingly dominate the ranks of sporting achievement. A 2019 report titled *Elitist Britain* by the Sutton Trust and the Social Mobility Commission showed that, in national school competitions across a variety of sports, state schools won only 53 per cent of them, even though they accounted for 86 per cent of competing schools.[12]

The Sutton Trust calculated that, among England's international cricket players, 43 per cent attended private schools (up from 33 per cent in 2014). The figure for rugby was 37 per cent. (For the traditionally working-class sport of football, only 5 per cent went to private schools.) So, elite schools accounting for 7 per cent of all students are increasingly Britain's training ground for professional sportspeople, just as they have been for senior judges (65 per cent attended private schools), permanent secretaries (59 per cent), diplomats (52 per cent) and newspaper columnists (44 per cent).[13] (Bloodworth reported evidence from Britain showing that prestigious professions, senior military ranks and cabinet positions are heavily dominated by the 7 per cent who attended private schools.)[14] As the authors drily observed: 'The prospects of those educated at private schools remain significantly brighter than their peers.' More bluntly, for professions that have the most power and influence and attract most admiration (sports players and actors), attendance at private schools is a fast-track to the top. Of course, the trend means that children from poorer families with no access to elite coaching and world-class facilities are finding it more and more difficult to break out of their circumstances. Moreover, when government sports funding agencies channel funding to those identified as medal prospects, young people from wealthy families receive a disproportionate share.

Australians might think these data reflect the English class system, but the growing private school lock on top-class sport is taking place in Australia too. After a sharp increase in the 1990s, the share of privately educated players in Ashes cricket teams has been hovering around 45 per cent.[15] If top-class players are made by intensive coaching as teenagers, this is not surprising when we see the lavish sporting facilities at schools such as Wesley College in Melbourne and the King's School in Parramatta, which boasts of its seventeen sporting fields.

It's true that around 40 per cent of high school students in Australia are enrolled in private schools. However, there is a very wide gap in fees, facilities and prestige from the lowest (mostly in the Catholic system) to the highest (mostly non-evangelical Protestant schools). The elite private schools in Australia – including the elite eleven members of the Associated Public Schools (APS) grouping in Melbourne, the eight belonging to Sydney's Great Public Schools grouping plus a couple of dozen others – correspond to the private sector in England. (In colonial mimicry of England's elite private schools, these nineteen private schools in Australia refer to themselves as 'public schools'.)

It's not only in Western Australia that elite schools have come to dominate the top ranks of Australian rules football, once seen as the sporting code that crossed all class barriers. The eleven APS schools (around 0.2 per cent of all high schools in Victoria) provide around a quarter of players drafted into AFL clubs each year.[16] In 2019, Caulfield Grammar (fees A$35,746 annually in Year 12) alone was the source of nineteen AFL players in the league and Haileybury (A$35,920) supplied twenty players. In addition to top-class facilities and coaches drawn from the ranks of celebrated former players, one of the key factors has been the decision from around 2000 to aggressively recruit talented teenagers from state schools and put them on scholarships. Using the talents of working-class kids to enhance the reputation of privileged schools is similar to the function of Indigenous scholarships (see chapter 5). In fact, the two often overlap.

Children with wealthy parents *and* sporting talent are especially prized. Beyond its 'outstanding sporting facilities', Knox Grammar offers a special programme to support 'high-performance student athletes considering a career in elite sport'. They are promised personalised one-on-one mentoring by high-performance coaches, an individual performance plan and regular visits from experts.[17]

The gap between sporting facilities available to children from families of modest means and those from wealthy families is widening. While cashed-up private schools have been using tax-deductible donations from well-heeled alumni to build state-of-the-art Olympic swimming pools, local councils across Australia have been closing municipal pools because they cannot afford to maintain them.[18]

Across most sports, the arrival of more Indigenous players and the elevation of women's sports in traditional male bastions such as cricket, AFL and rugby has been welcomed. Yet the growing domination of the top levels of these sports by young people passing through the hothouses of elite schools suggests that improving gender and ethnic diversity is camouflaging declining 'class' diversity.

The story is similar in the United States. We saw in chapter 5 that students from wealthy families benefit disproportionately from college admissions based in part on sporting ability. Another longitudinal large-sample study found that success in top-level college sport, typically the feeder for professional sports players, is due as much to family wealth as to physical talent. Students from privileged backgrounds are three times more likely to be college athletes than those from the least privileged backgrounds.[19] Not only are children from wealthy families much more likely to do well enough to be admitted to college, but they also have the advantages of private coaching and the best facilities. The authors write that 'narratives of disadvantaged Black youth thriving in sports receive outsized attention; our findings suggest that higher levels of family SES [socio-economic status] enhance opportunities for playing college sports' for both black and white students. One of the authors put it starkly: 'Wealth and privilege are important to succeeding in sports just as they are in other parts of society.'[20]

Honours for privilege

In Britain, nothing signifies society's official esteem more plainly than a knighthood. Corporate leaders covet these awards because they signal respect and trustworthiness and open doors to the most powerful circles. As the highest form of symbolic capital, they are worth spending a lot of economic capital to obtain. Niche companies specialise in providing advice and assistance to the well-heeled as to how best to achieve an honour. However, it may take years and a great deal of strategic investment. Business activity is never enough; one must prove one's commitment to the social good by way of sustained involvement in cultural institutions and charitable causes. Donations are the key to the door. Some wealthy people have attempted to take a short cut by buying a knighthood or a peerage. In previous years, a substantial donation to the party in power, or, better still, a loan that did not need to be declared but could be forgiven later, was enough. The most recent attempt to convert economic capital into symbolic capital without the delay and uncertainty of going through the formal process was in 2021, when a Saudi billionaire made donations to then Prince Charles's charitable trust in the expectation he would be knighted in return.[21] However, exposure of various 'cash for honours' scandals, notably in the Blair years, has cut off this route.

In Australia, perhaps no form of symbolic capital is purer than an Order of Australia, instituted by the Whitlam government in 1975 to replace the imperial honours system.[22] It has four levels, Companion (AC), Officer (AO), Member (AM) and Medal (OAM), in descending order. ACs are rare, often fewer than ten in a year, and highly coveted. AOs are highly regarded and difficult to obtain, with around 100 awarded each year. AMs are awarded for service to a particular field and are more common. OAMs are given mostly to volunteers at local sports clubs, youth groups, charities, and so on – everyday people who serve selflessly as community glue (and are therefore, in the eyes of many, far more deserved than the top 'gongs' awarded to the great and the good, often for just doing their jobs).

Decisions are made by the Council of the Order of Australia, comprising a diverse membership of well-regarded community members and state government representatives. Candidates for honours must be nominated and endorsed by four or five respectable people. Higher awards require references from eminent persons; the more eminent, the higher the chances of success. The Council commissions its own independent referees' reports from people in the same field, and a negative report from an enemy or critic can sink an application. Decisions often take two years or more from the time the nomination is submitted. Within certain professions, notably medical and scientific research, there is a culture of nominating and supporting your own for awards. Inspection of award lists over a few years suggests that medical researchers are grossly over-represented.

The structure of Council of the Order of Australia and its arms-length from politics makes cash-for-honours scams virtually impossible. However, there is more than one way to skin a cat. Wealthy people can still convert economic capital into an AO, or even an AC, through judicious allocation of funds to the right causes over several years, along with joining the boards of non-profits (a process explored in chapter 7 on philanthropy). The time and money may be well spent, as a higher honour can instantly transform the way others see you. When the former president of the Australian Medical Association, Dr Mukesh Chandra Haikerwal, was awarded an AC (a 'C' to those so elevated), he said: 'I never saw it coming and it's still taking some adjustment. The enormity of such an award – it really is remarkable.'[23]

Business executives speak of how the awards open doors, including doors abroad.[24] A business journalist at the *Australian Financial Review* remarked on how highly prized these awards are 'in boardrooms and other institutions at the big end of town'.[25] When, for a short period, Prime Minister Tony Abbott reintroduced knighthoods and dames in 2014, many ACs were angry, according to the secretary to the governor-general at the time. 'Many of them contacted Government House, commenting sharply that they had accepted what they thought was the highest honour!'[26] A lapel pin, very small but all-too-conspicuous to those in the know, comes with the award. A Council insider said of it, 'the pin is the thing. In the Qantas Chairman's Lounge, the eyes are looking.'[27]

For decades, award of the top honours was skewed heavily to older white men. In recent years, diversification to women and people from culturally diverse backgrounds has succeeded. Today, the proportion of awards going to women is approaching parity. Yet no one is advocating for more class diversity. The lowest award, the OAM, typically goes to working-class people in local communities, but at the higher levels networks of privilege can determine who receives the top honours. To be in the running for a top award you need four or five high-level referees, preferably with ACs themselves. How many people, even very accomplished ones, know five distinguished people willing to write a reference? An analysis by *Sydney Morning Herald* journalists in 2021 revealed that a quarter of the richest 200 people in Australia have awards, overwhelmingly the higher-level honours. Directors of major corporations are strongly represented, and the recipients of the top awards, AOs and ACs, are heavily concentrated in the country's wealthiest suburbs – sixty-seven residents of Toorak had them, fifty-seven in Mosman, forty-five in South Yarra, thirty-four in Kew, and thirty-nine in Vaucluse. The honours system, they concluded, 'is arguably just as class-based as ever.'[28]

We examined the educational backgrounds of the sixty-three people awarded Australia's highest honour, the Companion of the Order of Australia (AC), over the four years 2019–22. Of those whose high schools could be identified, thirty-four (71 per cent) attended private schools and fourteen (29 per cent) public schools.[29] Of those who attended private schools, they were overwhelmingly elite ones (twenty-seven of the thirty-four).[30] It's hard to avoid the conclusion that those born into privilege hog society's highest symbols of esteem.

Has elite bias in the award of top honours improved or worsened in recent decades? We compared data for the recent four-year period, 2019–22, with the four-year period 1986–9 – that is, thirty-three years earlier. In the earlier period, sixty-four ACs were awarded, compared with sixty-three in the later period.[31] The share going to private school graduates rose from 66 per cent in the earlier period to 71 per cent in the recent period, with the share going to graduates of expensive private schools rising from 47 to 56 per cent. Public school graduates received 34 per cent of ACs in the earlier period and 29 per cent in the recent period. On this evidence, class bias has become worse.

After decades of domination by white men, there has been a welcome trend towards awarding honours to women. In the earlier period, fifty-nine of the sixty-four ACs went to men and five to women; in the recent period, men received only thirty-three of the sixty-three awards and women thirty. While we congratulate ourselves on greater gender diversity, the continuing domination of these most prestigious awards by wealthy elites goes unnoticed. While the clamour for gender diversity is loud, demands for more class diversity cannot be heard.

Rhodes scholars

Described as 'the world's best known and most prestigious academic grant', the Rhodes scholarship has been a glamorous stepping stone on the career paths of presidents and prime ministers.[32] The cachet of the two-year sojourn at the University of Oxford is as highly valued in the business world as the political one. Graduating Rhodes scholars have been the primary recruiting ground for McKinsey and Co.[33] Apart from Cecil Rhodes's reputation as an imperialist, the award has always had an image problem. 'To many Australians', wrote Aaron Patrick in 2018, 'the Rhodes Scholarship symbolises not only an intellectual elite but encompasses the social elite of private schools, rugby playing fields and smoky common rooms.'[34] It's a characterisation that has been close to the mark, although today the common rooms are smoke-free.

To win this prize the applicant needs to meet four criteria. The first, of course, is outstanding academic achievement, typically provable only by those who are enrolled at the 'sandstone' universities. (In the USA, Harvard students have won 10 per cent of Rhodes scholarships. Add in Yale and Princeton, and the figure is 23 per cent.)[35] Until recently, exceptional sporting prowess was essential (a university blue was *de rigueur*), but today success in the arenas of music, debating or theatre can substitute. Applicants must also provide evidence of selflessness and 'sympathy for and protection of the weak', along with 'moral force of character and instincts to lead'.[36]

It takes time and mentoring to develop character and leadership; as we saw, these qualities are actively cultivated and provided for by elite private schools, reinforcing the habitus, absorbed over years, of the children of wealthy families. At university, demonstrating leadership and commitment to selfless service through engagement with student societies or charities takes time away from studies, time that poorer students are more likely to be spending at their part-time jobs or caring for a family member with an illness or disability.

Short-listed candidates are interviewed by a selection committee, which in Australia is chaired by the state governor. Of course, elite schools consciously and unconsciously impart to their students the ability to perform with confidence before a committee of eminent persons. In this intensely competitive race, aspirants must submit polished applications responding to the criteria, along with five to eight references testifying to their 'intelligence, character, morals, and values'.[37] Apart from academic mentors, the best referees are the kinds who move in the world of privilege.

In the United States, the short-listed are invited to a social engagement where they mingle with the selection panellists, other applicants and former Rhodes scholars. Having practised their talking points, it is expected they will 'make a lasting impression on the panellists'.[38] In Australia, hopefuls arrive for a dinner or lunch at Government House, always a grand colonial mansion in the most prestigious city precincts. For short-listers from poorer backgrounds, training in how to behave in the presence of the governor is available – 'primers on using the silverware', as it has been put.[39] Of course, for certain young people, an education in how to comport oneself in such a rarefied environment is absorbed over years, so a primer the week before a reception can only be a quick-and-dirty lesson in how to fake it.[40] In short, the odds are stacked against students from working-class families.

What do the data tell us? We examined the schooling of Australian Rhodes scholars over the four decades 1983–2022. Data are systematically collected for three states only – Queensland, Western Australia and Tasmania.[41] Given that exclusive private schools are more powerful in Sydney and Melbourne than elsewhere, we expect our results, if anything, to understate the bias.

The first observation to emerge from the data is increasing gender equality. In the first two decades, 1983–2004, 28 per cent of recipients were women, while in the second two decades 41 per cent were women.[42]

Across the whole period, 31 per cent of Rhodes scholars attended state schools. Over those decades, around 70 per cent of all secondary students in the three states attended state schools. Thirty-nine per cent of Rhodes scholars attended high-fee schools and 30 per cent attended schools with medium-low fees.[43] Comparing the two periods, 1983–2004 and 2005–22, the situation deteriorated. The share of scholarships going to state school graduates fell from 36 per cent to 27 per cent.[44] The share of scholarships going to students from the most exclusive schools, accounting for about 5 per cent of all students, rose from 33 per cent to 45 per cent.[45]

As we found with recipients of Australia's highest honour, the AC, the dominance of elite private schools over the most prestigious academic awards has grown over the last forty years. Graduates of elite private schools are around twenty times more likely to win Rhodes scholarships than those who went through the government system, even though their academic performance is no higher when account is taken of socio-economic status (see chapter 5). Once again, while society's highest rewards are increasingly available to women, improving gender equality has masked worsening class equality. As we will see next, the same pattern emerges in appointments to Australia's highest court.

The judiciary

In the legal world, 'privilege' has more than one meaning. In 2021, a twenty-year-old man found himself in court after he had punched a woman in the face because she had pushed back against his drunken insults in a pub[46] (he had called her a slut and told her to 'put her tits away'). Defending the man before the judge stood one of Sydney's very best silks, Robert Boulton SC, a former president of the NSW Bar Association and a barrister-of-choice for the city's rich and powerful.[47] After hearing an account of the incident and the man's admission of guilt for the assault, the judge decided to record no conviction. His honour's judgement referred to the fact that the man had attended Knox Grammar, an elite school in Sydney's leafy northern suburbs (Year 12 annual fee A$36,840).[48] His reasoning was from start to finish exculpatory, suggesting the woman's clothing 'might have been perceived by a 20-year-old former student from Knox to be provocative' and that his action in punching the woman was 'an aberration'. He wished the defendant good luck and advised him to 'keep your nose clean, young man'.

In Britain, 65 per cent of senior judges on the bench in 2019 had attended private schools.[49] In the United States, Supreme Court judges come overwhelmingly from three Ivy League law schools, Yale, Columbia and Harvard, admission to which favours students from wealthy families. An analysis published in 2010 noted that eight of the nine sitting justices had attended one of these law schools.[50]

New data show that the same elite school bias prevails in Australia. Since the end of the Second World War, forty justices have been appointed to Australia's highest court. If we divide them into two periods, each with twenty appointments, we see a welcome increase in diversity on the High Court bench.[51] In the first period, 1946–87, all the justices were men; in the second period, 1987–2022, seven of the twenty appointments were women. However, this growing gender diversity conceals a decline in class diversity. In the earlier period, 60 per cent of the High Court's justices had been educated at private schools, with 45 per cent at expensive private schools, bringing to the bench the worldview absorbed at those places. In the second period, 80 per cent passed through private schools, with fully 60 per cent the products of the most privileged schools. The last ten appointments since 2009 show no improvement. While five have been women, only three of the ten attended public schools, with seven the products of elite private institutions.

Although judges are required to make decisions without bias or prejudice, they are human beings. Today, when judges make comments or rulings that are explicitly sexist or racist, an uproar often follows, which isn't to say that they do not make judgements that are implicitly sexist or racist. Similarly, and perhaps more insidiously, judges from privileged backgrounds may be prone to what has been called by a US chief judge 'unselfconscious cultural elitism'.[52] Studies show that judges favour wealthy litigants over poor ones, in part because they may have 'a fundamental misunderstanding of the lives of poor people.'[53] When asked whether the appointment of female judges makes a difference to judgements, Lady Hale, then president of the Supreme Court in the UK, said, 'Where you start from can have an effect on where you end up,' which applies as much to class as it does to gender.[54] Lady Hale's words might serve as the epigraph to this book.

Most discussion of judicial diversity asks whether female judges are more sympathetic to female litigants. If they are, that does not mean female judges from elite backgrounds will be more sympathetic to working-class litigants, which would echo the long history of criticism of middle-class feminists by Black women.[55]

Legal and judicial cultures vary across countries. The hierarchy of status among lawyers is especially stark in the United States, where 'it is well known that elite law firms shut their doors to students who lack elite credentials'[56] (think *The Good Wife* versus *Better Call Saul*). In Britain, the recruitment practices of leading law firms show a strong class bias despite their public commitment to diversity.[57]

Given the preponderance of Australian High Court justices from elite private schools, perhaps it should be no surprise that, according to one estimate, nearly two-thirds of the highly sought-after positions of judge's associate went to law graduates who had attended private schools.[58] In an opaque process, appointments are made by the judges based on personal recommendations.[59] As in the United States, without high levels of social capital (strong networks) and cultural capital (the right habitus), entry to the most prestigious law firms is extremely difficult. Winning intensely competitive clerkship positions involves interviews that 'are akin to social vetting', according to insiders, favouring those 'most well versed in the middle class art of managing small talk with a canapé in one hand and a drink in the other.'[60] As Bourdieu and Passeron wrote, judgements are made using 'the unconscious criteria of social perception of total persons, whose moral and intellectual qualities are grasped through the infinitesimals of style or manners, accent or elocution, posture or mimicry, even clothing or cosmetics.'[61] Conformity becomes the requirement that the candidate must 'fit in' with the result that, as another close observer put it, 'the majority of law graduates hired through the pool of summer clerks come from a concentrated selection of privileged schools and postcodes.'[62] It's not that merit plays no role; it's just that exaggerated claims of merit and comforting notions of 'fit' are used to conceal a cultural bias towards the privileged.

Summary

In 1992, two Australian historians, Mark Peel and Janet McCalman, posed the question 'Where do our top people come from?' To answer, they studied all of those listed in the 1988 edition of *Who's Who*, 'a fairly comprehensive guide to leadership in Australian society'.[63] They asked where the almost 9,000 people listed went to school. The results of their labours were condensed in a feature article published in *The Age*,

Melbourne's main daily newspaper. It began as follows. 'Australians are governed and informed, financed and educated, analysed and preached to by an exclusive elite. We are ruled by an oligarchy dominated out of all proportion by the products of the nation's Protestant private schools.'[64]

Among other questions, this book asks how much has changed over the last three or four decades. The evidence here for rule by elites – measured by the increasing prevalence of graduates from expensive private schools in top-class sport, honours, Rhodes scholarships and the judiciary – suggests not much.[65] In fact, in contrast to sharp improvements in gender diversity and probably racial diversity, 'class diversity' has deteriorated. With wealth inequality growing over recent decades, perhaps this is not so surprising; but it sits uncomfortably with the ideals of meritocracy promoted so heavily in the neoliberal era. Hereditary advantage has found another way to work.

While social movements demanding women's equality, racial equality and gay rights have made significant progress since the 1970s, demands for more equality in wealth and power have fallen on stony ground.[66] Elite privilege has gone from strength to strength so that the 'exclusive elite' identified in the 1992 study, while less male and less white, remains 'an oligarchy dominated out of all proportion' by the products of the nation's expensive private schools. Apart from the ascendancy of an elite worldview among those in positions of power and influence, the most obvious harm from this rule by a few is that many talented people not from privileged backgrounds are relegated to lesser positions.

CHAPTER SEVEN

The Power of Giving

Philanthropic hyper-agents

As we've seen, the power of wealth and the privileges that go with it can be protected and magnified when combined with networks of influence and symbols of esteem. Philanthropy is a surprisingly effective means of acquiring both. The research evidence reviewed below shows that those who have accumulated power in the economic sphere can use giving to extend their influence into the social, cultural and political spheres. Taken together, philanthropy widens the power disparities between the rich and the rest. While the use of donations to influence politicians and policy decisions has been intensively studied, few have looked closely at how elite philanthropy, typically presented in the media as a sign of elite benevolence, is being used to change society in ways compatible with the worldview and interests of the super-rich.

Politically progressive philanthropists are a minority, almost a boutique circle. They are sometimes the black sheep of conservative families. In Britain, the hedge-fund billionaire Sir Christopher Hohn has funded the radical activist group Extinction Rebellion, as has Aileen Getty, the granddaughter of oil tycoon J. Paul Getty.[1] In Australia, philanthropic trusts associated with the Kantor family, related to Rupert Murdoch, stand out for their progressive giving.[2] The existence of a few progressive wealthy givers cautions against excessive generalisation; nevertheless, most giving by wealthy elites serves to reinforce the system that generates extreme wealth and entrenches disadvantage.[3] In 2020, the largest four private foundations in Australia, accounting for nearly half of the donations of the top fifty, all had a conservative political worldview.[4]

On the face of it, elite philanthropists give away some of their power and privilege when they give away some of their money. In practice, though, elite philanthropy is rarely driven by altruism, serving instead as a means of converting financial capital into other forms of capital. In addition to the enhanced reputational glow and the honours conferred by states (symbolic capital), the expanded networks (social capital) built by giving can be converted back into greater wealth and influence. Noting that, because of tax concessions, private philanthropy is near half funded by the public, four experts have argued that it can be seen as 'an unjustifiable form of state conferred elite privilege'.[5]

The motives for philanthropic giving by the wealthy should be distinguished from the vast number of small gifts made by everyday citizens. Summarising a decade of research, Paul Schervish concluded that what separates the very wealthy from the average giver is that the former 'invariably want to shape rather than merely support a charitable cause.'[6] In what might be a definition of elite privilege, the very wealthy see themselves as *hyper-agents*. Hyper-agency is 'the enhanced capacity of wealthy individuals to establish or control substantially the conditions under which they and others live.'[7] While most people seek the best way to live under the conditions in which they find themselves, the wealthy set out to expand the range of possibilities in which they can choose to live, to construct worlds to inhabit. Schervish describes hyper-agency as 'the empowering class trait of the wealthy'.[8]

It is this world-building capacity that some of our focus group participants alluded to when they defined privilege as more than the ability to live free from everyday constraints, 'to not have to worry about money'. They can shift the constraint boundary that limits others. As one put it: 'the top 1 per cent operate in a pretty different world than you or I. So it's different rules for those sort of people' (Luke, average income, younger, Melbourne).

To live by a different set of rules, wrote Schervish, 'is the fundamental endowment of wealth'. They see themselves as demigods able to burst the bonds of normal agency. 'The hyperagency of wealth holders is contingent upon a constellation of emotional, intellectual, and moral dispositions that provide great expectations, the confidence about one's ability to pursue them, and the responsibility to accomplish them.'[9] These characteristics are as conspicuous among tech tycoons as the super-rich in other domains. If, for the very rich, using wealth to shape one's world is an expression of one's self, using one's wealth to support a cause can also be an expression of one's self. Just as wealth allows its owners to set their own agendas in their business and private lives, so large donations to charities come with the expectation that the donor can set or at least influence the agendas of recipient organisations – or indeed an entire field of charitable concern.[10]

After a thorough review of the scholarly literature, Mairi Maclean and her co-authors concluded that, by design or in effect, elite philanthropy makes wide disparities of wealth and power more palatable and legitimate. 'Philanthropy provides elites with a justification for extreme inequalities that cannot otherwise be ethically or rationally justified, enabling them to "hide" behind emotionally charged discourses of giving at scale.'[11] The truth of this claim depends on a plausible account of how the processes by which elite philanthropy serve to make an unjust system more legitimate and acceptable. We argue that these processes include:

- setting the terms of public debate and the policy agenda;
- promoting an ideology of individual effort and choice;
- skewing social movements in more conservative directions;
- extending the power of wealthy elites in society; and
- making extreme wealth appear benevolent.

Setting agendas

It is said that no major decision is made at the World Health Organization without first asking how the Bill and Melinda Gates Foundation would react.[12] Health officials around the world are afraid to speak up for fear of losing the foundation's support, a phenomenon nicknamed the 'Bill Chill'.[13] The Gates Foundation provides 10 per cent of WHO's budget, second only to the United States, and has undoubtedly done much good. One consequence, however, is that an organisation set up by the international community for the public benefit, in the words of Lawrence Gostin of Georgetown University, 'is beholden to a largely unaccountable private actor'.[14] Lindsey McGoey, a former WHO adviser, has shown how the Gates Foundation distorts global health priorities, especially by funding programmes that have quick and measurable results so that the benefits of billionaire philanthropy are conspicuous.[15]

Bill Gates may be one of the more benign of the ultra-rich (and Melinda Gates more so) but, like all Silicon Valley billionaires, Gates favours technofixes over systemic change. 'I think more like an engineer than a political scientist,' Gates declared, as if engineering can solve the problems that politics cannot. Typical of mega-donors, Gates believes that business methods work best; after all, his own success came from his quick-footed and ruthless methods as an innovator in the marketplace. In the health arena, Gates's attitude is 'Big Pharma is awesome', as one critic put it.[16] To the immunisation task, where his foundation has spent most of its money, he brings what Manjari Mahajan calls a 'techno-cratic expertise and power rather than a discourse of human rights and activism'.[17] He succeeded, for example, in blocking WHO's plan to waive patents on Covid-19 vaccines so that poor countries could obtain them cheaply.[18]

The Bill and Melinda Gates Foundation is an extreme case, but it exemplifies the power of the hyper-agent. Gates and the ultra-wealthy who commit funds to the Giving Pledge, set up by Gates with Warren Buffett to persuade billionaires to give, can be thought of as the elite within the elite, those 'whose power and networks extend beyond corporate boundaries into society at large' – in fact, into the global community.[19]

The pressure from major donors on charities to conform is felt relent-lessly; but there are always those that insist on their independence. Some elite philanthropists bypass resistance by creating their own charities. The mining magnate Andrew Forrest (net worth US$20 billion) is a salient example.[20] Close observers agree that Forrest is driven first by money, but he also craves fame. And he is obsessed with image management.[21] His Minderoo Foundation has turned him and his wife Nicola into 'Australia's most celebrated benefactors'. (Like Bill and Melinda, Andrew and Nicola are what is known as a 'golden couple' in the philanthropic world, although in 2023 they announced their separation.)

The Walk Free Foundation, created by Forrest's Minderoo Foundation, presents itself as 'an international human rights group', akin perhaps to Amnesty International. It is committed to use 'a business-like global strategy to end modern slavery'. Its origin story lies in a visit by Forrest's daughter Grace to Nepal at the age of fifteen, where she was shocked at what she saw and heard, and a subsequent family discussion around the dinner table.[22] Grace Forrest is billed as Walk Free's founding director and head of strategic communications.

While the commitment to end modern slavery is admirable, the Walk Free campaign is not without its critics in the anti-slavery movement (nor is Forrest himself, who has been accused of 'an aversion to paying tax').[23] The Walk Free Foundation seemed to want to take charge of the myriad anti-slavery groups around the world 'by building a global movement of over eight million community activists'.[24] When in 2014 Forrest's Global Freedom Network gathered world religious leaders together at the Vatican to sign a pledge to end modern slavery, Pope Francis was a prominent supporter, and images of the pontiff and the philanthropist appeared in the newspapers. A year later, however, the Vatican withdrew, with its spokesman accusing Forrest of exploiting the pope and using the network to advance his own business interests.[25]

The law professor Janie Chuang characterised Walk Free's approach as 'legitimising the status quo by simplistically portraying slavery as a localised problem of poor countries failing to protect their people from slavery,' as if trade and investment flows between rich and poor countries had nothing to do with it[26] (Walk Free subsequently put more emphasis in its promotional material on the complicity of rich countries).[27]

In a commentary on the 'new, highly corporatized anti-slavery movement', the legal expert Anne Gallagher criticised WFF's *Global Slavery Index* as a 'metrics-focused strategic philanthropy in defining the "problem" and directing responses'.[28] (Forrest apparently took advice from Bill Gates, who told him: 'If you can't measure it, it doesn't exist.') Gallagher says it's a business-driven approach of key performance indicators and measurable outcomes that distorts the nature of the problem. She is disturbed by the self-censorship of anti-trafficking experts. 'To what extent does fear of exclusion from the deep-pocketed, high profile and increasingly glamorous "modern slavery" club, that counts movie stars and presidents amongst its members, play a role?'[29] The self-censorship is akin to the 'Bill Chill'.

Philanthrocapitalism

In a previous age, elite philanthropy was a form of charity for the poor; in more recent times, the super-rich believe they are uniquely placed to solve social and environmental problems, a phenomenon known as philanthrocapitalism. Increasingly, the view has spread that wealthy philanthropists, along with corporations and social entrepreneurs, are best placed to solve the world's biggest problems, either in place of governments or alongside them. This 'impact investing' uses market-based thinking and methods to solve social ills, relying on the investment savvy and entrepreneurial skills of the super-rich. It's the view from Davos, where billionaires gather to consider the world's problems. Philanthropy is a favourite topic of conversation.[30] (One participant observed: 'So at Davos you've got all these people who earned their money through exploitation, rent-seeking, you name it, and then they do a little bit of philanthropy to distract from all of that.')[31] Philanthrocapitalism aims to fix the flaws in rather than challenge the system, the one that enables massive fortunes to be made. Even defenders of philanthrocapitalism concede that 'giving back' by the super-rich is widely seen as 'a public relations attempt to put lipstick on a (capitalist) pig'.[32]

Convinced that social well-being and the pursuit of profit can work in harmony, leading advocates of philanthrocapitalism Matthew Bishop and Michael Green claim that it is 'a minimal requirement of a new social contract that will be needed to address the growing tensions caused by rising inequality and the rise of the One Percent'.[33] They believe that effective responses to poverty, slavery, climate change, and so on, can be solved by the business experience and life philosophies of the super-rich. They can do things that governments can't. It's a worldview that often disdains elected governments; Warren Buffett's view is that the Gates Foundation can spend his money more wisely than the government.[34] A critic, Linsey McGoey, reports that some philanthropists believe their giving is a form of 'self-tax' that excuses them from paying other taxes.[35] It's common for wealthy people, when challenged publicly about tax avoidance, to speak of how much they give to charity, convinced that their voluntary giving exempts them from the normal duties of citizenship.[36] After all, if you are saving the world from catastrophe – as Jeff Bezos is with his plan to move industry into space and as Elon Musk is by colonising Mars for human settlement – you are operating on a higher plane that normal citizens.

In a reprise of 'greed is good', McGoey sums up the worldview of the philanthrocapitalists.

The new philanthropists are increasingly proud, triumphant even, about the private economic fortunes to be made through embracing philanthrocapitalism. Not only is it no longer necessary to 'disguise' or minimize self-interest, self-interest is championed as the best rationale for helping others. It is not seen as coexisting in tension with altruism, but as a prerequisite *for* altruism.[37]

The danger to civil society and democracy represented by this new 'disruptive philanthropy' is described by the policy analyst David Rieff.

> … it has become the conventional wisdom that private business – the most politically influential, the most undertaxed and least regulated, and, most importantly, the least democratically accountable sector among those groups that dispose of real power and wealth in the world – are best suited to be entrusted with the welfare and fate of the powerless and hungry.[38]

Skewing movements

Summarising the sociological research on foundations in 2021, Jeanine Cunningham and Michael Dreiling concluded that, 'in general, corporate and elite foundations often aim to temper social change by moderating issues and movements in a manner that preserve larger, hegemonic relations in the society.'[39] In her doctoral research, Zurina Simm adopts a Gramscian approach to understanding the influence-building of elite philanthropy.[40] Wealthy elites achieve 'hegemony' not so much through force as through their intellectual and moral leadership, by means of which their view becomes normalised as commonsensical. Through alliances with cultural, academic and charitable institutions, philanthropists can take moral and intellectual leadership of vital public debates. Building on earlier studies, Simm writes that foundations can 'indirectly control movement activities by subtly steering social movements into specific forms of action and discourses.'[41] One effective means is to stack the boards of charities with people who share the worldview of the philanthropists funding them.

The influence of the super-rich on public debate through donations to think tanks is well documented, and we won't go over it here.[42] We might note, however, that for years in Australia philanthropists and corporations pushing a right-wing agenda poured money into the Institute of

Public Affairs. It was money very well spent, as the IPA played a central role in promoting the ideas of neoliberalism, modelled on the efforts of think tanks such as the Mont Pèlerin Society in the United States. After the victory of the neoliberal revolution, mainstream business moved more to the centre. Now, major corporations and philanthropists no longer fund the IPA, which failed to adapt and is now supported only by very right-wing billionaires such as Rupert Murdoch and Gina Rinehart.[43] The 'moderates' now support the Grattan Institute, Australia's most influential think tank. Its major funders, from whom many board members are drawn, include BHP, National Australia Bank, and three philanthropic trusts – the venerable Myer Foundation, the conservative Scanlon Foundation and a foundation created by the tech tycoon Grant Rule.[44] With a worldview broadly consistent with that of its philanthropic and corporate funders, the Grattan Institute shapes the nation's policy agendas on health, energy, education and the labour market.

Another potent but neglected mechanism for shaping social and political agendas is philanthropic support for 'moderate' or system-compatible charitable groups in the non-profit sector while marginalising more radical ones.[45] The evidence shows that wealthy foundations 'either avoid funding organizations that might threaten the established power structure or actively support moderate organizations as a way of mollifying public dissent.'[46] In the environmental domain, for example, the evidence shows that funding from foundations strongly favours more conservative groups. While some foundation giving has supported more critical groups, 'funding is overwhelmingly directed toward mainstream environmental discourses, such as preservation, conservation, and reform environmentalism.'[47]

Of all the social movements in recent decades, the environment movement has arguably posed the greatest threat to the prevailing system, with influential thinkers arguing that ecological destruction is built into industrial capitalism as such, a message repeated by young climate protesters with such slogans as 'System change, not climate change'. It is not surprising, therefore, that most grants have flowed into those organisations whose ideology and campaigns are most compatible with maintaining the privileged position of wealthy elites. Much of it has been 'dark money'.[48] In the climate change domain, foundations are perhaps best known for their aggressive funding of climate science denial and campaigns in favour of fossil fuel interests. Among those who accept the science, detailed analysis by Cunningham and Dreiling of giving networks reveals complex subgroups within elite philanthropy expressing varying preferences; but grants to organisations that challenge the system are rare. 'Large-scale elite gifts overwhelmingly favor forms of environment and animal giving that are socially and politically moderate, or even conservative.'[49] Elite philanthropy not only steers funding towards more conservative groups but channels protest into less threatening domains, such as promoting green consumerism, backing system-preserving technologies such as 'clean coal' and supporting green-washing activities.[50]

Co-opting charities

When wealthy elites come together to defeat reforms aimed at making the distribution of wealth more equal, they mobilise all resources at their disposal, including anyone who has benefited from their largesse – politicians, think tanks, academics, media outlets *and* charities.

The power of big donors was on display in Britain in 2012 when the Conservative chancellor George Osborne proposed capping the amount of tax relief the wealthy could gain from their charitable donations.[51] Many saw these donations as tax dodging in the guise of benevolence; Osborne himself said he was shocked by the extent to which multi-millionaires were using loopholes in donations law to avoid paying tax. Some of the richest were paying virtually nothing. In response, one wealthy donor complained that presenting the Osborne measure as a crackdown on tax dodging was 'insulting' because 99 per cent of giving is 'from the goodness of their hearts'.

Mairi Maclean and Charles Harvey described the campaign mounted by powerful elites to defeat the measure.[52] Rather than risk being presented as rich people defending their own financial interests, wealthy philanthropists mobilised three charitable organisations to 'mastermind' their campaign, targeting influential parliamentarians. One charity executive, interviewed later by Maclean and Harvey, admitted that he'd told philanthropists to keep quiet: 'It's much better that the charity sector fronts this discussion because as soon as philanthropists do it, it will always be attacked as rich people's playthings.'

Two of the three organisations were seen to be left leaning, the National Council for Voluntary Organisations and the Charities Aid Foundation. The three organisations mounted a tug-on-the-heartstrings campaign focused on how much their ability to give to the poor would suffer if tax subsidies to the wealthy were capped. They claimed the loss would be £500 million a year. The head of the Charites Aid Foundation denounced Osborne's criticism of tax avoidance: 'We should recognise and celebrate today's great philanthropists, not brand them as wealthy tax dodgers.'[53]

With reputable charities arguing that Osborne's measure would hurt the most vulnerable, the media were won over and Osborne backed down. Maclean and Harvey sardonically observed: 'The fact is that the sole occasion the British philanthropic field had united, it had done so not to protect the poor but to defend the rich.'[54] Charities themselves are wheels in the machinery of privilege.

A similar story unfolded in Australia in 2008 when the Treasury reviewed the operation of a type of philanthropic foundation known as private ancillary funds, or PAFs. The episode was exposed and analysed by Elizabeth Cham in a doctoral thesis.[55] Most philanthropy by wealthy families is channelled through these foundations because they can closely manage their giving and benefit from generous tax provisions.[56] There are now more than 2,000 PAFs, with assets of A$7.6 billion, handing out around A$500 million each year.[57] Instead of simply donating to a good cause, PAFs allow wealthy families to control their giving more tightly, maintain secrecy, accumulate tax benefits and pass the whole thing on to their children.

The Treasury was concerned that PAFs (previously called PPFs) were failing to give away their funds and accumulating too much. It raised particular concerns about lack of transparency. Even basic facts such as the names and addresses of the funds were kept from the public, as well as how much they spent and on what.[58] In some cases the funds were being operated as businesses, with their untaxed assets used to purchase houses and cars for their founders and family members.[59] Its discussion paper summarised the problems.

> As the Government effectively provides a subsidy of 45 cents for each dollar donated to a PPF, the Government expects that this revenue forgone will be

directed to the charitable sector in a relatively short period of time. ... [And] the public should be able to identify the PPFs and be satisfied that PPFs are operating in an acceptable and transparent manner.[60]

The Treasury did not anticipate how passionately the rich would defend their 'right' to operate out of the public gaze. Elizabeth Cham reported that the reactions from some of the owners verged on the frantic; the sense of outraged entitlement from the philanthropists was perhaps supercharged by the conviction that their funds were established so that they could 'assist those in need'. Fury was vented at the idea they should have to publicise their existence. 'Your proposal to publish my contact details is also totally unfair,' wrote one. Many complained they would be 'inundated' with requests for funding. (Most have no staff to assess applications, so grants are made at the whim of the trustees.) They did not want to have to respond to charities seeking funds; they wanted their *privacy*.

As we'd expect, the professions that gather around and feed off elite philanthropy uniformly backed their benefactors. In a revealing comment, an investment banker said: '[Philanthropy] gets us alongside the families and the succeeding generations. If we do our job properly, we have an over-the-horizon engagement with the whole family and its assets, not just the corner where the philanthropic funds lie.'[61] Less predictably, Cham revealed that charities were recruited to side with the philanthropists against the Treasury and the public interest. They opposed the 15 per cent annual distribution rate proposed by the Treasury and backed rules allowing the funds to operate in secret.[62] Cham noted that charitable organisations that applied pressure on behalf of wealthy families included the Sydney Opera House and the large Christian charities Mission Australia and Anglicare. Some arts organisations admitted that they had been leant on to make a submission in favour of their benefactors. Some recognised that they would benefit in the short term from the proposed 15 per cent minimum rate of distribution but were persuaded that their sponsors would give less to them in the longer term.

The Treasury is the most powerful department in Canberra and usually gets its way. But, in the face of united opposition from the rich and charities for the poor, it backed down. The episode illustrates how elite philanthropy, whose ostensible purpose is to help the poor and vulnerable by funding good works, is typically driven by self-interest.

Power networks

In their study of elite philanthropy in Britain and the United States, Maclean and her colleagues found that wealthy philanthropists move in an ecosystem of influence.

> The research team identified several incentives for elite philanthropists, including the amassing of 'social and cultural capital', such as receiving honours like knighthoods in the United Kingdom for their services to charity. Viewed in this light, donors can effectively buy their way into circles of influence and networks. Tax advantages also play a part.[63]

One mechanism for buying networks of influence is the appointment of high-powered individuals to one's philanthropic trust. The board of the Minderoo Foundation of Andrew and Nicola Forrest includes Allan Myers AC. Myers has been president of the National Gallery of Victoria, chair of the Grattan Institute and chancellor of the University of Melbourne and in 2021 had a net worth of A$834 million. He is joined by Andrew Liveris AO, a former CEO of Dow Chemicals, former chair of the Business Council of Australia, and president of the 2032 Brisbane Olympics Organizing Committee. Forrest has also appointed well-connected people to the staff, including a former premier of South Australia (along with a chaplain, a tax manager, and his daughter, Grace).

Some elite philanthropists seek the company of famous intellectuals and use their money to ingratiate themselves with important academic institutions. A donation of several million dollars to a prestigious university, very often Harvard or Oxford, is the entry price they pay into the world of high-powered thinkers. One billionaire investor created a kind of salon for celebrated Big Brains whom he flew around in his private jet and traded deep thoughts with over dinner. The circle included the evolutionary biologist Richard Dawkins, psychologist Steven Pinker, philosopher Daniel Dennett, Harvard mathematical biologist Martin Nowak, Harvard law professor Allan Dershowitz and Harvard president Larry Summers.[64]

Unluckily for them, the billionaire whose generosity they enjoyed was Jeffrey Epstein, and the jet he flew them around in was the infamous 'Lolita Express'.[65] Commenting on the strange circle, David Wallace-Wells wrote of the white, male intellectuals' 'sense of their own world-historical significance. They were special people, deserving special acclaim and, of course, special privileges.'[66]

When stories began to emerge of Epstein's crimes, some of his intellectual friends defended him. The eminent evolutionary biologist Robert Trivers, famous for his work on self-deception and a hero of Richard Dawkins and Steven Pinker, exonerated Epstein in 2015: 'By the time they're 14 or 15, they're like grown women were 60 years ago, so I don't see these acts as so heinous.' The cosmologist Lawrence Krauss relied on his superior powers of observation. 'I always judge things on empirical evidence, and he always has women ages 19 to 23 around him ... So as a scientist ... I would believe him [Epstein] over other people.'[67]

Although Epstein had not attended a university, as a very rich person he was 'unable to see any world he felt unqualified to enter'.[68] World famous intellectuals were no exception. 'Epstein used his money and influence to brand himself an avant-garde intellect, a sparkling autodidact dedicated to the pursuit of knowledge on the far-out edge of human perception. In large part, it worked extraordinarily well.'[69] Like some other billionaires – Elon Musk and Peter Theil come to mind – Epstein saw himself as a social prophet, with a fascination in genetic engineering and transhumanism. For these social prophets the future is a libertarian one of 'freedom', entrepreneurship and bold technological feats; in other words, they aim to make the world after their own image, one ruled by hyper-agents where people like themselves extend their reach from the economy into the domains of social and cultural change and beyond.'

The science writer Adam Rogers argued that Epstein's philanthropy:

> illuminates how the connections among a relatively small clique of American intellectuals allowed them, privately, to define the last three decades of science, technology, and culture. It was a Big-Ideas Industrial Complex of conferences, research institutions, virtual salons, and even magazines, and Jeffrey Epstein bought his way in.[70]

In the upper echelons of the super-rich, there was nothing exceptional about the way Epstein operated, other than the fact he was a paedophile, and it is thanks to the extraordinary scrutiny to which his crimes gave rise that we have gained a rare insight into that world. Rogers concluded that studying Epstein's network shows:

> the impregnable, hermetic way class and power work in America. In private rooms, around tables full of expensive food, middle-aged white men agree to help each other out. They write complimentary books about each other, they introduce each other to people who can cut seven-figure checks, and they trade yet more invitations to other, even more private rooms. These are the places where power in America gets apportioned.[71]

Beyond forming gratifying friendships with celebrities and rubbing shoulders with famous intellectuals, giving away money is used to build powerful networks for reputation management and political protection. Via donations to politicians, universities and charities, Epstein used his fortune to surround himself with a global power elite, both before and after his 2008 conviction and jail time for sex crimes against minors. In his 'black book', dated 2005 could be found the phone numbers of Tony Blair, Bill Clinton, Donald Trump, Melania Trump, Prince Andrew, Steve Bannon, Michael Bloomberg, Richard Branson, Andrew Cuomo, Steve Forbes, Ted Kennedy, John Kerry, Henry Kissinger, Rupert Murdoch and Chuck Schumer.[72] He subsequently formed a friendship with Bill Gates, an association brokered by senior executives of Epstein's bank, JP Morgan, and a proposal by Epstein to raise billions of dollars for health charities.[73] The two bonded over philanthropy (a bond cited by Melinda Gates as a reason for separating from her husband). While some of Epstein's contacts were mere acquaintances, others were friends who enjoyed sumptuous hospitality at his New York home, on his private island and in his jet. Some ignored or justified his crimes; others appeared to provide protection from legal and media scrutiny.[74] Steven Pinker contributed an opinion to Epstein's legal defence, which was run by the Harvard law professor Alan Dershowitz.[75]

Cultural capital

In addition to prestigious universities and famous intellectuals, cultural institutions are one of the main centres of elite philanthropic attention. While a genuine desire to help the arts can be a motive for giving, the arts field is also an ideal place for privilege to be supercharged by accumulating cultural and social capital. Cultural capital is acquired by entering into the 'life-world' of the institutions and those who move through them. Social capital is accumulated through entry into new networks of influence whose impact rises with the prestige of the cultural institution. The boards and councils of major arts organisations are stacked with the rich and powerful, thereby becoming some of the most exclusive and rewarding clubs for elites to join.[76]

At the apex, the foundation board of the National Gallery of Australia sparkles with the elite of the elite, figures such as the Packer family matriarch Roslyn Packer, the Fairfax dynasty scion Tim Fairfax and the media and mining mogul Kerry Stokes. Each has donated millions to the gallery and has been rewarded for their generosity with an AC, the nation's highest honour. Board members mingle with the gallery's council, a power network that includes Nicholas Moore, the former chief executive of Macquarie Bank; Ilana Atlas, ANZ bank and Origin Energy board member and the wife of the former chair of the corporate regulator ASIC; Judith Neilson, billionaire and powerful philanthropist; and the former president of the Liberal Party Richard Alston. Handily, the former secretary of the Council of the Order of Australia, responsible for managing the award of Australian honours, is also a member (the council boasts four AOs). The membership highlights the interlocking of elites in the corporate, government and non-profit worlds revealed by research in the United States.[77]

The council of the National Gallery is chaired by Ryan Stokes, the son of Kerry Stokes, an example of the way dynastic succession nowadays involves 'preparing the children for the money' not only with financial and management skills but also with deep networks and cultural capital.[78] While the grooming of children to take the reins of businesses is well studied, the role of philanthropy in passing on elite privilege should not be neglected. Placing sons and daughters on the boards of charitable trusts and cultural institutions can be seen as a way of accelerating their acquisition of social and cultural capital – parental legacies more valuable, more 'legitimate' and certainly less corrosive than a huge inheritance.

Dangling before donors the carrot of tax-deductibility, leading cultural institutions help keep the machinery of privilege ticking over. The high-end ones solicit money with the implicit promise of exclusive entry to their club of powerful benefactors, known as donor circles.[79] Donor circles provide a sense of belonging to an elite group, its uniqueness reinforced by special events such as exclusive previews of blockbuster exhibitions.[80] Invitations to gala nights for patrons are eagerly sought. Of course, the institutions reject such a mercenary characterisation of the system. The director of the Sydney Opera House, Louise Herron, turns her nose up at the transactional approach to donor circles, as if they were 'a kind of gym membership'.[81] It's not marketing, she sniffs, it's *philanthropy*. The Sydney Opera House is clearly on a higher ethical plane than those non-profit organisations that hire specialists to advise them on how best to understand a potential donor's motives and how to manipulate them psychologically into giving.[82] (If there has been a death in the family, the specialists suggest framing it as 'an opportunity to express empathy and to explore what this relationship meant to your donor.')

Wealthy young philanthropists – giving away their parents' money or their own from early success – appear to reject the traditional image of patrician wealth giving to establishment institutions. The donor circle for twenty- to forty-year-olds at the Museum of Contemporary Art promises those 'ready to start your philanthropic journey' that they'll 'be the first to know about emerging contemporary art and artists', offering the street cred of making friendships with 'emerging artists'.[83] In addition to private gallery tours, the promised benefits include networking with like-minded people. A founding member of the young donors' circle of the Sydney Writers' Festival is upfront; donors pay for connections – that is, they donate to build social capital.

Dynasties have emerged in the arts philanthropy world. The daughters of the billionaire investor and philanthropist Kerr Neilson ('Australia's Warren Buffett') and his former wife Judith Neilson have become arts philanthropists. For Paris and Beau, we learn, 'It's time to give back.' The children of major donors Gene and Brian Sherman, Ondine and Emile, take turns chairing the family foundation, with Ondine's husband Dror also involved.[84] Some cultural institutions recognise that children may not want to mimic the ways of their parents. The Australian Chamber Orchestra, for instance, responds by 'creating events where the parents are not in the same room.'

In sum, behind the headlines announcing each big donation to a cultural institution lies a complex, subtle and evolving process of calculation and strategising by donors and recipients so that each can maximise their returns and pass on to their offspring the advantages of wealth.

Reputation laundering

In their study of the ways very wealthy people craft 'philanthropic identities', Maclean and Harvey comment on how the very rich co-opt ethics in pursuit of a preferred image of the self.[85] Their generous giving – often triggered by a 'liquidity event' – expresses their virtuous nature. They not only manifest the benevolence of giving but present themselves as crusaders for social justice and defenders of freedom. One of the common tropes in this image-making is a stress on how, beneath it all, we are all the same, all equal, except that a few of us need a helping hand. Maclean and Harvey ask whether working on these self-projects is 'the price of addressing the politics of envy to maintain the status quo'. It's a bad faith motive for philanthropy, but one defended by Tony Blair when he said, 'We need philanthropy to lessen hostility towards the rich.'[86] (Counter-intuitively, charitable giving by the wealthy *declines* as inequality increases.)[87]

However, it would be churlish and against the evidence to insist that elite philanthropy is nothing more than image-building, self-advancement or a payment for social insurance. Like everyone else, the privileged elite construct an image of themselves as 'a good person', faulty perhaps, but ultimately virtuous. For super-rich individuals who have oftentimes succeeded in a rough game where only the ruthless survive, building a philanthropic self can be redemptive, a means of putting one's sins behind or to the side and building a new version of the self. They want to leave a noble legacy. So identities constructed through elite philanthropy may be authentic, in that the philanthropist identifies with the person recognised by their peers or the public for their generosity and goodwill, someone who does, when all is said and done, love humankind.[88]

For his part, Andrew Forrest was unaffected by becoming a billionaire. He explained that his drive to help comes from his experiences as the skinny kid at school who was bullied. 'All my life, I am a campaigner against unfairness. I'm not a philanthropist as such, I'm a campaigner against unfairness.'[89] The sincerity of the philanthropic identity may be doubted when the virtues are proclaimed too loudly, and few lay it on more thickly than Andrew Forrest. In its value statement, the Minderoo Foundation is positively saintly.

> Everything we do is driven by a deep care for people and a mission to improve the world for future generations. ... Forgive and support each other, and always be kind. ... Treat others how you hope to be treated yourself. Always demonstrate respect and embrace differences in others.[90]

Its list of values begins with 'Humility, Courage and Determination'. 'Andrew and Nicola' believe that 'in the eyes of God you are no more – nor less – valuable than anyone else.' In case anyone doubted their sincerity, they conclude with a promise: 'We act with integrity when we display all values, all the time.' Forrest prides himself on being the hardest of hard-nosed businessmen, yet his philanthropic persona seems to belong to the world of the inspirational speaker leavened with new age wisdom. He urges us to work towards 'being the best person you can be ... Be brave and vulnerable in your relationships. ... [and] put love into action.'

Love in action was not the experience of the Yindjibarndi people, the traditional owners of the land on which Forrest's company wanted to mine. Unwilling to pay adequate compensation, Forrest's company mined anyway then fought the traditional owners through the courts, eventually losing. Forrest's company was found to have worked actively to divide the community, leading to much bitterness.[91] Unrepentant, Forrest's company, while still mining the land, continued to fight in the courts, including against the traditional owners' compensation claim.[92] As is true of other elite givers, Forrest's ruthless business practices sit uneasily with his philanthropic persona.

Grace Forrest, founding director of the Walk Free Foundation, seems to have learned humility from her father. After telling a journalist that she hates the term 'philanthropist' because it's so elitist, the 24-year-old went on: 'I was at this event the other night with this amazing art collector from New York and she says, "Oh Grace, I've actually heard of you, you are the global slavery chick aren't you? I heard about you from Bono."'[93] Bono had apparently offered to be a referee for Grace if she wanted to do an MBA at Harvard. She told the journalist that growing up in a billionaire's mansion didn't affect her. 'I was still buying all the clothes from the op shop when I was in high school.'

Elite philanthropy is sometimes pure cynicism. It is now part of the PR agent's playbook to arrange for disgraced corporations, celebrities and business executives to make highly visible donations to charity.[94] In London, a PR niche has developed to help fugitive Russian kleptocrats launder their reputations.[95] Chatham House describes the three tactics. First, make powerful friends through donations to political parties. Second, use legal threats to silence critics. Third, donate to charities to elevate your moral standing. Oligarchs have discovered that giving to prestigious universities, such as the University of Cambridge, is also effective.[96]

Glowing headlines announcing hefty donations by celebrities and the super-rich generate popular goodwill towards the donors, improving their standing in political circles, which smooths the way for lobbying against measures they oppose, such as changes to tax laws. But those who showcase their moral concerns also attract scrutiny. U2's front man Bono won deserved praise for his work with the Live Aid charity. Yet cynics such as Owen Jones pointed out that his band avoided tax when it shifted its affairs from Ireland to the Netherlands. Bono himself appeared in the Paradise Papers, which exposed offshore bank accounts by the world's rich and secretive. Neither in themselves implies wrongdoing, but some asked, if Bono, with estimated net worth of US$700 million, is so concerned about the poor, why does he not pay his fair share of taxes? Jones reported that Bono said of U2's tax affairs it was 'just some smart people we have ... trying to be sensible about the way we're taxed' – another instance of rising above cognitive dissonance.[97]

Some among the ultra-rich do not see any need to reconcile their money-making selves with their desire to be a good person because, for them, the act of making a fortune is good in itself. Occasionally, they call it as it is. In 2021, touching down after an eleven-minute trip into a low-Earth orbit costing US$5.5 billion, Jeff Bezos thanked his underpaid employees and Amazon customers for his 'best day ever'. 'You guys paid for it,' he said. Bezos has been heavily criticised for paying virtually no tax, so his $100 million gift to Dolly Parton to give to charities of her choice, part of the billionaire's 'Courage and Civility' award, was met with some derision.[98]

For those not acting in good faith, Gaztambide-Fernández and Howard have argued, the poor can serve as the site where the elite can perform their benevolence and good citizenship.[99] One opportunity for this performance is the CEO Sleepout organised each year by the St Vincent de Paul Society to raise awareness of, and funds for, homeless people. The genius of the CEO Sleepout is that, by asking business leaders to make a 'real' sacrifice, a night of rough sleeping, it signals true commitment, whereas a straightforward donation can be just an expression of privilege. Not all CEOs are wealthy and, for some participants, joining the Sleepout is a genuine expression of compassion.[100]

Even so, for some the charity event also serves to entrench a certain ideology and provide an opportunity to build social capital. One CEO who slept out confessed to being homeless himself early in life during a period of mental illness.[101] He was rescued, he said, when an 'act of kindness gave [him] a moment of clarity', allowing him to 'make one good choice', to find accommodation. He could return to the streets, he said, 'if [he] made enough wrong choices'. The story, although inspiring, reaffirms the neoliberal model of success and failure as the result of an individual's 'choices'. Viewed from this standpoint, CEOs sleeping out are helping the homeless to 'make better choices in life', or overcome their bad luck, instead of challenging a system that allows homelessness to coexist with great concentrations of wealth. Ethnographic research into homelessness by Cameron Parsell and Beth Watts concludes that provision of services such as mobile showering and laundry services may do more harm than good because they entrench the lack of agency of homeless people, reinforce perceptions of their deficiencies, and excuse society from confronting systemic inequities.[102]

A major sponsor of the event is the owner of the leading business newspaper the *Australian Financial Review*.[103] One of its journalists,

Aaron Patrick, noted that the CEO Sleepout had become 'one of the new staples of the executive calendar', an event that 'gives participants a better-than-usual shot of being recognised for their participation'.[104] 'There was a touch of excitement for some of the biggest names in the business arena, who tonight unrolled their sleeping bags around the country. ... Hugh Marks [a media conglomerate CEO] said "I wouldn't call this a networking event, I do know some of them from business ... whatever we can do to help."'

The bank boss Nick Reade was also alive to the side benefits. 'We all have a responsibility to give back to our communities. And it can be good for your business too.'[105] But it was left to Alexander Koch from Pinstripe Media to win the 'Sydney humblebrag trifecta of networking, booze and real estate': 'We bedded down in sleeping bags with million-dollar views of Barangaroo across the water. Tomorrow, I'll be having dinner with friends, drinking French champagne. But they'll still be there on the street.'

Summary

Elite philanthropy is an effective site for the conversion of financial capital into social and symbolic capital and using them to accumulate further wealth. Unlike small donors, wealthy philanthropists typically want to shape the work of the charities to which they give. Some aim to set the agendas in global arenas such as health and the environment. The super-rich today believe that, because of their business experience and life philosophies, they are uniquely placed to solve the world's problems, an ideology known as philanthrocapitalism. Its effect is to strengthen the system that made them rich and make inequality more palatable.

This new phenomenon is a danger to civil society because the welfare of the poor and vulnerable is increasingly entrusted to the rich and unaccountable. Moreover, the objectives of social movements are sometimes skewed towards system-preserving goals by rich donors, who support 'moderate' organisations and marginalise more critical groups, a trend especially evident in the environmental movement. Wealthy donors have been known to recruit charities for the poor to their campaigns to protect tax concessions.

It is not unusual for wealthy elites to use donations to buy their way into powerful circles of influence, which in turn enhances their ability to shape society. Boards of respected charities and trusts often appoint former government ministers and top civil servants, along with high-powered individuals from business and think tanks. Some wealthy donors like to move in the world of big ideas by donating to prestigious universities and favoured research programmes.

Eminent cultural institutions, for example national art galleries, serve as fattening yards for elite privilege by offering big donors entry into exclusive 'clubs' where potent networks can be built and symbols of esteem, such as honours, can be acquired. And they function as places where privilege can be passed on to the next generation.

For some among the super-rich, giving is a justification for not paying taxes. For others, charitable giving is an established means of laundering stained reputations. The non-profit sector also serves as a site for the super-rich to create an image of selfless benefaction and build a legacy veiling less admirable behaviour.

CHAPTER EIGHT

The Privilege Blender

Networking at the top

My kids went to a very good school, and you just see the networking between the parents. Everyone in the school is either a judge or a surgeon or something or other. And the children are, how can I put it? ... They get referred for jobs because their [father's] mate is allowed to put on five graduates or whatever at his law firm so they definitely get doors opened that other people wouldn't. (Farah, average income, older, Melbourne)

For some parents, the high fees paid to send their children to elite schools are not only an investment in their progeny's prospects but also an investment in building their own stock of social capital. As one focus group participant observed, 'Some parents are, in fact, paying for that influence and access to the upper echelons of businesses and politics and so forth' (Patricia, average income, older, Sydney). Another, who himself went to one of Australia's most expensive schools, spoke of how parents see their children's schools as avenues for building their own networks.

My manager's son goes to ... the one that everybody's kids go to [at the firm]. So, for example, he managed to get himself into that birthday party and from there met quite a few people and opens an opportunity for himself as well. Not just the kids benefiting from going to that school, but parents networking opportunity as well. *What kind of opportunities?* Exclusive investment opportunities and private equity deals. (Cliff, wealthier, younger, Sydney)

Networks of relationships demand a certain investment and therefore investment strategies, whether consciously executed or not. Time and energy must be devoted to working out who could be most useful to befriend and then cultivating and maintaining the relationship itself. Effective networking requires certain kinds of competence and, noted

Bourdieu, 'an unceasing effort of sociability'.[1] Lilla (average income, older, Sydney) had worked in what she called elite media executive management in Australia and in the United States.

> [There was] an eagerness to meet and create connections with people that have the same level of privilege through wealth, power, influence and access as each other so they can form a wider network across quite a large range of different sectors. There's a degree of reciprocity about the exchange of services, social capital, decision-making across finance, media, telecommunications and banking, a wide range of different sectors. So they basically create almost like this kind of higher level of influence in Australia.

We do not want to emphasise unduly the role of cold calculation in the cultivation of social networks. Much of it is carried on unconsciously or reflexively, and some is for reasons of pure sociality or 'emotional investment', even if some of the relationships acquired for that reason pay off in more material ways.[2] Of course, the time and effort put into building relationships does not always pay off because of the 'essential ambiguity of social exchange', which may involve bad faith, self-deception and misrecognition.[3]

On the other hand, in the rarefied world inhabited by billionaires, a laser-like focus on mutual enhancement of material interests is standard operating procedure, according to an intimate observer. Brendan O'Shannassy spent two decades captaining super-yachts owned by the ultra-rich and so had a bird's-eye view of how billionaires think and act. 'When billionaires meet, it is for their solar systems of knowledge, information and access to intertwine and grow. It is implicit in every interaction that their sharing of information will benefit both parties; it is an obsession with billionaires to do favours for each other.'[4] Owning a super-yacht is 'all about the guests'. The guests are all selected because their presence can benefit the billionaire owner. As for the enormous cost, one billionaire guest said: 'One deal secured on board will pay it back many times over.'[5]

Citing decades of research, Maclean, Harvey and Kling confirm that forming and exploiting social networks is at the core of leadership in the modern corporate economy.[6] They identify the most powerful among the power elite as those with networks that spread across the various dimensions of the 'field of power' – that is, the social domain that transcends individual fields and serves as a 'metafield of contestation for dominant agents'. They often compete, but they also form coalitions when matters of mutual interest, such as laws affecting taxation or corporate accountability, are in the offing.

For this elite among the elites, Maclean and her colleagues use the term 'hyper-agents', a term like the one used in chapter 7 to describe those who are able not only to enjoy privileges within the boundaries limiting others but to shift the boundaries for themselves. These dominant actors 'possess the capital needed to influence the rules of the game and accumulate power.'[7] The most powerful hyper-agents are invited to join the boards of the biggest corporations and most prestigious non-profits – major art galleries, symphony orchestras, old universities, and so on.

For those at the top of the corporate and financial fields, boards, including boards of non-profit organisations, are perhaps the foremost venues for strengthening social capital. In her study of interlocking directorates, Claire Wright used network analysis to identify 'pockets of very dense connections' and the directors who linked one centre with others.[8] These hyper-agents transcend business and are at the centre of efforts by the elites to change government decisions, shape public opinion and direct resource flows. Their role as 'purveyors of legitimizing narratives designed to inform collective systems of meaning' is especially enduring. For example, the contemporary characterisation of business owners as 'wealth creators' and 'employment providers' has replaced the former language of 'exploiters' and 'capitalists'. The narrative serves to legitimise the elites so that they are represented not as greedy and selfish but as civic-minded. They therefore have an interest in disinterested activities such as sitting on the boards of cultural, educational and sporting institutions.[9]

Indeed, the forensic study of elite business networks by Maclean et al. confirms that, to enter and maintain a position within the field of power, building social capital through appointments to the boards of both large corporations and prestigious non-profit organisations is the most effective strategy.[10] Membership of a board, even more so if acting as chair, can serve as symbolic capital, a marker of esteem that can be parlayed into other advantages, further building one's capital. In other words, to give is to receive, as we saw in our consideration of philanthropy.

The networks of hyper-agents cross into the fields of politics, administration, media, private schools, universities and philanthropy. In Australia, one of the most influential hyper-agents is David Gonski, a close associate of the most powerful tycoons and media magnates in the country and a confidant of premiers and prime ministers.[11] Known as the 'chairman of everything', the consummate networker has chaired the boards of some of the nation's biggest corporations as well as the boards of an elite private school, the Art Gallery of New South Wales Trust, the Sydney Theatre Trust, the Australian Stock Exchange and Australia's sovereign wealth fund, among others.[12] He was appointed chancellor of a prestigious university, awarded the top honour, and selected by a Labor government to conduct a landmark review of school funding. The symbols of Gonski's power and influence cross-fertilise with his deep networks and his own wealth. Since he possesses such *convening power* among elites, it's not surprising he's described in the business press as 'a key player in the network of directors, executives, politicians and philanthropists that pull the levers on Australia's corporate and cultural life.'[13]

In a study of Fortune 500 executives, Stern and Westphal found that success at obtaining prized board positions includes the ability to ingratiate oneself with colleagues, but to do so in subtle ways so as not to prompt cynicism.[14] Senior executives from upper-class families are more successful with these tactics. A privileged upbringing has a powerful indirect effect on the ability to form corporate networks, because cultural capital acquired at home and at elite educational institutions improves one's chances of being invited on to prestigious non-profit boards.[15] Along with elite networks, a habitus of power – that is, a disposition arising from the internalising of confidence and expectation of life success – is the royal road to membership of the power elite.[16] It is nepotism's mode of operation for the modern era.

Research on Britain's business elites has shown the vital role in advancement of networks built through sport, clubs and arts charities.[17] Interestingly, Harvey and Maclean conclude that (in contrast with France) 'it is difficult to overestimate the importance of sport' in the British context. Among Australia's power elite, one of the year's most prized tickets is for the pre-game luncheon at the Australian Football League grand final, held in the Olympic Room at the Melbourne Cricket Ground, said to be an 'extremely tight guestlist'. To inveigle a place on the guest list is, according to close observers, 'to be included among an annual snapshot of hierarchy and status in the vaunted realms of business, sport and politics'.[18] At the 2022 luncheon, the prime minister and state premiers networked with corporate heavyweights from finance, infrastructure and media, including Lachlan Murdoch and Kerry Stokes.

Are tech bros different?

Does the rise of super-rich tech entrepreneurs, famed for breaking moulds, represent a split from this view of a closed social group formed by old school ties, interlocking directorates and sporting clubs?

Mike Cannon-Brookes made his A\$20 billion in the software sector and is best known for his campaign to hasten Australia's shift to green energy. With his long hair and everyday attire of jeans, black T-shirt and baseball cap (peak at the front), he sets himself apart from the common-or-garden billionaire. On his Twitter account, he records his CO_2 age (338.96 ppm) and lets it be known that he eats schnitzels with his kids at the local ex-servicemen's club.[19] In short, he's an unpretentious dude.

Yet Cannon-Brookes grew up in Australia's wealthiest postcode. His father was an international banking executive, and he was educated at the very exclusive Cranbrook School. 'Global issues were a topic at the dinner table', according to a profile of his father, 'and the children were used to crossing the globe during school holidays.'[20] From his parents he learned 'globality' (his father's term). It was this worldview and self-understanding, absorbed by young Michael at home, that provided his real start-up capital.

Despite his anti-establishment dress, Cannon-Brookes has a penchant for buying some of Sydney's most desirable and high-priced mansions, earning the description, along with his business partner, as 'the reigning royals in Sydney's exclusive harbourside suburbs'.[21] He has also splashed out on a private island, his own jet, and a series of sprawling estates in the rolling hills of the Southern Highlands. Although Cannon-Brookes presents himself as a CEO as far as one can get from the image of the whisky-sipping patrician at a gentlemen's club, he mostly resembles other rich listers by way of his habitus and his extraordinary network – a network that includes Elon Musk and Bill Gates as well as his father's global investment banking links. To finish it off, he jointly owns a glamorous football club with Hollywood actor Russell Crowe and former casino mogul James Packer. Hardly the 'accidental billionaire' of the business press.

The stereotypical tech entrepreneur's rags-to-riches story – beginning with a clever idea, developed by a penniless start-up operating out of a garage, powered by grit, self-belief and luck and finally paying off in the billions – does not stand up to scrutiny. Typically, the successful start-up in the garage has a lot going for it before work begins. Iconic figures like Bill Gates and Elon Musk had supportive, well-connected and affluent families. Often, the funding for the early stages of the start-up comes from family members and friends. One study found that 'the income of someone's parents is the factor that correlates most to entrepreneurship, with higher wealth connected to a greater likelihood of being a start-up founder.'[22] Indeed, parents' income is a more important determinant of success in the tech world than mathematics ability. In other words, inherited advantage overrules merit.

In Britain, one start-up founder spoke of how, in the beginning, he had to work from his family home. As it happened, his family home was a grade II listed mansion, and his family and friends lent him £1.2 million. The tech titans often graduated from private schools and attended Oxbridge or one of the Russell Group of universities or were educated abroad.[23] Although working-class business success stories, for example that of Alan Sugar, attract the headlines, the truth is that few working-class young people can compete with the privileges attending an upper-middle-class upbringing.

'The gap isn't about money', wrote Nicole Kobie in *Wired* magazine in a thorough look at start-ups, 'but role models; poorer people simply don't know as many entrepreneurs, inventors or start-up founders, so their children aren't aware these routes are possible.' They also lack the cultural capital to mix easily with and impress those who can facilitate successful transition from a good idea to a viable business.

> … pitching isn't easy when it's a room full of wealthy rich white men and you're female, black, disabled or something else they're not. 'If you're a working-class person pitching someone who all went to the same universities, and even the same schools, that's going to be just as alienating an experience as if you're a young woman pitching a group of all men,' Clifford says.[24]

Gender versus class

In an intriguing ethnographic study of elite London, Luna Glucksberg analysed the distinct but tightly bound hierarchies of class and gender.[25] She exposed the role of gendered labour in the intergenerational transfer of accumulated capital, in particular the role of wealthy men's wives in reproducing elite privilege and power. She argued that good, enduring marriages, in which wives sacrifice careers and produce children, along with doing 'women's work' of home-making and expending intensive efforts to ensure children receive the best education, are vital for allowing their husbands space for continued capital accumulation. Moreover, by 'preparing the children for the money', they create the conditions for dynasty-making. Being a wife to a powerful man is a demanding job, more so because their husbands, who surround themselves at work with efficient staff, expect the same at home.

Ostrander too considered the conflicted category of 'rich wives', concluding that (in Glucksberg's words) 'the push towards gender liberation was never strong enough to overcome the fear of losing class positioning by challenging their husbands' upholding of patriarchal norms.'[26] In short, the attractions of elite privilege were not worth giving up in pursuit of their own female empowerment. Oppression by men is the price they pay for submitting to the family enterprise of wealth accumulation. In a different context, a study of the role of 'girls' as bodily capital in the male-dominated VIP party circuit, Ashley Mears reached a cognate conclusion, describing 'the cultural incompatibilities of femininity in elite men's social spaces'.[27] One implication of the work by these scholars is that patriarchal attitudes and behaviours are more entrenched at the top than lower down the social hierarchy.

What about women who do not sacrifice their careers but want to develop their talents in the world dominated by men? Here they confront the power of men's networks.

Researchers have considered two explanations for why men prefer to select from their own networks. Social identity theory stresses 'homophily', the tendency to prefer people like oneself – of similar gender, ethnicity and social and cultural background.[28] Our focus group participants often referred to the way privileged people seek out other privileged people because 'they have more in common', or because they feel more comfortable mixing with their own kind. Research shows that homophily influences, sometimes strongly, decisions about hiring as well as appointments to boards, so that people who are 'not a good fit' are excluded.[29] Male directors feel more comfortable working with people like themselves, so that, even when women are appointed to boards, they still feel unwelcome.[30]

Against this explanation, or perhaps complementing it, social network theory argues that selection is governed by people's networks, built up from school, working life, clubs, other boards, and so on. In these networks, there is formal or informal gender segregation. In a thorough recent study, Isabelle Allemand and her co-authors found that old boys' networks are indeed 'the major reason for the low representation of women on boards'.[31] Not only are women's networks less powerful, but research indicates that women, both for moral reasons and through 'gendered modesty', are more reluctant to exploit their networks for personal gain.[32] The power of networking therefore works to exclude women from boards. When regulations require corporations to appoint more women to boards, women continue to feel excluded or marginalised.[33] Deb Verhoeven and her colleagues found that mandated appointment of more women to boards does not increase their influence or reduce the power of men in the networks that count.[34] An approach to gender equity of 'just add women and stir' does not work.

It's fair to assume that women who resemble the male directors in characteristics other than their gender will be preferred. In other words, homophily comes into play. Harvey and Maclean write that they 'are struck continually by the power of cultural reproduction in organiz-ations, the reassertion of social and cultural patterns often in the face of apparent change.'[35] This suggests that, if networking is at the centre of the reproduction of elite privilege, then greater inclusion of women in networks is unlikely to change elite privilege. Indeed, the research shows that the appointment of more women to boards is not in itself likely to change the culture and character of the organisations.[36]

Another way of looking at the intersection of gender and class at the top is to study elite businesswomen and how they construct and understand their success. Maria Adamson and Marjana Johansson took a unique approach, a discourse analysis of best-selling autobi-ographies written by four highly successful British businesswomen (a research method known as prosopography).[37] These contributions to what they call 'the burgeoning cultural genre of business celebrity autobiographies' illuminate the way in which 'success' is framed in popular discussion.[38] They reference research showing that, through books like these (by men and women), corporate executives extend their influence not only into politics and policy-making but also into cultural understandings of wealth, inequality and privilege; in other words, they help shape 'a society where corporate leadership has become the model for transforming not just business, but all spheres of life.'[39]

We will say more in the next chapter about some of the justification strategies that are found in these autobiographies. Hard work and determination as the foundation of success is ubiquitous, although there is a gendered aspect to it because the four women stress the social and cultural barriers they had to overcome. Struggles with family duties, the work–life balance, and so on, suggest Adamson and Johansson, are important ways for engaging their mostly female readers with the message of 'I'm just like you'. The researchers chose two celebrity businesswomen with working-class backgrounds and two with middle-class backgrounds. For the former, the humble beginnings theme is used to explain their determination to escape their origins, but also to justify their wealth. Who wouldn't want to escape the grind of poverty? They had to make *extraordinary* efforts to overcome the disadvantages they were born into. The middle-class women could not plausibly adopt this approach. Adamson and Johansson observe: 'Unlike being working class, capitalising on a middle-class background is not as appropriate, as it may call into question the legitimacy of one's achievement. Hence, rather than an emphasis on extraordinary efforts, the trope of constructing *ordinariness* was prevalent here.'[40]

One of the middle-class success stories, unable to build on her own humble origins, reached back to the humble origins of her mother and father. Her enrolment at a private school was the result of their 'hard graft'. She made another claim to ordinariness – growing up, she had no special talents and wasn't especially good at anything, a theme also taken up by the other middle-class high achiever. Adamson and Johansson read these as attempts to balance extraordinary achievement with feminine modesty.

Both approaches, working-class hard graft and middle-class ordinariness, have the effect of erasing class.

> … class is written in and out [of their stories] in different ways … Class background is either constructed as a resource to draw on (which however should ultimately be left behind) or framed as irrelevant, with individually based characteristics and efforts heralded as the key conditions for success in both cases.[41]

Throughout their stories, the women appeal to the shared experience of their gender, subsuming class differences. Their politics are the politics of feminist *empowerment*, one that allocates responsibility for success to the personal efforts of women (albeit with the moral support of their sisters) without challenging the broader gender and 'class' orders through which they journeyed.

The final means by which these high achieving women justify their privilege is to repudiate the importance of wealth for wealth's sake. One or two concede that earlier in their lives they were obsessed with money and spent wildly. But they grew out of that immature and dangerous mode of living, seeing in the end that happiness comes from loving families ('Your heart costs nothing', one opined), and found more appropriate ways of living with wealth. This way, they could draw a symbolic and moral boundary between themselves and the women who pursue riches and fame for shallow reasons (think Kardashian). So, their wealth should not set them apart; they are just like other women, a claim that belies the class division between the wealthy elite and the rest.

In the end, write Adamson and Johansson, 'the discursive repertoires of ordinariness, universal gender struggle and unimportance of wealth' all combine to erase class from these women's stories and rewrite on to society an understanding of striving and success as the product of individual effort.

'The misogyny pipeline'

In 2020, Chanel Contos, a graduate of an exclusive girls' school in Sydney's up-market eastern suburbs, learned that some of her friends at the school had been sexually assaulted by boys at nearby private boys' schools, just as she had.[42] A year later, when she asked online for other girls to relay their experiences, she was overwhelmed with the number of stories – 6,000 testimonies in three weeks. She launched a petition for consent education in schools, one that received enormous support and prompted immediate action by political leaders.

The episode illustrates how elite privilege intersects with and magnifies male privilege. Celebration of gender equality and empowerment within the culture of elite girls' schools, and the broadening of the life possibilities of girls from the upper-middle classes, confronts the reality of the violence they experience at the hands of boys of their own class.[43] Of course, rape culture is not confined to elite private schools, not by any means. However, there are characteristics of the elite private school milieu (explored in chapter 5) that make it especially pernicious – the sense of entitlement boys' schools naturally create, the presumption among students that they are special and more powerful, and the belief that the rules do not apply to them, that they have a kind of moral impunity.

Contos is conscious of her privileged upbringing (she lived in Vaucluse and attended Kambala School), the wealth that dwells in those leafy suburbs, and the opulence of the schools her friends and their assailants attended (Cranbrook and Scots College featured prominently). 'We've created a situation', said Contos, 'where, particularly for young men in private schools, their entitlement outweighs their empathy'[44] (prompting a Facebook group of mothers of sons at the elite boys' schools to complain, 'How dare this spoilt brat try and take down my son').[45]

When boys from elite schools transition to university they carry with them the same combustible mix of entitlement and misogyny. It's a vital step in what Jane Kenway calls 'the misogyny pipeline',[46] a pipeline that leads to powerful positions in business, the professions, politics and wherever privilege finds an opening. She argues that toxic behaviours are worse among boys from exclusive private schools because their misogyny is supercharged by their sense of power and entitlement. The argument receives support from a father of a Year 9 student at the King's School, who said elite schools cultivate a culture of entitlement and privilege which leads to a lack of sensitivity towards others. 'They teach these kids they're the best, they're the chosen ones, they're going to run Australia, they're going to conquer the world.'[47] It is expressed as contempt for women of their own class and for everyone outside it. Kenway refers to a variety of research on 'hegemonic masculinity', which elite schools help to produce, not least through sport.

Kenway asks whether these elite boys' schools could sustain class privilege without also reinforcing misogyny. She believes they couldn't, in part because their customers, wealthy parents, would not allow it. They send their sons to the schools so they can learn how to make the rules of entitlement work for them.[48] The schools themselves react to public exposure of bad behaviour by reasserting their 'values' and announcing punishments of individuals caught out. The punishments often do not fit the crime, and the schools put more effort into damage control than cultural reform.

An investigation by anti-rape activists into sexual violence and hazing at Australian universities, particularly evident at residential colleges at the University of Sydney, concluded that the culture that gives rise to these behaviours becomes entrenched in elite private boys' schools. 'There are close ties between particular private boys' schools in Sydney and certain colleges. For example, St Paul's College has high numbers of students who attended schools such as Trinity Grammar, The King's School, St Joseph's College, and Cranbrook School.'[49]

In 2017, spooked by bad publicity over incidents of sexual harassment and assault, the University of Sydney and its colleges commissioned a review by the former Sex Discrimination Commissioner Elizabeth Broderick.[50] Broderick's report on the culture of residential colleges put much of the blame on alcohol rather than any culture of misogyny and entitlement. It was accused of being a whitewash. The journalist and anti-rape activist Nina Funnell wrote: 'There is virtually no discussion of class, and the words "privilege", "wealth", and "entitlement" do not appear once. (The word "elite" does appear, but only in relation to "elite sport".) Nor is there any discussion of the college's religious affiliations.'[51]

The same was true of a separate report for St Andrew's College. It considered the diversity of students by geography, sexuality, disability and race but said nothing about social class.[52] Broderick (herself once head girl at the exclusive Meriden School)[53] chose to emphasise that the college 'has a strong and proud heritage and boasts a vibrant, high-achieving community.'

Similar observations have been made about elite schools in Britain. Students at London's Westminster School, the most difficult to get into after Eton and Harrow, are told they are the 'crème de la crème of this country', yet the school is notorious for reports of racism and rape culture. A female graduate said: 'My experience at school was that class privilege combined with male entitlement in the most toxic and destructive ways. There was rampant sexism and bullying. There was regular cocaine use in the school toilets, and among the very bright, very high-achieving girls, there was widespread bulimia, anorexia and self-harm.'[54]

The Times revealed claims of a 'private school bubble' in which boys from elite schools would 'form alliances of rich sexual predators'.[55] The culture is one of impunity, the belief that laws and norms apply to others while rich boys are exempt. As one student put it: 'This behaviour is implicit in the narrative which the school teaches the boys: that they are the best, the brightest, the future leaders of the world and therefore untouchable.' A formal review commissioned by the school concluded that, within the school, there is a strong sense of social hierarchy 'where some male pupils' status was dictated by familial wealth, academic success and charisma.'[56]

Kenway's misogyny pipeline is all too evident in private schools in the United States too, a phenomenon exposed to public scrutiny in 2018 when Christine Blasey Ford accused the Supreme Court nominee Brett Kavanaugh of attempting to rape her when he was a student at the exclusive private Georgetown Preparatory School. Blasey Ford's testimony sparked intense debate about male power, the privileges of wealth, and the way the elites live by different ethical rules.

An alumna of the Georgetown Prep's sister school, which Blasey Ford had attended, observed that the more privileged the boys were at elite boys' schools (with richer and more powerful fathers) the more they treated girls as sexual objects.[57] A male graduate of another exclusive school spoke of 'the surety that they wouldn't be held accountable, it fed their smugness when tormenting vulnerable kids.'[58] Another wrote of how the boys who abuse and assault girls are welcomed by the most elite colleges before becoming 'government officials, business leaders, possibly even Supreme Court justices', taking with them the attitudes, behaviours and memories made in the school culture.[59]

Elite, white and male privilege

In an influential intervention in 2003, Nancy Fraser argued that struggles over inequality had shifted over the previous three or four decades from a focus on *redistribution* – that is, income-related inequalities and their remedies – to *recognition* – that is, identity-based inequalities related to gender, ethnicity and sexuality and their remedies.[60] She drew a distinction between the 'social politics of equality' and the 'cultural politics of difference' (now referred to as identity politics), while maintaining that the two (economics and culture) are in fact connected in complex ways. Today, the politics of identity dominate the politics of redistribution, notwithstanding the brief flowering of the Occupy movement and denunciations of the 1 per cent.

Some scholars analyse elite or class privilege employing the same framework they use to analyse white, male and other forms of identity-based privilege.[61] This tends to collapse the social politics of inequality into the cultural politics of difference, as if one's position in the socio-economic hierarchy can be understood as a kind of identity. In our view, this is a category error. Eliteness due to wealth and influence is on a continuum; it can be modified, enhanced or curtailed, whereas gender and race describe categories to which people are assigned.[62] And whereas the notion of 'normativity' attaches to maleness, whiteness, heterosexuality, and so on, the wealthy elite is not the 'normal' against which the non-elites are judged.

Nevertheless, and as we have seen, in practice the two kinds of inequality intermingle. While we have been concentrating mainly on the privileges linked to wealth and influence, and in that sense are returning to the preoccupations of the redistribution era, we do so in a post-identity way, recognising that privilege associated with wealth and influence often intersects with gendered, racial and other forms of disadvantage. In other words, after the shift in emphasis from economic difference to cultural difference, we are turning the spotlight back on to the economic but doing so in a culturally inflected way.

The surge in scholarship on the politics of recognition allows us to return with a deeper insight into the politics of redistribution, not least with our stress on *doing* elite privilege. We have a clearer understanding of its interpersonal side, an awareness that the structure of elite–non-elite domination is, as Bob Pease writes, psychically embedded, so that 'psychosocial interventions need to be examined alongside structural and cultural changes.'[63] Similarly, we are now in a better position to understand that domination 'operates on three levels: the personal, the cultural, and the structural.' A white boy from a wealthy family undoubtedly occupies a culturally and structurally dominant position, but he may still be bullied at his elite school if he is different in some way. It is therefore legitimate to say, as Pease does, that 'almost everyone at some point in their life experiences both privilege and oppression.'[64]

In recent decades, social movements in some societies have successfully contested the exclusive privileges enjoyed by certain kinds of dominant groups.[65] In particular, as we saw in chapter 6, the women's movement has achieved important victories (in employment rights, divorce law, reproductive rights, services for women, political representation, and so on), eroding some of the privileges enjoyed by men. And following the important achievements of previous generations of civil rights and Indigenous rights activists, the granting of privileges exclusively to white people are now much more difficult to defend. The evidence indicates, however, that this kind of social progress has not eroded or undermined the privileges enjoyed by the wealthy elite. In fact, the opposite has occurred. As a result, the privileged position of wealthy white men, while declining in relation to their whiteness and their maleness, has been improving because of counterbalancing social and economic changes. The effect of the neoliberal revolution has been to enhance the wealth, power and influence of the '1 per cent' and so the privileged position occupied by this elite.

Compared to the 1950s and 1960s, male privilege and white privilege today are greatly diminished even if there remains a long way to travel. On the other hand, by any measure elite privilege is no less prevalent than it was in those times. Considering the changes brought by the dominance of market liberalism, elite privilege is perhaps more entrenched now than it was fifty years ago. Certainly, the rich are much richer than they were, and more powerful. While some capitalist societies are marked by substantially less racial discrimination and patriarchal attitudes than others, it is hard to imagine a form of capitalism without a wealthy elite wielding a great deal of power and enjoying many privileges, even if a social democratic form of capitalism were to mandate some income redistribution. It is true that in Western countries the wealthy elite remains dominated by white men, but that is not the case globally. Some 40 per cent of the world's billionaires are from countries other than the United States and Europe, mainly from China and India. Around 13 per cent of the world's billionaires are women.[66]

Summary

Among the power elite, networks are everything. Boards, both corporate and non-profit, are among the foremost venues for building social capital. The networks of these hyper-agents extend well beyond business, into politics, the media, universities, sports clubs and cultural institutions. The subtle skills needed to build powerful networks are usually passed on by upper-class family life and elite schooling. Although tech titans appear to reject the usual methods of corporate success, the same rules apply. Founders of successful start-ups usually come from affluent, well-connected families.

Patriarchy and elite privilege are intertwined in complex ways. 'Women's work' by the wives of super-rich men is often vital to their husbands' success. Women who want to succeed in the domain of powerful men are held back by their less powerful networks. Gender inclusivity in corporate life is unlikely to dilute elite privilege. Explaining their success, women CEOs discount their socio-economic backgrounds, instead emphasising their own hard work and determination.

Jane Kenway has described a 'misogyny pipeline' that channels boys from affluent families through exclusive private schools whose culture supercharges their sense of entitlement and privilege, giving rise to especially toxic forms of masculinity.

The framework used to understand white, male and other identity-based forms of privilege cannot easily be adapted to analyse elite or class privilege, although its insights help illuminate elite privilege. While there has been significant progress in challenging male and white privilege in Western societies (albeit with a long way to go), the power and influence enjoyed by wealthy elites has been expanding in recent decades.

CHAPTER NINE

Hiding and Justifying Privilege

Sociologists have spilled a great deal of ink over the question of how unequal and unjust societies can 'stably reproduce themselves over time'.[1] The puzzle has deepened in recent years as the distribution of wealth and life opportunities, now more unequal than they have been in decades, has met with no serious reaction. Social media vents on the topic, but nothing seems to be done. Occupy Wall Street always looked as though it would fizzle out. If anything, the reaction to injustice came in the form of Trumpism, a response to perceptions of elite privilege. In 2019, Chicago's mayor, Rahm Emanuel, formerly President Obama's chief of staff, wrote that the 'full-on middle-class revolt against the elites and the privileges they hoard' is the most important political dynamic of our era.[2] (In the United States, 'middle class' often refers to those without college degrees.) The perception, Emanuel went on, is that the elites get all the breaks and know how to work the system to their advantage, while 'ordinary people are forced to pay full freight.' That the revolt was led by a billionaire celebrity is testament to Trump's ability to reframe economic problems as cultural ones.

Here we explore why the continued reproduction and display of privilege meets so little resistance in putatively meritocratic societies, focusing on three mechanisms – naturalisation, camouflage and justification. They work to make great wealth more acceptable or less visible. Compared to wealth disparity, privilege needs extra naturalisation, camouflage and justification because it seems more unjust when those at the top leverage rights and benefits denied to others. We also consider how elites justify their wealth and privileges to themselves.

Naturalising

Naturalisation refers to the framing of elite privilege as a natural and unchangeable feature of social life. Bourdieu referred to 'the ability to make appear as natural, inevitable, and thus apolitical that which is a product of historical struggle and human invention.'³ The related idea of normalisation refers to the processes by which elite privilege becomes an accepted state within a given social context, a normal state of affairs. When elite privilege is normalised, protest against it appears to be quixotic.

Several mechanisms or processes serve to naturalise or normalise inequality and privilege. Ideology, the beliefs and values that shape people's understanding of the world around them, is used to justify and reinforce prevailing power structures. The spread of neoliberal ideology of free markets and limited government has advanced the belief that, when people are free to pursue their self-interest in a free market, the most talented and hardworking individuals rise to the top. It is closely aligned with the older idea of meritocracy, a society in which success is based on individual merit rather than inherited roles or structural barriers so that inequalities in outcomes arise from differences in talents and drive. We have seen many instances throughout this book of discriminatory practices that favour elites but are covered over and obscured, leaving the impression that success and failure are due to given and unchallengeable factors.

Cultural norms can also naturalise inequality and privilege. Gendered norms assigning roles to men and women have been thoroughly deconstructed by feminists and are now everywhere challenged. The same has been true of beliefs about natural racial hierarchies. Belief in hierarchies resulting in inequality, even gross inequality, have clung on more tenaciously; in fact, with the decline of social democracy, the taken-for-grantedness of wealth hierarchies has become more embedded. With fewer adults having the language and arguments to critique the system that gives rise to inequality and elite privilege, children from a young age learn to accept them as normal, both as characteristics of society and as defining their own roles. When driving past an opulent private school with grand buildings and acres of playing fields, what does a parent of modest means say when the child in the back seat asks, 'Why can't I go there?'. As Bourdieu wrote, people learn to adapt their subjective expectations to their objective possibilities.

Public discourse, from the media to politicians, reinforces daily the view that the way society is structured and power is distributed is given and unchangeable, except at the margins. 'The economy', for example, is presented as an enormous, remote and autonomous institution that decides people's fates according to its own inexorable logic. And the neoliberal fetishisation of 'choice' has seen the demand for personal choice invading non-market domains such as education and health care with the result that the 'freedom' to choose eclipses the ability to choose.

Before we look more closely at these mechanisms, it's worth getting a sense of the contours of naturalisation in popular thinking. The focus group conversations showed how tolerance of inequality and unfairness softens their sting. As one participant put it: 'Listen on the radio, you can hear it. You can see it everywhere. It's just our system of living. And it's just a part of what's been created in our lifestyle today. We all get used to it and we all go along with it' (Tony, wealthier, older, Sydney).

When the privileges of elites are seen to be part of the natural or normal order of things, they contain their own justification.[4] After mentioning a wealthy man who went unpunished after breaking lockdown rules, Phillip (average income, older, Melbourne) said resignedly, 'because that's how it is when you're privileged.' Agreeing that there are some at the top and some at the bottom of the social hierarchy, Dylan (wealthier, younger, Melbourne) said: 'That's how it is, how society probably has to run, realistically.'

Differences in taken-for-grantedness explain why a high level of inequality in one society may spark widespread protest while the same level of inequality in another society may be accepted as normal. Economists measure 'tolerance of inequality' to help explain why some societies seem more relaxed about high levels of inequality than others.[5] However, while most people accept some disparities in income, even wide disparities, few accept unfairness, and when elites enjoy privileges denied to others it is widely felt to be unfair.

Our national survey and focus group results reveal that Australian society is marked by a sharp division between those who view inequality and privilege as corrosive and unfair and those who accept them as part of the natural order. In our survey, we asked which one of the following statements better reflects their view:

In Australia, there's one rule for the rich and another rule for the rest.

Overall, the rules are applied fairly in Australia.

Fifty-one per cent chose the first and 37 per cent nominated the second, while 12 per cent couldn't say. Men are substantially more likely than women to believe the rules are applied fairly. For men there's an 8 per cent gap between the first and second option (49 versus 41 per cent) while for women it's 19 per cent (53 versus 34 per cent). University-educated, fully employed men with higher incomes living in capital cities are somewhat more likely than others to believe that, overall, the rules are applied fairly. In other words, the beneficiaries of the system are somewhat more likely to say the rules are applied fairly, while women, those on lower incomes, and those who did not go to university are more inclined to believe that there's one rule for the rich and another rule for the rest. And while 54 per cent of people who attended public schools believe there's 'one rule for the rich', only 42 per cent of those who attended non-Catholic private schools agree. Still, a substantial minority of those who do not benefit from the system believe the rules are applied fairly.

The national survey also asked respondents how often, if ever, they have felt angry or resentful about wealthy people or celebrities getting special treatment. Forty-six per cent said they never (15 per cent) or only occasionally (31 per cent) feel angry or resentful, while 49 per cent said they feel angry or resentful sometimes (28 per cent) or often (21 per cent). These percentages do not vary significantly across gender, income, education level and age (except in the over sixty-fives, who are a little less likely to feel those emotions). The only notable division is between the broader community and graduates of expensive private schools, who are less likely to experience angst over special treatment – 24 per cent said they never feel it (as opposed to 15 per cent in the wider community) and 17 per cent said only occasionally (31 per cent in the wider community).

Social media and newspaper comment sites reveal an often bitter subterranean contest over elite privilege. Some see through naturalisation and are cynical and resentful about the privileges enjoyed by elites. This tension also showed up in the focus group conversations.

... society just turns a blind eye to that, and these rich people just keep on living their privileged lives. And I think that's just really, really bad. (Naomi, wealthier, older, Sydney)

On a day-to-day basis, the levels of connections, social connections and networks formed by groups of privileged people ... [create] quite a wide chasm to cross for people to be able to have the same access to society and the same influence as this group of people do. (Lilla, average income, older, Sydney)

The alternative view was also expressed. 'I don't think there's anything wrong with being highly successful if you've worked your way up ... That's what's important' (Lynette, wealthier, older, Sydney).

Meritocracy

One pervasive means of naturalising privilege and the benefits that go with it is to claim that elite preferment arises from natural ability or hard work rather than special treatment due to an inside run, powerful networks or cultural affinity. In our focus group conversations, for example, some wealthier participants said that wealth should not be criticised as 'privilege' if it has been acquired by 'hard work' as opposed to having it 'handed to you on a plate'. Working hard for your wealth gives it legitimacy.

Leah said that she had worked for 'a really successful man'.

So he's extremely privileged, has a very lavish lifestyle. But he works for it. It's not like it was just given to him. ... So you get to see both sides to the story where, yes, you can be privileged, but there's also a lot of work and not everyone gets things handed down to them. So I guess it's all about perspective. ... Is it really privilege or are you just good at what you do? (Leah, wealthier, younger, Sydney)

Peter, a doctor, believes privilege and wealth go together. However, 'I don't begrudge people that are high up in society because they invariably have worked hard to achieve what they have. They have made probably a lot of sacrifices in their private lives as well to focus on their business. So I don't begrudge it' (Peter, wealthier, older, Sydney).

As neoliberal ideology supplanted social democracy, social and cultural discourse became increasingly dominated by the view that we live in a society where anyone can make it if they work hard enough.[6] As we have seen, however, the social and cultural capital acquired in families of origin and elite schools load the dice of success in almost every area. In his best-selling denunciation *The Meritocracy Trap*, Daniel Markovits assembled the US evidence to argue that meritocracy had become what it was intended to combat: 'A mechanism for the concentration and dynastic transmission of wealth and privilege across generations. A caste order that breeds rancor and division.'[7] Although it does at times breed rancour and division, meritocracy more often conceals the enormous benefits of elite incumbency behind a façade of equal opportunity. Rancour and division must then find expression in other, darker forms, looking for others to blame for their discontent.

Sports stars frequently declare that anyone can achieve their dreams as long as they try hard enough. So common has this trope become that we are inclined to forget how absurd it is. Yet the ideology of success due to personal effort infects the highest levels. The former chief justice of Australia's High Court, Susan Kiefel, told high school students: 'You can usually do whatever you determine to do. The constraints or limits placed upon a person's life and career usually come from themselves.'[8] Kiefel's neoliberal ideology of personal achievement leaves no room for the systematic oppression of Indigenous people, for example. Nor does it account for the way individuals are enabled by political struggles. Kiefel herself rode the women's movement to success, treading a path blazed by Mary Gaudron, the High Court's first female justice, appointed in 1987 by a Labor government influenced by years of feminist agitation. We read that Kiefel left her state school at fifteen to become a legal secretary, then returned to night school and university, prompting the *Sydney Morning Herald* to opine that 'Justice Kiefel's rise is a great example to every child, male and especially female. Barriers can indeed be overcome.' In this narrative of personal triumph, marvelling at the one who transcends difficult circumstances, everyone else is responsible for their own failure, rendering invisible the discriminatory structures of gender, race and class.

This meritocratic narrative was discernible in the focus group conversations, particularly among the older, wealthier participants. Success was viewed as the outcome of competence so that the wealth and privileges that go with it have been *earned*. Indeed, the argument goes, successful people are not properly described as 'privileged'; the privileged are those who have acquired wealth without earning it, and that might include the children of the rich.

> … privileged is like some of these kids that their parents have worked really hard and so the children benefit from that and then some of them, excuse my French, become just total brats because they're privileged, because mum and dad have money. So therefore mum and dad buy them the flash cars and some people even buy their kids houses and that sort of thing. *Those* are the privileged ones. (Naomi, wealthier, older, Sydney)

Whereas poverty, unemployment and disadvantage were once understood as structural problems demanding social change, nowadays they are typically seen as afflictions of the affected individuals or families. A focus group participant put it bluntly. 'I think the worst part of it is that when we say to people, "Well, you're just making excuses because in this country anybody can do anything." I think that's a myth' (Glenn, average, older, Melbourne). The meritocracy discourse has an atomising effect on conceptions of society when success is due solely to personal effort and hierarchizing structures are occluded. The point of view of the dominant elite becomes the dominant point of view.[9]

Obliviousness

For those steeped in privilege, the advantages that flow from it can become so normalised within their social milieu that they are oblivious to its inherent unfairness. Interviewed in 2022, the ABC's newly appointed head of news, Justin Stevens, remarked that 'No one should ever feel entitled to a job.'[10] Stevens, a graduate of the exclusive St Ignatius College in Lane Cove and a 'rugby tragic', went on to describe how he got his break in journalism. At the age of fourteen he managed to get a week of work experience with the prominent Channel Nine newsreader Peter Overton. He told of how his father, an oncologist, bumped into Peter Overton's father, another oncologist at the same hospital, in the tea-room and asked if he could help out his son. It all unfolded from there.

Medicine seems to be a hotbed of favours for the privileged. Phil Gould, the renowned rugby league coach, told of frantically phoning his billionaire friend Nick Politis in the middle of the night to tell him his mother was gravely ill in hospital. Politis, who made his fortune from car dealerships and is known as 'the Godfather', is owed many favours. He contacted one of Australia's leading neurosurgeons, who got out of bed and went to the hospital in his dressing gown to attend to the woman.[11] Gould later posed a pertinent question: 'Just what makes a leading surgeon say "yes" to Nick Politis?'

Work experience and internships are now seen as essential to career prospects, so competition is intense. In 2022, senior partners of Boston Consulting Group flew their children to London for 'an exclusive week-long work-experience programme'.[12] When staff heard about it, they complained about 'super-nepotism' and objected to having to 'babysit the bosses' kids'. They pointed out that the company has forty applicants for every internship. In reply, the company said the work-experience programme was 'designed to help children [of top managers] have a broad educational and professional experience'. Tone-deaf to the use of privilege, a senior partner whose children had attended wrote: 'We are paying our own way if we want our children to go.'

For many years, during which wealth and income inequality in Britain deteriorated and 'austerity' caused distress to those at the bottom, the *Financial Times* seemed oblivious to the offence caused by the title of its luxury consumption magazine, *How to Spend It*. In May 2022, two years into the pandemic and with a war raging in Ukraine, the editor announced that the magazine, packed with advertisements for private jets, super-yachts and ultra-luxe holiday escapes, and once referred to as 'hard-core wealth porn', would be changing its name. Apparently, the title's 'irony … has sometimes failed to land', and so henceforth it would be known as *HTSI*.[13] Even so, she wrote, the magazine would carry on promoting hedonism and 'a slightly escapist lifestyle' because '*HTSI* has never been, and never will be, one for the hairshirts.'[14] In her world, it seems, the alternative to a super-yacht is a hairshirt.

Concealing with shared symbols

Erving Goffman once noted that a society's *collective symbols* 'serve to deny the difference between categories in order that members of all categories may be drawn together in affirmation of a single moral community.'[15] These unifying symbols help to camouflage the role of privilege in structuring societies that are essentially discriminatory and unfair.

In Australia, the often trumpeted values of egalitarianism, mateship and a fair go for all (together wrapped into the 'Anzac spirit') tend to cover over and suppress social distinctions. The government itself declares to potential immigrants that the nation is defined and shaped by the values of 'freedom, respect, fairness and equality of opportunity'.[16] A couple of focus group participants referred to this means of camouflaging privilege. 'It's the myth of the battler ... the myth that we're all Australian, we all cook our barbies on Australia Day, we all go to the beach. ... it's that "we all call Australia home" sentiment, which is just a lot of marketing' (Josh, wealthier, younger, Sydney). Glenn, a Melbourne solicitor, put it more pointedly: 'One of the ways it's hidden is by perpetuating myths of egalitarianism and equality. I think that makes it crueller for those that are excluded. They don't know what they're actually missing out on' (Glenn, average income, older, Melbourne).

Marketing messaging that bolsters the sense of a people united by their shared national culture are everywhere, from Qantas's angelic children's choir singing 'I still call Australia home' to the ABC television promo featuring a group of Pitjantjatjara women standing in a spectacular gorge in Arrernte country singing 'I am Australian'.

We are one, but we are many
And from all the lands on Earth we come
We share a dream, and sing with one voice
I am, you are, we are Australian.[17]

The song is heart-warming and it's easy to allow one's chest to swell with love for the nation; yet, objectively, the sentiment is untrue and takes on a special poignancy when expressed by Indigenous women. We were reminded of the disjunction between the 'we are one' messaging and the harsh reality of social difference during the Covid lockdowns. In the early days the sense was widely shared that the lockdowns were an epochal social leveller. Giorgia (average income, younger, Sydney) was optimistic. 'When the pandemic first hit in 2020, I was like, okay, this would be the great equalizer. ... We're all in this together ... maybe this is what's meant to happen on some level because there might be a fairer balance of wealth or whatever.' Disillusionment soon took hold: 'I was fairly quickly proven wrong in the sense of I do feel [the privileged] definitely would have had a very different experience, I think, in every sense. Specifically financial privilege. ... My naivety was quickly proven wrong.'

Hiding wealth

The consumption practices of the super-rich, presented to us as an exotic species, are an endless source of fascination. It is the unobtainability of their lifestyles that pulls us towards them, whether we react with admiration, envy, distaste or contempt.

The variety of reactions creates a problem for the super-rich when it comes to leveraging their status to gain access to a privilege. On the one hand, squandering money in grotesque displays is common enough. When a one-percenter flies their friends to a private party in Las Vegas and pays a small fortune for Beyoncé or Rod Stewart to perform, the objective is to impress. However, according to a person responsible for booking acts such as Cold Play and Celine Dion: 'They do it discreetly and for 30 to 50 friends, and they'll have a million-dollar artist perform 45 minutes before they have a celebrity chef prepare a dinner. That's the kind of thing we've seen more and more of.'[18]

Performers sign strict confidentiality agreements, and some hosts instruct their guests to leave their phones at the entrance to prevent videos being made. In a world of popular pushback against the super-rich, these displays are conspicuous only to the desired few, unless images leak out.[19] The paparazzi are the bane of the super-yacht-owning billion-aire's life, suggesting the snappers provide a valuable social service.[20]

Paradoxically, although wealth and privilege may be concealed in these ways, it is also true that, to leverage the advantage of wealth and influence into the granting of a privilege, status must somehow be displayed. West and Zimmerman wrote about male privilege display that it 'must be finely fitted to situations and modified or transformed as the occasion demands.'[21] Likewise, doing elite privilege requires subtle management of one's signalling to suit the circumstances.

The concealment of privilege is partly explained by the reluctance of the wealthy to identify themselves as such, the more so in societies where the egalitarian myth is entrenched, where signalling 'I am better than you' is likely to attract a sharp rebuke. 'Stealth wealth' conceals itself, at least in certain settings. Emma Spence's doctoral research included employment with a firm brokering the sale of super-yachts at a yacht show in Palm Beach, Florida. Her task was to station herself at the end of a gangplank and decide whether those wanting to go aboard to inspect the yacht were potential customers or in a lower financial league. She had to learn the subtle semiotics of the very rich. 'I had little comprehension of how difficult identifying the superrich through dress alone would be,' she wrote, and followed her supervisor's instruction: 'Every person who approached my station was to be treated with the utmost respect, so as not to inadvertently insult or put off a potential client.'[22] She chatted amiably with a mature woman wearing trainers and a denim jacket, deciding she failed the rich test. Yet when the same woman arrived the next day to inspect a yacht, she turned out to be the wealthiest woman at the show.

Spence's supervisor handed her the business card of a man who'd been allowed on board. The card was black, shiny and made from metal. Emma was impressed. 'It's hideous,' her supervisor exclaimed. 'It is very ostentatious. Quite embarrassing.' The business card made the man stand out, but it signalled a desire to exaggerate his wealth, something most seriously rich people do not feel the need to do. Dressing down avoids unwanted attention, but there are other ways of communicating one's status. When another nondescript man wandered by, Emma's more experienced co-worker rushed down to tell her she had spotted, through her binoculars, the man's $100,000 watch, and she pursued him as a potential customer. One must move in the realm where watches like that are recognised and appreciated.

Origin stories

The third strategy for protecting the system of elite privilege is legitimation, achieved by several means. Some super-rich people are embarrassed to admit to their privileged family origins. The Australian mining billionaire Andrew 'Twiggy' Forrest tells a log cabin story. In the words of Jane Cadzow's probing profile, he 'has always presented himself as a knockabout bloke made good,' a kind of inadvertent billionaire.[23]

Despite his carefully curated presentation as an ordinary bloke, Forrest comes from a blue-blood pastoralist family in Western Australia. The Forrests have supplied a number of MPs and the state's first premier (Andrew Forrest's great-great-uncle). Forrest himself was sent to two of Perth's most elite private schools, Christ Church Grammar School and Hale School, yet he reframes his schooldays as a time of bullying and victimisation and his ability to rise above it. Since becoming rich, he once said, his lifestyle is unchanged. 'I haven't changed my wife, my house or my car.'[24]

In a study of British professionals and managers from middle-class backgrounds, Sam Friedman and his colleagues noticed that many misidentify their origins as working-class and poor.[25] They feel the need to legitimise their positions of privilege with a story of ordinariness that erases 'the structural privileges that have shaped key moments in their trajectories'. The authors offer three explanations as to why they might feel this way.

First, claiming working-class roots or ordinariness can fend off accusations of pretentiousness and snobbishness. Secondly, downplaying their privileged background disarms those who might accuse them of having an unfair advantage. They deserve their success because it was won through talent and hard work. Thirdly, while sociologists typically classify people by their immediate family of origin, people often tell life stories that extend back before their parents' generation. Multi-generational narratives are used by the wealthy and successful to construct a family identity rooted in a deeper class history of deprivation.

The last-mentioned may explain the pride some Australians take in their convict origins, as if something of their authentic self can be found in the harshness and injustice of the British system of colonial deportation. Among the descendants of more recent migrants, great wealth is often legitimised by stories of the hardships experienced by parents or grandparents arriving penniless from war-ravaged Europe or after weeks adrift on a boat. Their success is the result of an often romanticised family narrative of grit, determination, self-sacrifice and inherent talent, the raw materials of upward mobility.

In Friedman et al.'s study, subjects who told humble origin stories 'often presented themselves as classed outsiders, who had overcome significant barriers within their elite occupational environments.'[26] They might retain or affect certain classed characteristics, such as regional accents, modes of dress, unpolished manners and rough edges. Some adopt a stance of mateyness towards manual workers to mark themselves as 'just like them'.

In sum, Friedman and his co-authors conclude, origin stories that obscure or downplay privileged upbringings enable those who tell them to present their career success as taking place 'against the odds' and reflecting personal commitment and hard work. These stories not only obscure their origins to others but blind the privileged to their own favoured upbringings. Curiously, perhaps, the authors add: 'We do not mean to imply that these accounts are somehow disingenuous, or cynically strategic.'[27]

Among Australians, a 2015 survey found that four in ten identified themselves as 'working class', while half (52 per cent) identified as 'middle class'. Two per cent said they were 'upper class'.[28] If upper-middle- and lower-middle-class categories are included, then 75 per cent become 'middle class'. Yet among the wealthy elite the urge to tell stories of humble origins seems irresistible. Australia's former conservative prime minister Malcolm Turnbull was at times referred to, even by some in his own party, as 'Mr Harbourside Mansion'. A merchant banker and venture capitalist with a network of powerful friends, he was elected to parliament to represent the wealthiest electorate in the nation. So as prime minister he had an image problem. His justificatory narrative was a textbook example of disavowing privilege. When under attack from the Labor Party opposition in parliament, he owned up to his wealth. 'Everyone knows I am wealthy,' he said, before recruiting his wife into the story. 'The fact is, Lucy and I have been very fortunate in our lives. ... We've worked hard, we've paid our taxes. We've given back. My wealth ... is entirely a function of hard work.'[29]

Pre-empting the obvious criticism, he then acknowledged that there are taxi-drivers and cleaners who have worked hard and who do not have much money. 'This country', he went on, 'is built upon hard work, people having a go, and enterprise. Some of us will be more successful than others. ... There's a lot of luck in life.' Of course, the hard-work plus luck discourse erases the role of privilege – privilege reflected in Turnbull's teenage habitus of confidence and authority and the extraordinary network of powerful people he was able to develop from early adulthood. Yet he narrated an origin story of emotional hardship in modest circumstances – he was raised in Sydney's leafy eastern suburbs by his lone father after they were abandoned by his mother when he was nine.[30] (His mother, Coral Lansbury, would later become Distinguished Professor of English at Rutgers University.) For a time, he said, they ate their meals sitting on boxes, for want of chairs. He was sent to boarding school on a partial scholarship – in fact, one of the most esteemed private schools, Sydney Grammar, alma mater of three prime ministers, seven High Court judges and twenty-eight Rhodes scholars.[31] At the University of Sydney, the academic ability and other qualities he displayed won him a Rhodes scholarship.

Service work

Researchers studying white and male privilege have reflected on how hard it is for many, even the well intentioned, to recognise and own up to their privilege. The same phenomenon is true of elite privilege; in fact, we suggest, it is harder, because eliteness is typically less evident and more deniable than whiteness or maleness. On the other hand, there are some among wealthy elites who are aware of their privilege and feel conflicted about it. They know that the rich are glamorised but also often scorned, the more so in the presence of poverty and disadvantage and when privilege puts itself on display. Wealth itself has long been associated in the popular mind with moral corruption. 'Filthy lucre' can be found in the Bible, and today we might refer to someone as 'filthy rich'. Shakespeare was scathing about the way gold conceals moral corruption, of how it 'will make black white, foul fair, / Wrong right, base noble, old young, coward valiant.'

For some among the wealthy elites, this presents a conundrum: how do they preserve the sense of being a 'good person'?[32] The moral struggles of the rich have been the subject of sociological research. Katy Swalwell studied how privileged students at an elite but progressive-minded school in North Carolina responded to their teacher's call for them to engage in social justice projects.[33] When asked how they would defend their elite education, one student replied: 'In the long-term, because we have privilege, we're going to be able to do things [for the common good] that, you know, kids in other communities might not be able to accomplish.'

It's a belief that explains why the most expensive private schools all place stress on the 'service' programmes they run – to demonstrate the school's commitment to producing good citizens. As Howard and Kenway noted, a commitment to social justice 'is crucial to the public image of most elite educational institutions and for elites in demonstrating their "good moral character".'[34] The schools therefore cater to the moral as well as the academic and social needs of the students whose parents can afford to send them.[35] Their service programmes contribute to the construction of the self as a good citizen and augment CVs that testify to superior character. The evidence reviewed by Swalwell suggests that cultivation of the character traits that define good citizenship neglect critical reflection on how privilege emerges from family circumstances and institutions. In other words, the cultivation of character serves the status quo.

For descendants of some wealthy dynasties, it may be implausible to cover over the facts that way. Carrillo Baillieu Gantner, for example, is the grandson of Sidney Myer, founder of the large retail chain. Everyone knows he moves at the heart of the Melbourne establishment. He acknowledges he was born into privilege and says he has 'a responsibility to repay that privilege by service',[36] an obligation he has turned into a 'distinguished career' in philanthropy and arts administration. Gantner is loath to use the word 'philanthropist' because it is 'wanky'.

Perhaps a little too cynically, Rubén Gaztambide-Fernández and Adam Howard represent benevolent benefaction in these terms: 'Positioning themselves as part of the solution through acts of charity, the merito-cratic logic mobilizes other people's suffering as a way to construct a self that is caring, knowledgeable, and cosmopolitan.'[37]

Modest consumers

Elites are diverse in many ways, including their attitudes towards consumption. Extravagance and wanton luxury are fodder for media stories, both celebratory and reproving, amplified in the age of celeb-rities, influencers and selfies. For more liberal-minded elites, the imagery of 'lifestyles of the rich and famous' presents a moral problem, or at least a perception problem, the more so as the numbers of super-rich expand in lockstep with the numbers of homeless. And as the world enters an era of climate disruption, the disproportionate culpability of wealthy consumers is now part of the public conversation.

As we have seen, the means by which the possession of great wealth can be morally justified include 'giving back' through philanthropy and service, the construction of humble origin stories, and hard-work discourses. In a fascinating study of wealthy consumers in New York, Rachel Sherman describes a further strategy – distinguishing oneself from the 'bad rich' by choosing to adopt 'reasonable', even 'ordinary', lifestyles.[38] Through fifty in-depth interviews with wealthy New Yorkers – mostly highly educated and politically liberal, and with incomes mostly in the top 10 per cent of the city – she examined how wealthy consumers talk about their own consumption practices and understand their needs.

Sherman describes how they draw a symbolic boundary between themselves and those seen as morally illegitimate. The bad rich are those who attract public obloquy for their ostentatious, shallow and wasteful ways of living. Although her interviewees may belong to the same socio-economic group as the bad rich, they see themselves as belonging to a different symbolic group.

In practice, Sherman's wealthy New Yorkers spent a great deal of money, but they engaged in sometimes elaborate self-talk to resolve their discomfort with their privileges and practices, using discourses to frame their consumption as ordinary, as nothing special. They said they were only meeting their basic needs and that they were prudent in their spending. They looked down upon ostentation and described their lives as much like an ordinary middle-class family. (Sherman comments that, in the United States, to adopt the mantle of 'middle class' means to be classless, to belong to the amorphous mass.)

They wanted to be good people and give back to society in some way, and repeatedly spoke in ways to differentiate themselves from the extravagance of the bad rich. One father, with wealth exceeding $50 million, spoke of his frenetic life and of 'making peanut butter and jelly sandwiches'. One woman spoke of living modestly, 'I mean, I don't have jewels. … We're just normal.'

Sherman also interviewed thirty providers of lifestyle services to her interviewees, such as real-estate brokers and interior designers. One of the latter said that, when designing for the affluent, he always throws in a few pieces from Ikea or Crate. 'They love that. It makes them feel better.' For the expensive items, he makes sure the price tags have been removed so the housekeepers don't see them. (A wealthy interviewee admitted taking the price tags off purchases to hide the expense from the nanny.) The interior designer said that his 'obscenely' rich clients feel ashamed.

For the anxious affluent, Sherman concluded, there is no problem with having money; what matters is how one spends it. If they can persuade themselves that they are reasonable, prudent, careful consumers then their financial privilege doesn't count.

It is an open question as to how far conclusions drawn from New York's affluent can be applied to wealthy people elsewhere, although Sherman's conclusions ring true for some affluent people in other Western nations. Her study of boundary-building may be usefully compared with a study, published in the same year, of elite moralities among Finland's top 0.1 per cent of income earners, or at least a subgroup of them – those who made their fortunes as entrepreneurs by founding their own businesses. Anu Kantola and Hanna Kuusela were interested in how this very wealthy elite build self-identities based on moral boundaries not only to separate themselves from the 'bad rich' but also to elevate themselves morally above almost everyone else.[39] It is a particular challenge for very wealthy elites to justify their position in a nation such as Finland, with its historically strong commitment to equality and social solidarity. Even so, the modes of justification mirror those used in the United States.

Kantola and Kuusela's twenty-eight interviewees fell mostly into the class of ultra-high net worth individuals – that is, with assets over US$30 million. The image of the modern entrepreneur, in tech industries and beyond, is a supercharged one of hard work and risk-taking, and these were very prominent themes in the interviews. Both carry strong connotations of the entrepreneurs' moral worth, from which position they offered harsh criticism of 'lazy' wage earners, public servants and benefit recipients. Like Sherman's subjects, the rich Finns, although mostly from secure middle-class backgrounds, emphasised their humble origins and the ordinary lives they continue to lead. 'I participate in the cleaning of the house. I carry firewood,' said one. 'I consider myself a normal bloke,' said another. They distinguished themselves from the 'truly rich'. Contrary to the hard-work narrative, Kantola and Kuusela noticed that some of them had taken long breaks from work and lived leisurely lives.

Well, they had worked hard and paid their taxes; they had 'earned it'. The authors summarised their research.

> Overall, the entrepreneurs create symbolic and moral selves as hard working, risk taking, humble, ordinary blokes who do not show off their wealth. These moralities distinguish them from others and draw boundaries justifying their growing wealth. However, their actual lives contradict this moral self.[40]

Summary

How do societies built on inequality and elite privilege avoid social unrest? We argue that the machinery of privilege generates its own means of self-justification, ones that serve to quell the political emotions created by inequality and injustice. The belief that we live in a meritocracy, which dovetailed neatly with the rise of neoliberal ideology, naturalises social differences as arising from varying talents and individual hard work. Some successful women, for example, see their achievements as due to their own efforts, with no recognition of the opportunities opened to them by decades of women's activism. Today, any suggestion that gender and racial hierarchies are part of the natural order receives strong pushback, yet the hierarchy of wealth and privilege is widely, if not universally, accepted as just how the world is.

Still at the ideological level, a society's collective symbols of nationhood or national character unite people as one, but they also help to camouflage the differences. Elites promote these narratives, not least in advertising and marketing.

Other than ideology, the machinery of privilege shrouds its operation in more practical ways. Although conspicuous displays of wealth seem to be everywhere, to avoid unwanted attention displaying one's wealth is often reserved for one's own social group.

The stories elites tell about themselves are often crafted to mislead. It's common for elites to misidentify their origins, telling tales of humble backgrounds. Their 'ordinariness' erases the inherited advantages that helped them get ahead. Elite privilege is also justified through service work, which the wealthy use to preserve their sense of being a 'good person'. Presenting themselves as living an ordinary lifestyle sets a symbolic boundary between themselves and the 'bad rich'.

CHAPTER TEN

Psychic Harms

The landscape

Condescension, deference, shame, guilt, envy, resentment, arrogance, contempt, fear and mistrust, or simply mutual incomprehension and avoidance, typify relations between people of different classes.[1]

While privilege is often mentioned in public debate, rarely do we hear comment on how the exercise of privilege is *experienced* by those on the receiving end, the felt injuries when elites assert their social dominance. Our conclusion is that, in a society characterised by high levels of privilege for a few, the acting out of that privilege makes a deep impression on the emotional lives of others. In addition to those arising from direct interactions, psychic harms are more often the result of systems tailored to privilege simply taking their course.[2]

The sociology of emotion has a history going back to the 1970s. Reviewing the research, Eduardo Bericat wrote that sociology should aim 'to understand *the emotional nature of social life*, in other words, the *emotional structure* and *dynamics* present in the social phenomena that are the object of study [original emphasis].'[3] The rationale for the study of emotions is that we can read social processes and tensions by close study of individuals' emotional responses to phenomena witnessed or experienced.[4] That's why our focus groups and opinion survey were designed to elicit information on emotional responses to manifestations of privilege.

In an important British study of 2005, Diane Reay argued that, far from class consciousness disappearing, 'the emotional experience of being classed' defines a psychic landscape of social distinction.[5] Everyday social intercourse is steeped in affective meaning, so that 'emotions and psychic responses to class and class inequalities contribute powerfully to the makings of class.'[6] 'Class' is today not much used to understand political phenomena, but the psychological processes of reinforcing boundaries within the social hierarchy remain as strong as ever, even if they are visible. Although in this book we mostly eschew the term 'class' in favour of 'elites' and 'social stratification', the preceding chapters have already made many observations about the emotional experience of being classed – what it feels like to engage with others of different classes, to be excluded from certain places, to see another granted a benefit denied to you, to be treated unfairly, to be humiliated.

Studying this psychic landscape is valuable in itself, but we maintain that doing so can also provide insights into the structure and operation of privilege. We have noted that scholars have studied the elites' attitudes of ease, entitlement, superiority and natural confidence in their place in the world. When played out in daily life, the obverse of these attitudes become 'the everyday slights, indignities, put downs and insults' experienced by those at the other end of the social scale, or even those in the middle.[7] The idea of *microaggressions*, used primarily to understand everyday expressions of racial and gender dominance, can be adapted to class and social difference. Just as race- and gender-inflected microaggressions, often apparently trivial and unintended, can leave victims feeling humiliated, devalued and angry, so too class-inflected put downs and insults cause emotional distress to their targets. They also shape the victims' understanding of the social world – its structure, dynamics and justice.

Shame

We reported in chapter 5 that boys from the high-priced Shore School named Mount Druitt as Sydney's 'worst suburb' and scorned those who live there. They illustrated how the contempt of the elites for those below them is a reflection of broader beliefs about social hierarchy. However, in the psychic landscape of class, the deepest wounds are not inflicted only by the most privileged on the least privileged, judging by the public shaming of students at Mount Druitt High School following the release of their exam results. A front-page story in a Murdoch tabloid newspaper labelled the school the worst in the state and included an unauthorised photograph of the final-year class – in effect identifying the students as the worst in the state. There was an uproar, which soon passed, leaving the distressed, shamed and stigmatised students in its wake.

Several years later, one of the students in the photo reflected on the event: 'I will never forget the memories and hurt I felt on that horrible day.' Another said, 'People were actually pointing fingers, you could hear them talking behind your back ... that really hurt because I know deep down I wasn't a loser.'[8] Another student confessed she was too ashamed to return to her workplace: 'I was a disappointment, I'd embarrassed my family, my picture was in the newspaper, and I was too embarrassed to go back to work.' In 2010, a teacher at the school spoke of the trauma: 'It's so hard to convey the outrage, the anger, the hurt that we felt at that time and how hard it was to rebuild from that. ... The shame that those students went through was horrible ...'[9] All of those from Mount Druitt High School were stigmatised, as was the suburb itself. It damaged their job prospects. 'I don't actually say I come from Mt Druitt,' said one. 'I say I came from Oxley Park, you know, no one knows where Oxley Park is situated. I just, you know, lie a bit.'[10]

Col Allen, the tabloid newspaper editor who approved the story against the misgivings of some of his journalists, argued that it did the students a favour by drawing attention to the poor quality of their school and schooling. He had performed a public service. Allen was the most powerful newspaper editor in the country and went on to be appointed editor-in-chief of the *New York Post*. Defending the public humiliation of students from a disadvantaged area was an argument that could be made only by a person living in a bubble of privilege. Several of the students decided to sue the newspaper for defamation. They were advised against it; it would be too risky to take on Murdoch's News Ltd, a powerful and ruthless corporation with the best lawyers. The consequences of losing would be severe. But the students persevered. Eventually they won the case. They extracted an apology from the newspaper and were awarded damages, restoring a modicum of the dignity that had been taken from them.[11]

The story of Mount Druitt High is no more than a prominent instance of a daily drumbeat of shaming.[12] Places plagued by higher levels of social disadvantage are described by the media as 'suburbs of shame', tainting all who live there.[13] When their life conditions are judged by others, people feel ashamed not because they have committed any wrong but because they know they are being seen as lesser beings. People living in poor communities speak of how their hardship brings not only material deprivation but humiliation. They report feeling small and powerless, experiences in which their selves are 'painfully scrutinized and negatively evaluated'.[14] A range of emotions can follow being shamed – sadness, depression and isolation. The effect on the self can be devastating.[15]

Perhaps the most frequent microaggressions of class or status are those questions, explicit or implied, that attempt to establish a person's place in the social hierarchy. A direct question about one's school, suburb or occupation can be a means of establishing dominance. In our national survey, we asked respondents whether they at times had felt ashamed because of where they live, the school they went to, or their parents' occupation. Admitting to feeling ashamed is not easy, yet 31 per cent of Australian adults admit to having felt ashamed of their place of residence, their school or their parents' job.[16] Younger adults (aged eighteen to thirty-four) are much more likely to say they have felt ashamed (49 per cent) than older adults (22 per cent among those aged fifty to sixty-four and only 10 per cent of those over sixty-five). This may be because adolescents feel shame more intensely than adults,[17] and memories of the slights and humiliations associated with suburb, school and parents fade as one grows older. Bearing in mind that the emotional challenges of fitting in are especially acute in the schoolyard, parents in households with children living at home are much more likely to admit to feelings of shame (44 per cent) than those in households without children (26 per cent).

The focus group participants provided insights into how shame and embarrassment play out. Although a focus group with five strangers is not the place to express strong emotions, our observation is that people become more inclined to admit to feelings of shame when primed to do so by conversations about inequality, schools, suburbs, and so on. (If this is so, then the survey results may understate the proportions who have felt shame.)[18] Hence the poignant comments from a few about how, as children, they thought they were normal until someone denigrated their suburb or their school. Luke, for example, said: 'No play dates if they knew I was from Footscray.'

People lower down the social hierarchy admit to concealing where they live or where they went to school because of the negative reactions they receive. Luca (average income, younger, Sydney) said, 'People would cringe when I mentioned the western Sydney suburb I came from, so sometimes I'd pick another suburb, so they don't cringe.' Drew, from the same group, said that, when he mentioned his public school to a partner at the accounting firm where he works, 'he visibly recoiled. ... He looked at me differently.' *What was that like, when he recoiled?* 'It was pretty disappointing, but also not surprising.'

As a schoolgirl, Hana (wealthier, older, Melbourne) was billeted with a family in Toorak. When asked at the dinner table what her father did, she told them he worked at Ford, 'on the line'. 'And then it clicked. This family doesn't work on the line, and I felt embarrassed.' Nowadays, Hana said, she looks up to and admires wealthy people.

Rose said she does not tell people where she lives because 'Where I live is loaded with information.' Ashley too admitted, 'I don't mention that I grew up in Campbelltown' because people have firm ideas about the people who come from there. In chapter 4, we recounted the story told by Patricia, who lived in an up-market suburb, about herself and her colleague who did the same job at her workplace, a private bank. When her bosses and the customers learned that her colleague was from Mount Druitt, they treated Patricia in a friendly way while the co-worker with the wrong address was ignored, in effect ostracised, treated as a non-person.

Looking up, looking down

Relations between those up and down the social ladder are fraught with emotional effort and inner turmoil. When our focus group participants were asked whether they treat wealthy and influential people differently, the reflex reply was that they treat everyone the same. As one said, he prides himself on treating people on their merits. Probed further, some became more reflective, admitting that they do pay more attention to people they believe are wealthy or influential. Hana (wealthier, older, Melbourne), we saw, looks up to them even though 'I don't want to.' Lydia from the same group said that, if she knows someone has money, then she will 'give them more of a hearing than perhaps some other people, I must admit.' Paul (average income, older, Sydney) said that, if someone pointed out a billionaire at a party, then 'I think you may afford them a bit more respect.' All these comments were made more or less bashfully, as if looking up to the rich and powerful went against some inner principle or entailed a small sacrifice of dignity.

Jessica (wealthier, younger, Sydney) said that when you meet someone new you want to be on the same level, to have the same power. So, if she's introduced to a wealthy or privileged person in a bar or a restaurant, she changes her mannerisms, accent and language. Ashley (average income, younger, Sydney) assumes that a person from a privileged background has a 'completely different experience of life', so they won't have much in common. Luke (average income, younger, Melbourne) took a similar view: 'Definitely. I mean, there's a whole upper caste or class of society that probably moves and operates in ways that us plebs can barely fathom.' Monique, from the same group, reflected on the gulf between classes: 'If you've got someone of a high order and then you've got someone else that's a low-income earner, it's like they just don't meet.'

Some from a higher position in the hierarchy may want to be respectful and congenial in their relations with those below but risk being seen as condescending, disrespectful or unduly familiar. While Jessica talked about levelling up, Ben (wealthier, younger, Melbourne), who attended an exclusive school, commented that the adjustment works the other way, so that 'you might come down a notch or two.' But he has also discovered that the gulf between the elites and the rest sometimes takes the form of disdain from below. 'You get on really well with somebody and then they asked you that dreaded question "Where do you live? What school do you go to?" And the instant you say it, their face drops.' Ben's attempts at connecting by 'coming down a notch or two' may be a well-intentioned attempt to bridge a class divide in which he had no say. Reay distinguished between an *exclusivist* middle-class position, where a combination of arrogance, satisfaction, contempt and pride prevail, and an *egalitarian* middle-class position, with its mix of guilt, defensiveness, empathy and conciliation.[19]

We are not suggesting an equivalence between disdain from above and disdain from below. As Stephanie Lawler writes, the disdain for elites from those below doesn't count because 'they lack the social authority to make their judgements stick.' She quotes Kathryn Abrams's observation that 'a war of disgusts is one that those less socially privileged are unlikely to win.'[20]

Disgust is a strong word, although among the wealthy attitudes to those living in less salubrious suburbs it may include contempt. Leah (wealthier, younger), from Sydney's exclusive eastern suburbs, said she 'can't be bothered with' people from certain suburbs. She said she judges people by their postcodes, feeling the need to add, 'Don't get me wrong. I'm a decent person.' That kind of blunt contempt was rare in the wealthier focus groups, partly, we suspect, because it's unacceptable to express it outside trusted circles. Even among students at elite private schools, those who live in suburbs that are expensive but not in the same league as the 'best suburbs' report that they are looked down upon and derided, even if 'good humouredly'.

People in low-esteem suburbs are not the only ones to lie about where they live. We found some from wealthy suburbs admitting to deceiving others about where they live. Holly, from one of Sydney's most exclusive suburbs, Vaucluse, simply says: 'I don't talk about my suburb.' Amy attended an elite private school and is a social worker. She said that, when she tells people in her social group that she lives in an expensive suburb, they assume she was born with a silver spoon in her mouth. 'My credibility flies out the window.' Jessica, from a neighbouring elite suburb, tells people she lives in a more down-market suburb 'just to avoid the discussion, to not go down that track.' These disavowals are motivated by embarrassment rather than shame.

Rather than deceive people about living in an exclusive suburb, some make a point of signalling that, although they may live in an elite suburb, they are not like the stereotype. 'I didn't come from Mosman', one participant tells people, 'I just happen to live there.' Maddison, from an expensive Melbourne suburb, admits she lives there but adds that she lives in an apartment. 'When I first met my partner, he said "Oh" when I told him where I live. He didn't think we'd get along.'

Privilege in the playground

The injuries of social class are often felt most painfully in the school playground, among children yet to learn the rules of social inhibition or, indeed, respect for difference. (One of the functions of exclusive schools is to teach students more subtle ways of expressing their dominance.) Drawing on her extensive work in British schools, Diane

Reay writes that schooling 'is a fertile ground for exploring psycho-social and emotional aspects of classed identities.'[21] In schools, interactions among students and between students and teachers are beset by the everyday slights and humiliations associated with social and economic difference. Reay notes that the discourse of schooling now routinely reprimands sexism and racism but there are no protocols for dealing with 'classism'.[22] Even the language for parrying the microaggressions of class is absent.

While children are taught to understand sexism and racism 'politically', students do not have the linguistic tools to respond to class shaming. To illustrate, at a well-regarded public primary school from which many students are sent by their well-heeled parents to expensive private schools, a ten-year-old boy whose parents for ethical reasons planned to send him to a public high school was told by a classmate that he was going to a 'shit school' because it was not private.[23] This boy could readily call out racism but had no retort to his own shaming as it was not part of the classroom discourse.

It's not just the shaming of children by others within their school environments; the presence and behaviour of elite schools casts a pall over other schools. In response to a news story about public funds being paid to elite private schools, two of the 'most respected' comments were:

> And yet at my public school, we have to move the photocopier and desks in classrooms to avoid the leaky roofs. This is beyond a joke.

> Well that's a microcosm of the way things are in education in Australia. If you are entitled you are entitled to more. Helps the next generation of entitled know without a doubt which side their bread is buttered on.[24]

Every story about an elite school spending millions of dollars on grand buildings and world-class sporting facilities prompts a wave of disgust and resentment across much of the community and deepens the belief that Australia is a profoundly unfair country run for the benefit of the rich. In chapter 5 we mentioned the opening of Cranbrook's new senior school buildings in 2022. Cranbrook is regarded by some as the 'best' school in Sydney; it's certainly among the most expensive, with the wealthiest clientele. The cost of the new buildings was A$125 million.[25]

Each of these lavish projects is experienced as a slap in the face by many parents and students at public schools who can only dream of such facilities. The president of the teachers' union expressed a widely held opinion when he said that, while private schools invested in 'obscene building projects', public school students had to make do with 'demountables and in overcrowded schools that are in desperate need of refurbishment'. The slap was felt even more keenly when Cranbrook school leaders boasted about the facilities. The buildings, said the headmaster, will 'help ready students for university and life beyond the school gates', and the school council president declared that the Cranbrook boys, whose parents are paying A$40,000 each year, 'will find it really inspirational'. In the city's west, a child sweating through summer in a portable classroom might pause to reflect on last night's news story about Cranbrook's new buildings and feel the pang of injustice. Yet, resigning herself to her lot in life, she returns to her books.

Summary

The practices of privilege can cause abiding emotional harms to others. Diane Reay speaks of the psychic landscape of social class, a concept applicable to the acting out of privilege in a hierarchical society. The everyday slights and indignities visited by elites on those lower down the social scale can be understood as microaggressions, deliberate or unintended. Social media and news comment sites are evidence of widespread resentment over elite privilege.

Shaming people because of where they live, the school they attended, or their parents' occupation is commonplace. In a survey, half of young adults admit to feeling ashamed. Some adults report others 'cringing' when they mention their suburbs or the school they attended and admit to concealing where they live for fear of being looked down upon.

Focus group participants shyly admitted they treat wealthy and influential people with more deference. Others spoke of how they adapt the ways they speak and behave as they attempt to reach the same level as a member of the elite. For their part, some wealthy people 'come down a notch or two' when speaking to those below them on the social scale. Some residents of elite suburbs, out of embarrassment rather than shame, deceive others about where they live because they do not want to be stereotyped.

Extravagant spending by elite schools attracts widespread resentment and moral outrage. Young people are especially sensitive to the humiliations of schools and suburbs. Within schools there are protocols for responding to racism and sexism but not for the microaggressions of class. The peaks and troughs of the psychic landscape of privilege are impressed deeply on adolescent minds.

CHAPTER ELEVEN

Economic and Social Harms

Before considering the economic and social harms, it's worth asking how the harms arising from elite privilege can be differentiated from the harms due to economic inequality.[1] A thought experiment can help. Since virtually everyone accepts that some level of inequality is necessary and reasonable, we can imagine a society where the prevailing level of inequality is acceptable (say, Sweden in the 1960s) yet where many feel resentful at the privileges enjoyed by wealthier and more influential citizens. Perhaps this only illustrates how difficult it is in practice to separate wealth from privilege, since the wealthy will always seek to exploit their position for advantage. Still, we can imagine two societies with the same level of inequality but differing commitments to restraining privilege. Chapter 12 will consider some measures to limit the exercise of privilege that do not require redistribution of wealth and income, as well as some that do.

Distorting markets

In 2021, the Pandora Papers revealed that billionaires, business leaders, senior politicians and celebrities had enormous undisclosed assets hidden offshore in tax havens. Many called for crackdowns on the offshoring of wealth, including two US lawmakers, who declared that, after being laundered through these accounts, 'billions of dollars of dirty money belonging to adversarial actors are flooding the United States.'[2] In Australia, Tony Watson, a partner at the tax advisory firm Nexia, had seen it all before. 'Whenever these things happen there's always outrage and clamour for action. ... But as soon as our attention is diverted, vested interests begin their job of eroding the strength of the laws and the effectiveness of the enforcement process.'[3] The first move of the lobbyists, he said, is to persuade lawmakers that criminal prosecutions are excessive and undesirable.

Perhaps nothing preoccupies the rich more than ways to reduce the taxes they pay. Whole industries have sprung up to help them do it – tax lawyers, tax accountants, lobbyists, bank departments catering to ultra-high net worth individuals, agencies that create shell companies in tax havens. When they succeed, the revenue forgone must be paid by other citizens, those who do not have the privilege of accessing specialist advice or who accept that paying their fair share of taxes is the price they pay for living in a civilised society. Among the wealthy, the prevailing, if not universal, view appears to be the one expressed by the media billionaire Kerry Packer. 'I don't know anybody that doesn't minimise their tax,' he said, probably truthfully, adding, 'If anybody in this country doesn't minimise their tax they want their head read.'[4] Of course, Packer's aggressive tax minimisation was not what the average taxpayer does when they claim back the cost of a new computer.

Economic harm refers to the ways elites use their various forms of capital to gain unfair advantages in the economy, thereby imposing costs on others. As we have seen, elites use their networks and 'cultural capital' acquired through school, family and social groups to gain preferred access to internships, jobs, board positions, and so on, all of which help their finances and life opportunities. In these ways, elite privilege harms those who have the talents to obtain the internships and jobs but are beaten by less suitable others with superior networks and a closer 'cultural fit'. The harms are both economic and social.

Economically, the slowing of productivity growth in recent decades has been a topic of intense concern and speculation by economists. Maximising labour productivity depends on the market smoothly allocating workers to the jobs best suited to their skills, yet it is in the logic of privilege to favour elites on grounds other than their talents. By interfering in this process, preferment for elites due to their networks or discriminatory ideas of 'cultural fit' seems likely to be a factor in slowing productivity growth.[5] The extent of this effect is impossible to say, but if our focus groups' unanimous opinion on the prevalence of preferment is anything to go by then it must be significant.

Another way to think about the effect of elite privilege on the economy is by combining our analysis of the reproduction of privilege based on Bourdieu's theory of capital conversion with Thomas Piketty's analysis of how inequalities of wealth and income emerge and are passed on in rich countries, a phenomenon he called patrimonial capitalism. This is done in Appendix 3. In short, Piketty considers the factors that contribute to income inequality and those that contribute to wealth inequality. Growing income inequality has been driven largely by the extraordinarily high salaries paid to those at the top. Elite networks and habitus work to increase the dominance of elites in those highest income occupations. For wealth inequality, the evidence shows that wealthy parents tend to produce wealthy children. However, they do so not because they leave them large inheritances but because they invest in their children's social and cultural capital. So by the time the children inherit their parents' wealth, perhaps around the age of fifty, they are already wealthy from taking the highest paying occupations and their investments. Thus, our Bourdieusian story of elite privilege helps to explain, through a feedback loop, the growing inequality identified by Piketty.

Ressentiment

As for the social harm from elites taking internships, jobs and other positions from more talented others, to the extent that victims know they lost out due to unfair practices, this naturally causes resentment and disillusionment. Although it is impossible to measure, it seems reasonable to assume that the systemic and interpersonal occurrence of unfair advantage is so widespread that it shapes society, contributing to lower mobility across social strata. Its role in reproducing an unequal and unfair distribution of income, wealth and life opportunities gives rise to the cynicism and alienation, evident, for example, in our survey results showing that half of Australians believe that 'one rule for the rich and another for the rest' is a more accurate characterisation of their society than 'the rules are applied fairly' (preferred by a bit more than a third).

The psychic landscape of class is shaped not only by the microaggressions of privilege felt directly by the less privileged. Popular reactions to elite privilege tell us that it is a social and political phenomenon that has a discernible effect on the public mood and public understanding of systems of power, evident in the regular outpourings of resentment in social media. Resentment is the obverse of privilege's arrogance; indeed, in his study of political emotions, Jack Barbalet writes that 'resentment is taken to be the emotional apprehension of undeserved advantage.'[6]

It becomes a political emotion when resentment against privileged individuals spills into resentment against the system that grants exclusive benefits to elites.

Some commentators speak disparagingly of 'the politics of resentment'. Yet resentment, along with anger, have been the emotional fuel for all kinds of social revolutions. Expressions of resentment are a natural response to the felt injustices of privilege. It would be a strange society that did not feel indignation at the abuse of power and sustained exploitation of elite privilege. When systems of privilege are too visible, they generate a pervasive sense of umbrage towards elites. The efforts elites and those who serve them make to conceal their privileges reflects the degree of public indignation at the state of affairs. There are times when rampant entitlement takes a psychological toll on society at large, eliciting anger, resentment and, in extremis, depression, powerlessness and anomie.

As durable features of society, these suppressed feelings of resentment, envy and powerlessness in the face of entrenched privilege can give rise to *ressentiment*, a deep-seated desire for revenge or levelling of the social hierarchy.[7] Surging *ressentiment* in the United States helps explain the rise of Trumpism.

One of the most harmful effects of the privilege machine on society is the myriad ways it entrenches and rigidifies social hierarchies, making for a less fluid society in which mobility is limited and social divisions are exacerbated. Exclusive private schools are one of the primary vehicles for this stratification, accompanied by a growing reputational gap with state schools. The hardening of beliefs in the superiority of elite schools is reflected not only in the ways they undermine selection based on merit but also in the evidence that those who attended state schools find others 'cringing' or 'recoiling' when they mention them. Increasingly, it is becoming shameful to have attended public schools.

In other words, the proclaimed benefits of meritocracy – those with talent and application can realise their full potential – are corrupted by elite privilege, just as sexism has prevented women from reaching their full potential. One of the psychological costs is that those who miss out on chances in life because elites exercise their privileges – whether it is the failure to obtain an internship, being beaten to a job or missing out on a university course – see their lack of success as a result of their own shortcomings rather than the outcome of a system that favours the privileged. Sennett and Cobb described the feelings of disappointment, failure and, eventually, resignation as some of the hidden injuries of class.[8] The genius of meritocratic ideology is that, when individuals blame themselves for their lack of success, the structures of privilege are exonerated and resentment does not gain a political foothold.

Discourse power

Changing the language means changing how the world is understood. Wealthy elites shape the public discourse in ways that drown out other narratives. Most dramatically, this discourse power has been used to redefine freedom as personal choice, to weaken the appeal of social democracy, and to make competitive individualism the prevailing model of society. The long campaign to instantiate free market liberalism by mobilising intellectuals, think tanks, lobbyists, and media has been well documented.[9] In 2007, George Monbiot commented on its success, evidenced by the insinuation of its language into all parts of society. 'Nowadays I hear even my progressive friends using terms like wealth creators, tax relief, big government, consumer democracy, red tape, compensation culture, job seekers and benefit cheats. These terms, all invented or promoted by neoliberals, have become so commonplace that they now seem almost neutral.'[10] If you control the discourse, you win the argument, and the wealthy elites largely control the discourse.

Neoliberal ideas, while having an atomising effect, help elites draw social boundaries. The wealthy entrepreneurs of Finland, write Kantola and Kuusela, have a language that distances themselves from the rest of society.[11] An ideology of hard work coupled with consumerist self-gratification 'may produce an elite that uses a hard disciplinary discourse to justify income disparities and to deny any moral obligations or solidarity with others.' Cleaving to a neoliberal narrative that legitimises inequality and social stratification as natural outcomes of personal responsibility deepens the divide, even in Nordic countries. 'The moral boundaries wealth entrepreneurs construct by labelling the less well-off as lazy and undeserving of benefits contradict the moralities supporting the Nordic model, which sees all citizens as worthy of social benefits and less well-off individuals not as lazy but as disadvantaged.'[12] Marking moral boundaries in this way is used to legitimise social stratification and justify the unequal distribution of wealth and power.[13]

The discourse surrounding elite private schools is having the same effect, although their roles and public perceptions vary across countries. In Australia, neoliberalism supercharged and generalised the religious rhetoric of 'school choice', persuading politicians to direct more public funding to private schools, including elite ones. With the expansion of private schooling, a large constituency of parents of children at private schools, rich and poor, has sidelined the once near universal agreement that the state school system is and should be the bedrock of a merito-cratic and non-sectarian society.

The reputation of elite schools as superior, morally as well as academi-cally, is enhanced by the incessant derogation of public schools, often led by the media.[14] In our focus groups, participants repeatedly referred to expensive private schools as 'good schools'. This is only one of the ways elite schools live off state schools, beyond public funding and the draining of talented teachers, bright children and, increasingly, promising sports players.[15] All of these further enhance the reputations of expensive private schools as the best places to send one's children, if financially possible.[16]

Civic harms

Elite privilege means getting your own way in a variety of situations. Pierre Bourdieu observed that, to attain their freedom, aristocratic elites exempted themselves from 'petty rules and regulations'.[17] Mikael Holmqvist, in his study of an elite suburb near Stockholm, found that wealthy residents tend to see rules and regulations as applying to other people. A sense of entitlement and self-importance naturally inclined them to view restric-tions as obstacles to be overcome. A talent for getting around obstacles is admired in the business world, and businesspeople employ squads of accountants and lawyers to help them do it. Applying through the usual channels is irritating and time-consuming, even beneath their dignity. They are accustomed to going straight to the person in charge.

There is certainly a widespread perception that those at the top of the hierarchy operate according to a different set of rules, at least according to some of our focus group participants.

[During the lockdowns] the privileged and the ultra-rich were sort of, 'if I could bend the rules, I'd just go for it.' They didn't care about the penalties because they had so much wealth and it didn't matter to them. (Ben, wealthier, younger, Melbourne)

I guess the top 1 per cent operate in a pretty different world than you or I. So it's different rules for those sort of people, really. (Luke, average income, younger, Melbourne)

Societies governed by the rule of law depend for their stability on public trust in regulatory institutions. Impartiality and equality before the law means everyone, regardless of their wealth, status or influence, should be held accountable if they break the law. Yet elites are frequently not held accountable; they 'get away with it' – a kind of injustice that erodes faith in democracy. A US real-estate magnate bragged about how his wealth allows him to bypass democratic and regulatory systems. 'I can pick up the phone and call a congressman who's heard my name, and I can have the impact of one million votes on the issue with a phone call. … When I want something, [politicians] come here and meet me for breakfast, and I tell them what I want.'[18] Allowing for a degree of self-aggrandisement, this kind of truth-telling leaves a legacy of bitterness and cynicism in the wider public.

Wealthy elites not only regard themselves as above society's laws; they are also less strongly attached to their societies. Studies of gated communities indicate that distance from the rest of society reduces the sense of moral and social responsibility for others. 'The elite neighbourhood is an effective mechanism for creating such social distance,' concluded Ilan Wiesel.[19] Scholars have studied the social withdrawal of the 'globals' who live mobile lives with a degree of detachment from the ties that bind most people to their neighbourhoods, cities and nations – their homes, their gardens, their pets, their neighbourhoods, their friends, their children's friends, the shops they rely on, their exercise routines, the medical services they use, and so on.[20]

For some among the super-rich, these bonds are so tenuous that they can envision translocating to a yacht in another part of the world with a few days' notice. When the pandemic broke out in early 2020, those who owned yachts took to them. Wealthy Britons chartered super-yachts to escape lockdowns, planning to spend weeks or months at sea.[21] (While ports for cruise ships closed, marinas remained open.)

The super-yacht is the perfect vehicle for the privileged state of mind. Out on the ocean, the owner puts himself beyond the petty rules and regulations that govern the lives of everyday people. Much of the time, super-yachts dwell beyond the reach of ordinary law enforcement. They cruise in international waters, and, when they dock, local police tend to give them a wide berth; the boats often have private security, and their owners may well be friends with the prime minister.[22]

The term 'offshoring' is used to describe the parking of wealth in tax havens to avoid paying one's dues, but it can be thought of as a state of mind, one in which the ties that bind ordinary citizens to their locations are weak. It's a state of mind that makes for sail-in, sail-out citizens, those who feel free to escape the obligations of living in a society – that is, obeying local laws and regulations, supporting a community and paying one's dues.

In short, when segments of the wealthy elite exempt themselves from social norms and disengage from broader society, they contribute to the fragmentation of society, sharpening the divide between the privileged few and the rest. Civic trust and social cohesion rely on shared values, norms, and a sense of mutual responsibility, so, when elites remove themselves from the spaces where these rules apply, trust in institutions is eroded and a sense of unfairness spreads.

Summary

Economic harms arise when elites impose costs on others in the exercise of their privilege. These harms include the higher taxes others must pay when elites lobby to change laws or when they use schemes to avoid paying their fair share of taxes. This behaviour is mimicked by others, creating a larger constituency opposed to reform. When elites use their influence to secure positions such as internships, jobs and board positions, others are harmed. Privilege may reduce an economy's productivity when it interferes with market allocation of workers to the jobs best suited to their skills. Social and economic harms rise with inequality, and our analysis of privilege helps explain how wealth and income inequality have worsened.

Unfair practices used by elites to secure unwarranted benefits rigidify social hierarchies, denying opportunities to deserving others. Undermining merit as the path to success causes social resentment and disillusionment, entrenching the view that the rich work to different rules. Elites sustain their power through discourse control. When they prevail in the contest over the language used to understand society, their voice in the town square drowns out others. When elites use the language of merit to explain their wealth and influence, their success appears to elevate them morally.

Civic harms follow when elites regard themselves as above the law and exempted from society's rules. When authorities allow them to bend or ignore rules, public trust in regulatory institutions and democracy is impaired. Cynicism takes hold. Social cohesion is damaged when segments of the wealthy elite withdraw from society and the community, taken to an extreme with super-yachts, devices for 'mental offshoring'.

CHAPTER TWELVE

Contesting Privilege

Analysing the worsening state of wealth and income inequality in rich countries since the 1970s, Thomas Piketty wrote of how the emergence of a new patrimonial capitalism was made possible by the higher growth rate of wealth compared to income and, among other things, the cutting or abolition of inheritance taxes. In this book we have been arguing that it has not been only the cold laws of economics driving the emergence of patrimonial capitalism – Piketty's 'grand dynamics' of capital accumulation – but also what we have called the machinery of privilege. The machinery of privilege is responsible for the passing down of social and cultural capital as well as economic capital. The accumulation of social and cultural capital, with exclusive schools at the centre, are the foundation of a new kind of nepotism – that is, the practice among the rich and influential of unfairly favouring their children and people of their class with advantages such as jobs, board positions, inside information and much more. In fact, we believe, the patrimony of social and cultural capital may be more significant than inheritance of wealth. And it's a system in which everyone is implicated.

Elite privilege causes psychological, social, economic and civic harms, yet its continued reproduction and enhancement goes largely unchallenged. What then can be done to throw sand in the machinery of privilege, to slow it down and alleviate its harms? In this chapter, we propose some measures that restrain the three forms of patrimony – the inheritance of wealth, but also the unfair advantages conferred by the social capital and cultural capital passed on to the next generation by the operation of the machinery of privilege.

Perhaps nothing has done more to entrench and enable the growth of elite privilege than the sharp rise in inequality of incomes and wealth over the last forty years. A natural first response is to rebalance the distribution of incomes and wealth by increasing taxation of the rich and enhancing the rights and protections for those at the lower end of the income and wealth scales.

Thomas Piketty has shown that an important contribution to worsening inequality has been steep falls in top marginal income tax rates in OECD countries since the 1970s.[1] Taxes on wealth have also been declining, perhaps even more damaging to social harmony. In some countries, the collapse of taxes on inheritance has been especially marked. In the United States, the tax rate on the largest inheritances fell from 70 per cent in 1980 to 35 per cent in 2013.[2] In Australia, they were abolished altogether.[3] Inheritance taxes work against the intergenerational transfer of both wealth and privilege. The British economist Tony Atkinson proposed a system of progressive taxation of inheritances, with a top rate of 65 per cent on large estates, using the revenue to fund a minimum inheritance paid to all citizens on reaching adulthood.[4] The OECD agrees there are strong equity and efficiency arguments in favour of inheritance taxes.[5]

Radical tax reform is necessary, not least for weakening the political power of the super-rich, but it's also apparent from what has come before in this book that it is not just what elites possess that constitutes their privilege. A variety of social practices and processes sustain, legitimise and reproduce the wealth, influence and power of elites. In other words, privilege relies for its reproduction not just on the intergenerational transmission of wealth in privileged families but also on the transmission of social and cultural capitals within and between privileged families that begins early in life. In addition, it relies for its reproduction on a wider machinery of privilege, a set of social and interpersonal practices that operate in insidious ways, permeating educational, political, legal, cultural and public sector institutions to preserve, reproduce and enhance elite privilege. These all suggest more creative avenues are available to reshape the landscape of elite privilege. Below we suggest some measures aimed at disrupting the reproduction of privilege.

Perhaps nothing would do more to weaken the pervasive influence of elite privilege than a reduction of the resourcing gap between exclusive private schools and the rest. The children of the elites enjoy so many advantages in life that no government committed to social justice could provide any public funding for exclusive schools. That barely needs to be said, yet in most countries governments channel large public subsidies to elite schools by allowing wealthy parents to claim tax deductions for donations to their children's schools.

Tax deductibility means that the public pays out around half of the money used to build sumptuous facilities for the advantage of a tiny minority of already highly privileged children. In Britain, small compensation is provided by rules that require elite schools to open facilities built using tax-deductible donations for use by the public; yet the benefits of those facilities are still enjoyed mostly by the children on whose school grounds the gyms, pools and theatres are built. Tax deductibility for elite schools only subsidises privilege, adding ethical insult to the injuries of public school underfunding, and should simply be ended by removing their charitable status. Alternatively, donations could be capped at A$1,000 so that parents of children attending public (or low-fee private) schools might benefit from tax deductibility as much as rich ones do.

These means would make only a modest difference to the ability of wealthy elites to create exclusive schools to pass on privilege to their progeny. It would be more effective to abolish private schools altogether, a move endorsed by the British Labour Party's annual conference. Of course, the Swedish experience described by Mikael Holmqvist shows that even this would not be a complete solution, as public schools in the suburbs where the wealthy congregate soon emerge as 'superior' schools, if only because of the reputation they develop as institutions for rich kids. Even so, abolition would see educational resources distributed much more evenly, in a way more consistent with the principle that life chances should be based on merit.

Universities claim to be meritocratic, yet the sons and daughters of elites disproportionately fill places in prestigious universities and degree programmes.[6] When offering places, universities ought to favour students from schools without the extravagant facilities, small classes, hand-picked teachers, personal mentoring and culture of entitlement. One option would be to increase admissions reserved from students with educationally disadvantaged backgrounds or to limit admissions from exclusive private school graduates to their share of total students.

The same applies to scholarships such as the Rhodes. Today's selection panels make efforts to ensure gender and racial diversity, yet their selections heavily favour graduates of elite private schools – that is, students trained to excel in the qualities and skills that impress selection panels.

These panels should be challenged to justify rewarding privilege with more privilege.

Although elite favouritism crops up periodically in public debate, its consequence – the limited 'class diversity' in some organisations, professions, or sectors – is rarely recognised, and nothing is done to counter it. Leaders of public organisations and private companies have responded to pressure to promote gender and racial diversity with measures to counter discrimination against women and people from diverse cultures. As a result, male and white privilege in these organisations are declining while elite privilege is more entrenched than ever.

Private and public organisations with a declared commitment to social justice could begin a process of change by forming *challenge panels* to expose the influence of elite privilege throughout the organisation.[7] In recruitment for jobs and internships, this influence often takes the form of unconscious preferment afforded candidates with the right connections or 'cultural fit', a process described by Nicola Ingram and Kim Allen as the 'social magic' that 'transforms subjective judgments into seemingly objective assessments.'[8] The bias is often based on the schools they attended. Recruitment practices reinforce the elite cultural predisposition of those already at senior levels within the organisation. Challenge panels, or privilege review panels, would focus not on promoting 'class diversity' as such but on ensuring that processes and decisions about recruitment, promotion, performance, pay, and access to opportunities more broadly are equitable and transparent. They would identify and call out unfair advantages for elites, such as preferment for graduates of exclusive private schools. Apart from encouraging 'class diversity', effective challenge panels would enhance the morale of all workers in the organisation dispirited by unfair recruitment and promotion practices.

Nothing undermines public confidence in government more than the perception that the rich and powerful are subject to a different set of rules; yet the exercise of privilege is rife in public administration. The rich and influential are frequently given special treatment because they know the right people and understand how to exploit loopholes and exceptions in laws and regulations. If cultural change can sharply reduce gender and racial discrimination, then it can also challenge unconscious bias favouring special treatment to the rich and powerful. In addition to government employment and promotion practices, challenge panels could review rules and procedures that favour elites and initiate conversations within organisations about elite privilege and the conscious and unconscious biases that give rise to unjust practices. Such a cultural change may include training civil servants in how to resist pressure to give special treatment to the rich and powerful, having *first assured them* they will not be penalised but praised for upholding organisational values.

Data for the United Kingdom and Australia show that an excessive number of senior judges have had privileged backgrounds. They naturally, if unconsciously, bring their elite worldview to the bench. When making judicial appointments to higher courts, often on the advice of a panel of senior jurists, governments should be 'class blind', which in practice means they should have their eyes wide open for discrimination against candidates from non-elite backgrounds. A challenge panel would help counter this bias. In fact, challenging bias should begin in recruitment for clerkships and judges' associates, because that is where the first steps on a glittering career are taken.

Why are so many top honours – knighthoods in Britain and ACs in Australia – awarded to rich people who do no more than give away a small portion of their often inherited wealth? There is nothing intrinsically meritorious in that; all they have done is exercise their privilege and done so in ways that repay them generously – in enhanced reputations, lucrative networks and fawning recipients. Don't we admire them less than the everyday citizen who devotes herself to her community over many years with no expectation of reward? If she is acknowledged at all, she will receive the lowest of the orders, while the scion of a dynasty who has used his wealth to curry favour by strategically targeted giving will receive the highest honour. The wealth so used may itself be tainted and philanthropy employed as a means of laundering it. An official honour adds a cup of whitener to the washing cycle. Should we not be giving *demerit awards* to those among the rich who underperform in the philanthropic arena compared to their privileged position?

Apart from wealthy philanthropists, most top honours are awarded to scientists, medical researchers, business executives, arts bosses, civil servants and judges. As we saw, a high proportion have privileged backgrounds, giving them a long head start in professional life. Challenge panels could intervene in the process of recommending candidates for top honours (conducted by the Cabinet Office Honours and Appointments Secretariat in London and the Honours and Awards Secretariat in Canberra) to ask whether candidates are truly providing eminent service to the community *given the privileges they have enjoyed*. Indeed, in a society disinclined to reward privilege with symbols of esteem, the ordering of the annual honours list might be reversed, with tireless community volunteers at the top and philanthropists, business tycoons and professionals just doing their jobs at the bottom.

During the Covid lockdowns, the mass media drew readers with stories exposing a few of the more egregious instances of exclusive benefits being granted to the rich and famous, at a time when others endured the restrictions. Nevertheless, most newspapers and television networks, owned by power elites, consistently reinforce the ideas and beliefs that enable and justify elite privilege. They promote an individualistic worldview justified by an assumed meritocracy. They endorse conformist politicians and ridicule radical ones. They defend deep inequalities, dismiss those demanding higher taxes on the rich as 'class warriors' and blame poverty and disadvantage on the personal failings of those afflicted. At times, media outlets ridicule, humiliate and dehumanise people from disadvantaged communities. Like others, Britain's editorial code of practice requires journalists and editors to 'avoid prejudicial or pejorative reference to an individual's race, colour, religion, sex, gender identity, sexual orientation or to any physical or mental illness or disability.'[9] There is no requirement to avoid prejudicial or pejorative reference to an individual's 'class' or educational background or to avoid vilifying communities based on their socio-economic status. If those provisions had been included in the Australian code of ethics, then the journalists who had misgivings about the vilification of students at Mount Druitt High School (described in chapter 10) might have prevailed over their editor and averted a serious wrong being committed.

The kinds of institutional changes proposed above would provide the foundations for contesting privilege at the interpersonal level. Employees of private companies and public agencies often collaborate in granting exclusive benefits to elites, bestowing these privileges out of habit, to avoid unpleasantness, or simply from feelings of deference to the rich and powerful. In a society serious about countering elite privilege, these employees would have a social language for abstaining from unfair conferral of benefits on elites. Institutional changes could also give those at the sharp end of elite microaggressions the confidence to push back.

Just as language was developed to call out sexism and racism, the power of words can be used to oppose the power of elites. We hope this book will prompt a robust public debate about elite privilege, allowing the subterranean rumblings of discontent to surface as social critique – in other words, to convert manifestations of elite privilege from private troubles into public concerns.

The National Survey

The survey was conducted by OmniPoll in December 2021 and included a representative sample of 1,229 Australian adults aged eighteen years and over. Respondents were drawn from the online panel managed by Lightspeed Research, OmniPoll's online partner. Along with sex and age, sample quotas were set for each state, city and regional area. To help reflect the overall population distribution, results were post-weighted to data from the Australian Bureau of Statistics on age, sex, area and highest level of schooling completed (although not type of school attended).

The survey collected data on respondents' place of residence, age, sex, household structure, marital status, employment status, highest education level, and pre-tax household income. Note that, despite the measures taken to ensure representativeness, comparison with actual data shows that respondents who attended private schools are over-represented in the sample.

Interview schedule

1 Thinking about your last year at high school. Was the high school you attended a public school, Catholic school or other private school? (Select one answer)

[Public school/Catholic school/other private school]

2 [If attended a Catholic or other private school] Compared with other Catholic schools/private schools, as far as you know, were the fees paid at your high school higher than other Catholic schools/private schools, lower, or about the same?

[Higher/Lower/About the same/Can't say]

3 Do you agree or disagree with each of the following statements?

During the Covid lockdowns, wealthy people and celebrities found ways to get around the rules.

[Strongly agree/Somewhat agree/Somewhat disagree/Strongly disagree/ Can't say]

It's OK to use your connections to get around Covid lockdown rules.

[Strongly agree/Somewhat agree/Somewhat disagree/Strongly disagree/ Can't say]

Now some questions about things you may or may not have experienced in your life.

4 Firstly, how often, if ever, have you felt angry or resentful about wealthy people or celebrities getting special treatment?

[Never/Occasionally/Sometimes/Often/Can't say]

5 And how often, if ever, have you felt ashamed because of where you live, the school you went to, or your parents' occupation?

[Never/Occasionally/Sometimes/Often/Can't say]

6 Thinking again about your school. When you may have applied for jobs in the past, did any mention of the school you went to help or harm your chances of getting the job, or did it make no difference?

[Helped your chances/Harmed your chances/Made no difference/ Can't say]

7 Which one of the following two statements about Australia better reflects your opinion?

In Australia, there's one rule for the rich and another rule for the rest.

Overall, the rules are applied fairly in Australia.

Can't say

8 Thinking about expensive private schools in Australia, which one of the following statements best reflects your opinion?

They improve educational choice

They entrench inequality in society

Can't say

The Focus Groups

Eight focus groups of between 75 and 90 minutes' duration were conducted in May and July 2022. The conversations were conducted online with five participants and a moderator in each group. (One person was a late withdrawal.) Participants were recruited by Stable Research from its online panel composed of people, aged eighteen and over, who make a conscious decision to be invited regularly to participate in online surveys through a double opt-in registration process with the polling company. The panel is adjusted to be broadly representative of the Australian population. Participants received a fee of A$125 (all dollars below are Australian dollars). Standard processes were followed to gain participants' consent, including procedures to ensure anonymity. Focus group conversations were conducted by the authors.

Four groups were drawn from residents of Melbourne and four from residents of Sydney. For each city, participants were screened to provide four groups with the following demographics:

Older (50–65), high income/wealth
Older (50–65), average income/wealth
Younger (25–40), high income/wealth
Younger (25–40), average income/wealth

Of the participants, 21 were women and 18 were men.

Average income/wealth participants were included if they had annual household incomes between $70,000 and $150,000 and assets, excluding the residential home, of less than $1 million. High income/wealth participants were included if they had annual household incomes over $250,000 and assets, excluding the residential home, greater than $3 million. It was not expected that very wealthy people would be on Stable Research's panel or volunteer to participate.

Not unexpectedly, there were difficulties recruiting participants for the two younger/high wealth groups because younger adults have not usually had enough time to accumulate extensive liquid assets and are typically not old enough to have benefited from large inheritances. We therefore adopted a different screening process, asking younger adults if they had attended expensive private schools. Their incomes and assets, as well as their suburbs of residence, were also considered. (Two volunteers were excluded because, on checking, the private schools they nominated do not have high fees.)

Transcripts of the conversations were created using an AI technology and edited to correct mistranslations and other errors. The quotations used in this book have been lightly edited to exclude repetitions and space fillers such as 'you know' and 'like'.

A note on interpretation

In their paper 'Saying meritocracy and doing privilege', Shamus Khan and Colin Jerolmack discuss the traps of interpreting what elites say about what they do. At the elite school Khan studied, he noticed that what these privileged students said and did were often inconsistent, as if they knew intuitively how to construct a persona for interviews. 'The narratives they construct in an interview are at odds with [their] situated behaviour.'[1] They caution against construction of 'quote-driven' ethnography.

It's a caution we keep in mind when interpreting the words of our focus group participants, particularly those from the four wealthier groups. We detected some glossing of views and experiences and, at times, an evasiveness about their own behaviour. Others were unapologetic about the benefits they enjoyed as wealthier people and the advantages they gave their children.

In any case, our participants in the wealthier groups were not among the 'wealthy elite', the primary focus of our study. Based on the information we had, none had assets in excess of A$10 million. Some of them, however, had been in regular or periodic contact with the very wealthy – at elite schools, sharing exclusive neighbourhoods, working in high-end law and accountancy firms, at philanthropic trusts, or working directly for ultra-rich families. Some of our informants were insightful, even cynical, observers.

Piketty, Bourdieu and Privilege

Thomas Piketty's argument in *Capital in the Twenty-First Century* is that the history of inequality in developed countries over the last two centuries can be explained by the competition between two forces.[1] The first is the 'natural' tendency for wealth to grow faster than income, so that those with a lot of wealth will become even wealthier. This tendency is captured by Piketty's now famous formulation r > g – that is, the rate of growth of capital (or wealth), which is typically 4 or 5 per cent before tax each year in rich countries, is higher than the rate of growth of income, which is typically only 1 or 2 per cent.[2]

The second force, which tends to counteract the first, consists of shocks to the economic system that wipe out part of the value of wealth, shocks such as the wars and depressions of the twentieth century, and epoch-marking political changes that strengthen labour's bargaining power against capital, allowing wage and salary incomes to increase more rapidly. Higher taxes on capital, such as inheritance and capital gains taxes, also count among these counteracting forces. Increased power of labour and higher taxes on capital were in play in the three decades after the Second World War, explaining the shift to greater equality, which went against the longer historical trend, before the return of a new form of patrimonial capitalism in the last four or five decades.

Piketty argues that, setting aside shocks, the growth of wealth (r) and the growth of income (g) are influenced by independent processes. The growth of income is determined mainly by structural features of the economy – demographic and technological changes. The growth of capital 'depends on many technological, psychological, social, and cultural factors.'

We next consider the role of privilege in each of these processes, bringing together Pierre Bourdieu's analysis of the reproduction of elites through the transubstantiation of kinds of capital and Piketty's explanation of inequality summarised above.

Income inequality

Using standard neoclassical theory, Piketty argues that, up to a certain point on the wage and salary scale, inequality can be well explained by differing marginal productivities of workers, which in turn depend on 'the race between technology and education'.[3] The supply of skilled labour to meet the demands of employers adopting changing technology depends in large measure on the ability of the education system to supply enough workers with the right skills. However, account should also be taken of the 'rules of the labour market' set by governments and the relative bargaining power of workers and employers.

Of course, powerful elites can influence governments to change the rules to benefit employers, which is what they did as neoliberalism replaced social democratic thinking in the 1980s. Laws limiting collective bargaining weakened unions and workers, expanding the scope for outsourcing, short-term contracts and reduced employee protections.[4]

Piketty stresses that his explanation of wage and salary scale inequality breaks down at the high end of the income distribution (the top 10 per cent, certainly the top 1 per cent, and even more so for the 0.1 per cent of income earners), where there have been enormous increases in remuneration that simply cannot be explained by higher productivity of top managers. (This trend has been stronger in some countries than in others.) The explosive growth of salaries of top managers or super-managers has meant 'extremely high, historically unprecedented compensation packages for their labour' and can only be explained by institutional factors, notably the way in which the neoliberal revolution, concentrated in English-speaking countries, loosened the constraints within big companies on paying their top managers extraordinarily high salary packages.[5]

Exactly why and how these norms changed, writes Piketty, is 'a question for sociology, psychology, cultural and political history, and the study of beliefs and perceptions as much as economics per se.' He refers to 'meritocratic extremism' (a kind of cult of winners),[6] the failure of corporate governance, and 'the very large decrease in the top marginal tax rate in the English-speaking countries after 1980'. The very high incomes increased the political influence of the highest income earners (exercised through donations to 'political parties, pressure groups, and think tanks'), which allowed them to lobby to lower their taxes.[7]

Clearly, privilege comes into play here. Consider some of the highest paying professions – senior managers of large corporations, financial dealers, medical specialists such as surgeons and anaesthetists, top lawyers, judges and engineers. Who gets to fill these positions – the people best qualified or those with better connections and understanding of how to make their way in the system? Not everyone has an opportunity to develop their talents so that they can compete on an equal basis for these positions. Children from privileged families often prevail over others because they attended elite schools and grew up in families with connections and an understanding of how the system works (that is, in possession of Bourdieu's forms of capital). In short, those coming from elite backgrounds enjoy such benefits, in the form of habitus and social capital, that they have a distinct advantage in the competition for the highest paid professions. As we have seen, this is supported by several studies of recruitment practices by prestigious firms, and our focus group conversations were certainly peppered with examples of the privileged using their connections and their habitus to advance their positions at the expense of others.

It's reasonable to conclude that those Piketty calls 'the super-managers', the ones who pocket extraordinarily high salaries and make up the 1 per cent or 0.1 per cent of income earners, are drawn heavily from the already privileged elite. In addition, we suggest, the breakdown in norms, the failure of corporate governance, and the reductions in top tax rates that permitted the emergence of the class of super-managers came about as a result of the agitation and lobbying of the wealthy elite, supercharged in their efforts by the entrenchment of neoliberal discourse in society.

So we are suggesting that growing income inequality is due not simply to imbalances in supply and demand for skills but also, and perhaps much more so, to the operation of a system of elite privilege.

Wealth inequality

How do some acquire much more wealth than others, or, as Piketty puts it, what are the 'many technological, psychological, social, and cultural factors' on which the accumulation of wealth depends? It's a very complex question, although surely the 'primitive accumulation of capital' depends first and foremost on the possession of political power.

(Post-Soviet Russia provides an instructive example.) It's true that we are inclined to think of the vast fortunes made in the tech sector by lone entrepreneurs with foresight and a good idea. However, as was suggested in chapter 8, serendipitous innovation is typically turned into business success only with the help of the networks, seed capital and habitus that middle-class entrepreneurs can call on.

When income grows much more slowly than wealth – 1 to 2 per cent as opposed to 4 or 5 per cent – those with a large amount of wealth will rapidly outstrip those trying to accumulate by saving from their incomes. As Piketty puts it, 'wealth accumulated in the past is recapitalized much more quickly than the economy grows.[8] Wealth begets wealth. To the extent that high wealth and elite privilege go together, we can say that privilege begets privilege.

Piketty shows that the world wars and the deep depression of the 1930s destroyed vast amounts of wealth, bringing more equal societies after the Second World War. In the thirty years following the war, historically high tax rates on capital kept the return on capital closer to the economic growth rate, ushering in more equal societies. But the neoliberal revolution of the 1980s and beyond, coupled with financial globalisation, changed the political balance, resulting in sharp reductions in taxes on capital, including the reduction or abolition of inheritance taxes, widening the gap between the growth rates of wealth and income.[9]

Wealth is highly correlated across generations. Piketty shows that, in France in 2010, two-thirds of wealth holdings were inherited, and the trend is rising.[10] In the United States over the last thirty years, the wealth of high-income families doubled, while for low-income families it fell.[11] (Among the wealthy, as the number of children declines, wealth becomes more heavily concentrated.) On closer inspection, measuring the effect of inheritance on intergenerational wealth inequality turns out to be complicated. When children receive inheritances from their parents they are mostly in middle age, around fifty, and, depending on years in education, have had twenty to thirty years in the workforce to build their own wealth. When their parents die, poorer people with little wealth may receive a large boost in relative wealth (say, from $50,000 to $500,000) while already wealthy people may receive a much larger amount of inheritance that makes a smaller proportional increase to their wealth (say, from $10 million to $30 million). But that is immediately on inheritance. Over the next years, poorer people are more likely to spend their inheritance on consumption, while wealthy people are more likely to invest more of it. So after ten years the changes in wealth may be quite different.

However, children inherit more than wealth from their parents. Rich parents also transfer large amounts of (Bourdieusian) social and cultural capital in the form of educational qualifications and reputation, networks, attitudes towards work and money, and habitus generally. When put to use, these forms of capital can be transformed into financial capital, which is why children from wealthy families often have large amounts of their own wealth at the time they receive an inheritance from their parents.

To understand intergenerational effects, economists have developed a measure of the way a parent's position in society influences their children's position in society – in effect, a measure of how much wealth begets wealth. Known as 'intergenerational wealth persistence', it measures the effect of an increase in parents' wealth on an increase in children's wealth. A rise in this measure means a decline in social mobility. Studies in OECD countries have found that around one-third to two-thirds of intergenerational wealth persistence is due to inheritance of wealth.[12] The rest of the persistence of wealth is due to what can be called Bourdieusian factors – that is, parental investment in the social and cultural capital of their offspring while they are young and the opportunities these provide to accumulate wealth themselves. As Black and others put it: 'wealthier parents may invest more in their children's human capital, help their children get better jobs, provide funding for business startups, give financial gifts, or affect child preferences or attitudes.'[13] This is our reworking of Piketty's idea of patrimonial capitalism.

Notes

Chapter 1 Introduction

1 Rupert Neate, 'Super-rich jet off to disaster bunkers amid coronavirus outbreak', *The Guardian*, 12 March 2020; Jessica Green, 'Farewell poor people: how the rich are fleeing London – as millionaires offer up to £50,000-a-month to rent rural retreats', *Daily Mail*, 24 March 2020.

2 Lynsey Hanley, 'Lockdown has laid bare Britain's class divide', *The Guardian*, 7 April 2020.

3 Joshua Chaffin, '"The rich shouldn't feel like the enemy": is New York turning on the wealthy?', *Financial Times*, 6 April 2021.

4 See Australian Bureau of Statistics, 'ABS releases measures of socio-economic advantage and disadvantage', 16 March 2008, https://tinyurl.com/52ht8b3h.

5 Sarah McPhee, 'Schools email parents about "significant" increase in students attending class', *Sydney Morning Herald*, 1 August 2021.

6 See 'A unique outdoor education exclusive to Scots', https://scots.college/visit-scots/campuses/glengarry/; Michael McGowan, 'Students from exclusive Sydney school relocate to regional NSW campus during lockdown', *The Guardian*, 14 July 2021.

7 Jordan Baker, 'Redlands students escape lockdown for Snowy Mountains ski school', *Sydney Morning Herald*, 19 July 2021.

8 Sam Clench, '"People just don't care": Australians stranded overseas come to terms with their own country "abandoning" them', News.com.au, 13 July 2021.

9 Tiffany Wertheimer, 'India Covid pandemic: Girl, 5, reunited with mother in Australia', *BBC News* online, 18 June 2021; Herlyn Kaur, 'Six-year-old girl stuck in India amid COVID pandemic leaves Perth family with nervous wait', ABC News online, 9 July 2021.

10 Caitlin Fitzsimmons, '15,000 rich foreigners given visas to Australia during the pandemic', *Sydney Morning Herald*, 1 August 2021; Bryant Hevesi and Andrew Prentice, 'Australia's richest man is allowed to skip quarantine in notoriously strict Western Australia despite the billionaire mining mogul having tested positive to coronavirus', *Daily Mail*, 21 January 2021; Carrie Fellner and Nigel Gladstone, 'Thousands enter Australia for "holidays and business" as wait drags for stranded locals', *Sydney Morning Herald*, 1 July 2021; Caitlin Fitzsimmons, 'Pandemic no barrier to private jet arrivals in Australia', *Sydney Morning Herald*, 30 May 2021.

11 Alan France, Steve Roberts and Bronwyn Wood, 'Youth, social class and privilege in the antipodes: towards a new research agenda for youth sociology', *Journal of Sociology*, 54/3 (2018): 362–80, at p. 370.

12 Thomas Piketty, *Capital in the Twenty-First Century*. Cambridge, MA: Belknap Press, 2014.

13 Ibid., p. 173.

14 Nancy Fraser and Axel Honneth, *Redistribution or Recognition? A Political–Philosophical Exchange*. London: Verso, 2003.

15 We believe our argument applies, *mutatis mutandis*, to all liberal democratic societies. We are not sufficiently expert to comment on its applicability to other kinds of societies. Compared with the post-war decades when it was enthusiastically promoted as the means to build a

more equal society, today meritocracy is more often offered as a fig leaf. The mobilisation of meritocracy as a defence of inequality is done half-heartedly, perhaps because the demands for a fairer society have lost much of their fervency in the neoliberal era – that is, in the absence of a powerful alternative to liberal capitalism.

16 See chapter 6, note 1.

17 Indeed, in their book focused on private schools in Britain, Francis Green and David Kynaston describe these schools as 'engines of privilege' (*Engines of Privilege: Britain's Private School Problem*. London: Bloomsbury, 2019).

18 William Harvey, 'Strategies for conducting elite interviews', *Qualitative Research*, 11 (2011): 431–41.

19 Rachel Sherman, '"A very expensive ordinary life": consumption, symbolic boundaries and moral legitimacy among New York elites', *Socio-Economic Review*, 18/2 (2018): 411–33, at p. 415.

20 Adam Howard and Jane Kenway, 'Canvassing conversations: obstinate issues in studies of elites and elite education', *International Journal of Qualitative Studies in Education*, 28/9 (2015): 1005–32, at p. 1007.

21 Emma Spence, 'Eye-spy wealth: cultural capital and "knowing luxury" in the identification of and engagement with the superrich', *Annals of Leisure Research*, 19/3 (2016): 314–28, at p. 315.

22 Shamus Khan and Colin Jerolmack, 'Saying meritocracy and doing privilege', *Sociological Quarterly*, 54/1 (2013): 9–19, at p. 11.

23 Ibid., p. 12.

24 Howard and Kenway, 'Canvassing conversations', p. 1008.

25 Quoted ibid., p. 1015.

26 France, Roberts and Wood, 'Youth, social class and privilege in the antipodes', p. 370.

Chapter 2 Understanding Elite Privilege

1 See Erzsébet Bukodi and John Goldthorpe, 'Elite studies: for a new approach', *Political Quarterly*, 92/4 (2021): 673–81.

2 Michael Gebicki, 'Qantas Chairman's Lounge: inside the invite-only club that rejected Jacqui Lambie', *Traveller*, 31 May 2021.

3 Ibid. Pierre Bourdieu noted: 'One cannot admit into one's place a person of little repute without oneself losing repute.' Bourdieu, 'Symbolic capital and social classes', *Journal of Classical Sociology*, 13/2 (2013): 292–303, at p. 295.

4 'Inside the secretive Qantas Chairman's Lounge, Australia's most exclusive club', *Business Insider*, 25 January 2017.

5 Samantha Hutchinson and Stephen Brook, 'Qantas flyers see red over Chairman's Lounge snub', *Sydney Morning Herald*, 28 September 2021.

6 Chris C. [*sic*], 'Inside the secret world of VIP travel and invitation-only lounges', *Executive Traveller*, 28 May 2015.

7 Ingrid Fuary-Wagner and Ayesha de Kretser, 'What exactly is the Qantas Chairman's Lounge, and how do you join?', *Australian Financial Review*, 23 August 2023. When in 2023 Qantas CEO Alan Joyce was pressed to explain by senators, he said: 'I'm not making any reference to who is in the lounge or under which criteria that is granted.' Stephen Johnson, 'Astonishing moment Qantas boss Alan Joyce refuses to answer five questions from senators …', *Mail Online*, 28 August 2023, https://tinyurl.com/9scw6e2a.

8 At times our attention is focused on something like the 'ultra-high-net-worth individuals', often defined as those with assets worth more than US$30 million. In Australia, they were reported to number just under 21,000 in 2021 (Tom Burroughs, 'Australia's UHNW population keeps growing, shrugs off pandemic', *Wealth Briefing Asia*, 2 March 2022). In

their US study, Scully et al. define wealthy households as those in the top 5 per cent of net worth. Maureen Scully, Sandra Rothenberg, Erynn E. Beaton and Zhi Tang, 'Mobilizing the wealthy: doing "privilege work" and challenging the roots of inequality', *Business and Society*, 57/6 (2018): 1075–113, at p. 1076.

9 Thomas Piketty, *Capital in the Twenty-First Century*. Cambridge, MA: Belknap Press, 2014, p. 278, passim.

10 Piketty refers to the top 1 per cent as the 'dominant class' and the 9 per cent below them as the 'wealthy class', suggesting the former 'occupies a prominent place in the social landscape and not just in the income distribution.' Ibid., pp. 252, 254.

11 In the context of political power, John Higley, a prominent scholar, defines elites somewhat narrowly as 'persons with power to affect organizational outcomes individually, regularly and seriously'. John Higley, G. Lowell Field and Knut Grøholt, *Elite Structure and Ideology: A Theory with Applications to Norway*. New York: Columbia University Press, 1976, p. 17.

12 Alison Bailey, 'Privilege: expanding on Marilyn Frye's "Oppression",' *Journal of Social Philosophy*, 29/3 (1998).

13 Bob Pease, *Undoing Privilege: Unearned Advantage in a Divided World*. London: Zed Books, 2022.

14 Claire Maxwell and Peter Aggleton, 'The reproduction of privilege: young women, the family and private education', *International Studies in Sociology of Education*, 24/2 (2014): 189–209, at p. 194. They also write that 'the concept [of privilege] captures well the material, cultural and ideological resources accessible to this particular group, and their role in processes of social differentiation and hierarchisation.'

15 Ibid.

16 See, for example, Karl Maton, 'Habitus', in Michael Grenfell (ed.), *Pierre Bourdieu: Key Concepts*. 2nd edn, Abingdon: Routledge, 2014.

17 'Bogan' is a derogatory, although increasingly embraced, term used in Australia to describe 'an uncultured and unsophisticated person; a boorish and uncouth person' (Australian National Dictionary).

18 On Tinkler, see David Nichols, 'Review – boganaire: the rise and fall of Nathan Tinkler', *The Conversation*, 19 November 2013. The phrase 'cashed up bogan' reflects the assumption that bogans are meant to be poor. Nichols suggests that mining moguls Gina Rinehart and Clive Palmer also qualify as bogan billionaires.

19 Dylan Riley, 'Bourdieu's class theory', *Catalyst*, 1/2 (2017): 111.

20 Alan France, Steve Roberts and Bronwyn Wood, 'Youth, social class and privilege in the antipodes: towards a new research agenda for youth sociology', *Journal of Sociology*, 54/3 (2018): 362–80, at p. 370.

21 Claire Maxwell and Peter Aggleton, 'Becoming accomplished: concerted cultivation among privately educated young women', *Pedagogy, Culture & Society*, 21/1 (2013): 75–93.

22 Michelle Lamont, *Money, Morals, and Manners: The Culture of the French and the American Upper-Middle Class*. Chicago: University of Chicago Press, 1992, p. 370, n.2.

23 Aaron Reeves, Sam Friedman, Charles Rahal and Magne Flemmen, 'The decline and persistence of the old boy: private schools and elite recruitment 1897 to 2016', *American Sociological Review*, 82/6 (2017): 1139–66, at p. 1145.

24 In his overview of the sociology of elites, Khan wrote: 'To study elites, then, is to study the control over, value of, and distribution of resources. In simpler terms, this means studying power and inequality – from above.' Shamus Rahman Khan, 'The sociology of elites', *Annual Review of Sociology*, 38 (2012): 361–77, at p. 362.

25 Pierre Bourdieu, 'The forms of capital', in J. G. Richardson (ed.), *Handbook of Theory and Research for the Sociology of Education*. New York: Greenwood Press, 1986, pp. 241–58,

at p. 250. He added that non-economic forms of capital are 'never entirely reducible' to economic capital and are most effective when they conceal their roots in wealth, including from their possessors.

26 Ibid., p. 249.

27 Hutchinson and Brook, 'Qantas flyers see red over Chairman's Lounge snub'.

28 Bourdieu, 'The forms of capital', p. 243.

29 See Rob Moore, 'Capital', in Grenfell (ed.), *Pierre Bourdieu*, pp. 98–113.

30 In the United States, Khan and Jerolmack noted that 'Knowing how to eat is in many ways more challenging than knowing what to eat', and the same might be said about how to conduct oneself at a dinner party or in an art gallery or an office environment. Shamus Khan and Colin Jerolmack, 'Saying meritocracy and doing privilege,' *Sociological Quarterly*, 54/1 (2013): 9–19, at p. 16.

31 Maxwell and Aggleton, 'The reproduction of privilege'.

32 Ibid., p. 194.

33 Ibid., p. 198.

34 Bourdieu, 'The forms of capital', p. 253.

35 Patricia Thomson, 'Field', in Grenfell (ed.), *Pierre Bourdieu*, p. 70.

36 Some understand symbolic capital as a kind of meta-capital rather than an additional type of capital, one that arises from the reputation and legitimacy that goes with possession of financial, social and cultural capital. Bourdieu himself wrote of symbolic capital as 'the acquisition of a reputation for competence and an image of respectability and honour-ability ...' (Pierre Bourdieu, *Distinction: A Social Critique of the Judgement of Taste*. London: Routledge & Kegan Paul, [1979] 1984, p. 291). Here we interpret symbolic capital as all those recognisable markers (awards, titles, credentials, honoured positions) that signal prestige and authority.

37 Moore, 'Capital', pp. 100–1.

38 Frank Bongiorno, 'I get by with a little help from my friends', *Inside Story*, 23 May 2013.

39 Shamus Khan speaks of knowledge capital in narrower, Gramscian terms: 'Ideas, knowledge, and ideology are seen as central to the maintenance of elite power.' Khan, 'The sociology of elites', p. 370.

40 Faisal Devji, 'Celebrity academics', blogpost *Hurst*, 29 May 2020; Richard Miles, 'The rise of the super profs: should we be worried about celebrity academics?', *The Conversation*, 15 November 2012.

41 Candace West and Don Zimmerman, 'Doing gender', *Gender & Society*, 1/2 (1987): 125–51, at pp. 125, 126.

42 In their study of an elite girls' school, Maxwell and Aggleton write that the concept of privilege 'captures well the material, cultural and ideological resources accessible to this particular group, and their role in processes of social differentiation and hierarchisation.' Maxwell and Aggleton, 'The reproduction of privilege', p. 190.

43 Too much emphasis on the 'structure of privilege' or 'structural forces' goes against our stress on the practice of privilege, the *doing* of privilege. Structures, while always present, are often attributed an independent existence rising above what is happening on the ground and taking on God-like powers, manipulating what is happening down below. We agree with Bruno Latour's critique of 'two-level' constructions in which a vague external force sits above the actual world and manipulates events, whether that force be science, the economy, class, society or God. We prefer to think in terms of concrete institutions, entrenched beliefs, and patterns of behaviour based on norms and habits, although we do speak of 'systems' to refer to aggregates.

44 This approach is consistent with the criticism that has been made of Bourdieu's use of

habitus, which is presented as *determining* practice rather than providing the actor with a disposition and qualities that 'can be used to navigate explicit and implicit expectations' in the face of 'the situational contingency that haunts performances of elite distinction.' The quoted phrases are taken from a very stimulating paper by Max Persson, 'Contested ease: negotiating contradictory modes of elite distinction in face-to-face interaction', *British Journal of Sociology*, 72/4 (2021): 930–45.

45 Piketty characterised them as among the wealthy 'nine per cent'. The highest rewards from labour arise from use of analytical skills such as intuitive problem solving, skills beginning with elite education. Y. Liu and D. B. Grusky, 'The payoff to skill in the third industrial revolution', *American Journal of Sociology*, 118/5 (2013): 1330–74.

46 Guy Standing speaks of the precariat's existential insecurity, with 'no occupational identity or narrative to give to their lives' ('Meet the precariat, the new global class fuelling the rise of populism', *World Economic Forum* blogpost, 9 November 2016, https://tinyurl.com /3nxs6h7x).

47 Mairi Maclean, Charles Harvey and Gerhard Kling, 'Pathways to power: class, hyper-agency and the French corporate elite', *Organization Studies*, 35/6 (2014): 825–55, at p. 834 (they do not say what 'workers' includes).

48 Lee Drutman, *Political Divisions in 2016 and Beyond: Tensions between and within the Two Parties*, Research report from the Democracy Fund Voter Study Group, June 2017. See also the Twitter (X) thread by Paul Krugman at https://tinyurl.com/59j6ja4b (16 April 2019).

49 Diane Reay, 'Beyond consciousness? The psychic landscape of social class', *Sociology*, 39/5 (2005): 912 (emphasis added).

50 Mel Campbell, 'So, you think you're middle class …', *Crikey*, 11 December 2014.

51 In 'Symbolic capital and social classes', Bourdieu rejects accounts that are solely objectivist or solely subjectivist.

52 On the very different meanings of 'middle class' in the United States and Britain, see Daniel Markovits, *The Meritocracy Trap*. London: Penguin, 2019, p. 297.

53 Mike Savage, 'From the "problematic of the proletariat" to a class analysis of "wealth elites"', *Sociological Review*, 63 (2015): 223–39.

54 Ibid., p. 230.

Chapter 3 The Micropolitics of Elite Privilege

1 Candace West and Don Zimmerman, 'Doing gender', *Gender & Society*, 1/2 (1987): 125–51, at p. 126.

2 The phrases are used by Bourdieu for habitus. See David Swartz, *Culture & Power: The Sociology of Pierre Bourdieu*. Chicago: University of Chicago Press, 1997, p. 103.

3 Status symbols and signs of distinction are similar, although not the same. A status symbol is a possession or characteristic that is highly valued in a particular society or social group and is seen as an indicator of one's social or economic status. A sign of distinction is a cultural marker or symbol that individuals use to demonstrate their social status or membership in a particular group. While both are used to convey social status and to differentiate oneself from others, status symbols are often material possessions or attributes, while signs of distinction can be both material and cultural. Cultural signs are harder to buy as they need to be acquired over time to attain authenticity.

4 Erving Goffman, 'Symbols of class status'. *British Journal of Sociology*, 2/4 (1951): 294–304, at p. 294.

5 'Staffer "crumbled" under pressure to change Iguanas story', *Sydney Morning Herald*, 23 June 2008. See also '"Don't you know who I am": MP forced to apologise after tirade', *Sydney Morning Herald*, 1 October 2009.

6 Goffman, 'Symbols of class status,' p. 300.

7 Ibid., p. 297.

8 Ibid., p. 303, n.2.

9 West and Zimmerman, 'Doing gender', p. 136.

10 Dee Michell, Jacqueline Wilson and Verity Archer (eds), *Bread and Roses: Voices of Australian Academics from the Working Class*. Rotterdam: Sense, 2015.

11 Karl Maton, 'Habitus', in Michael Grenfell (ed.), *Pierre Bourdieu: Key Concepts*. 2nd edn, Abingdon: Routledge, 2014, pp. 57–8.

12 Skills in navigating the rules of the game are an element of cultural capital.

13 Swartz, *Culture & Power*, p. 100.

14 Megan Blaxland et al., 'From being "at risk" to being "a risk": journeys into parenthood among young women experiencing adversity', *Families, Relationships and Societies*, 11/3 (2021): 321–39.

15 Karl Maton, 'Introducing LTC', https://tinyurl.com/mvy6ufyt.

16 Personal communication with the ambassador.

17 'NSW COVID-19 lockdown laws tightened, restricting travel from Greater Sydney after crisis Cabinet meeting', *ABC News* online, 13 August 2021.

18 Documents provided to the authors under freedom of information laws by the NSW Ministry of Health on 24 February 2022. See also Jordan Baker, 'Redlands students escape lockdown for Snowy Mountains ski school', *Sydney Morning Herald*, 19 July 2021.

19 A dissident parent at Scotch College said: 'These people who are in the [Scotch College] committee think they are of blue blood, and they are superior [to] others. Rules are for others to follow and everyone should make concessions for their group. They enjoyed making their own circles and running the association as their private club' (Stephen Brook, 'Mother wages four-year battle against Scotch College parents' association', *The Age*, 26 June 2022).

20 'Parents are advised to apply as early as possible', says Scotch College, 'as initial offers of places for Prep, Year 4 and Year 7 are mainly determined by the age of the boy on receipt of the initial application' (letter to parents concerning school places, https://tinyurl.com/mwctctwb).

21 The source for 'savvy parents' is a private communication.

22 In Britain's most exclusive schools, report Green and Kynaston, 'parents rush to register their children at the earliest opportunity after a child's birth, sometimes even before.' Francis Green and David Kynaston, *Engines of Privilege: Britain's Private School Problem*. London: Bloomsbury, 2019, p. 121.

23 It is hard to see how all of this is squared with Scotch College's declaration that 'Christian teachings underpin all that we do' (Scotch College prospectus, https://tinyurl.com/y9hdz7k9).

24 Personal communication.

25 Name dropping has been shown to be more effective with strangers because familiarity with someone's actual position may reduce its effectiveness. Thorn-R. Kray, 'On name-dropping: the mechanisms behind a notorious practice in social science and the humanities', *Argumentation*, 30/4 (2016): 423–41, at p. 432.

26 Documents provided to the authors by the Western Australia Department of Health on 7 December 2022. Hamish Hastie and Nathan Hondros, 'Billionaire Kerry Stokes exempted from strict quarantine rules after arriving in Perth from Aspen by private jet', *WAToday*, 23 April 2020; Hamish Hastie, 'Cleared for landing: Stokes' political clout unveiled as federal minister, premier discuss hotel lockdown exemption', *Sydney Morning Herald*, 23 July 2020; Hamish Hastie, 'McGowan dodges more questions over billionaire's hotel quarantine exemption', *Sydney Morning Herald*, 24 July 2020; Hamish Hastie, 'McGowan "doesn't recall"

if he tried to influence Stokes' anti-Palmer law coverage', *Sydney Morning Herald*, 3 August 2022. The 'most respected' comment on the last-mentioned was: 'The relationship between the state government and Seven West Media stinks more than a Christmas ham in August. Everyone knows this.'

27 Rinehart's US\$30 billion and Forrest's US\$20 billion dwarf Stokes's US\$4 billion fortune but, when you control public opinion, politicians take more notice. Stokes counts Xi Jinping among his friends (Clive Hamilton, *Silent Invasion*. Melbourne: Hardie Grant, 2018, p. 271).

28 Personal communication.

29 Rebecca Trigger, 'Texts between Mark McGowan and Kerry Stokes revealed in Clive Palmer defamation case', *ABC News* online, 9 March 2022; Andrea Mayes, 'WA Premier Mark McGowan's texts with billionaire media mogul Kerry Stokes a revealing insight into power and politics from Palmer defamation case', *ABC News* online, 12 March 2022.

30 Australian Miliary Medicine Association, 'Andrew Robertson', www.amma.asn.au/members /andrew-robertson/.

31 Caitlyn Rintoul, 'Kerry Stokes praises West Australians' immense generosity after bumper Telethon', *West Australian*, 28 October 2019.

32 Personal communication to authors.

33 Ilan Wiesel, *Power, Glamour and Angst: Inside Australia's Elite Neighbourhoods*. Singapore: Palgrave Macmillan, 2019, p. 59.

34 Jean-Pierre Daloz, 'Elite (un)conspicuousness: theoretical reflections on ostentation vs. understatement', *Historical Social Research*, 37/1 (2012): 209–22, at p. 216. Bourdieu referred to 'ostentatious discretion, sobriety and understatement' as a mode of distinction (*Distinction: A Social Critique of the Judgement of Taste*. London: Routledge & Kegan Paul, [1979] 1984, p. 249).

35 Pierre Bourdieu, 'What makes a social class? On the theoretical and practical existence of groups', *Berkeley Journal of Sociology*, 32 (1987): 1–17, at pp. 11–12.

36 Daloz, 'Elite (un)conspicuousness', p. 210, n.1.

37 Ibid., p. 211.

38 Ibid., p. 216.

39 Mikael Holmqvist and Ilan Wiesel, 'Elite communities and polarization in neoliberal society: consecration in Australia's and Sweden's wealthy neighbourhoods', *Critical Sociology*, 49/4–5 (2023): 767–82.

40 Daloz, 'Elite (un)conspicuousness', p. 220.

41 Mikael Holmqvist, *Leader Communities: The Consecration of Elites in Djursholm*. New York: Columbia University Press, 2017, pp. 31–2.

42 Swartz, *Culture & Power*, p. 107.

43 Lidia Katia Consiglia Manzo, 'Naked elites: unveiling embodies markers of superiority through co-performance ethnography in gentrified Brooklyn's Park Slope', *Urban Geography*, 40/5 (2017): 645–64.

44 Ibid., p. 657.

45 Ibid., pp. 659, 660.

46 In his poem 'Thank you for waiting,' the poet laureate Simon Armitage skews the fine-grained distinctions set by airlines.

47 Bourdieu, *Distinction*.

48 Rob Moore, 'Capital', in Grenfell (ed.), *Pierre Bourdieu*, p. 105.

49 'In reality, agents are both classified and classifiers, but they classify according to (or depending upon) their position within classifications.' Pierre Bourdieu, 'What makes a social class? On the theoretical and practical existence of groups', lecture at the University of Chicago, 9–10 April 1987, p. 2.

50 Bourdieu, *Distinction*, p. 272, passim.

51 Ibid., p. 282.

52 Mark Brown, 'Saatchi's scathing portrait of the art world: "Vulgar, Eurotrashy, masturbatory"', *The Guardian*, 3 December 2011.

53 Richard A. Peterson and Roger M. Kern, 'Changing highbrow taste: from snob to omnivore', *American Sociological Review*, 61/5 (1996): 900–7.

54 Ibid.

55 Vegard Jarness, 'Cultural vs economic capital: symbolic boundaries within the middle class', *Sociology*, 51/2 (2017): 357–73, at pp. 362–9.

56 Rob Beckett, 'Chavy B*stard!', https://tinyurl.com/44ttxafk, minute 2:30.

Chapter 4 *The Geography of Privilege*

1 Mike Donaldson and Scott Poynting, *Ruling Class Men: Money, Sex, Power*. Oxford: Peter Lang, 2007, p. 164.

2 Melbourne Cricket Ground, 'Private suites', https://tinyurl.com/3d9bubzd.

3 Sarah Lyall and Christina Goldbaum, 'When V.I.P. isn't exclusive enough: welcome to V.V.I.P.', *New York Times*, 30 November 2022.

4 Evan Osnos, 'The haves and the have-yachts', *New Yorker Magazine*, 25 July 2022.

5 Ibid..

6 Ibid.

7 Howard Walker, 'James Packer Gets the Keys to His New 108-Metre Benetti Gigayacht', *Robb Report*, 28 July 2019.

8 Jonathan Beaverstock, Philip Hubbard and John Rennie Short, 'Getting away with it? Exposing the geographies of the super-rich', *Geoforum*, 35/4 (2004): 401–7.

9 Donaldson and Poynting, *Ruling Class Men*, p. 240.

10 Knight Frank, 'Australia's "Harbour City" – the new mecca for the super-rich', https://tinyurl.com/mryjubk5.

11 Lucy Macken, 'Sydney private schools go on $100 million buying bonanza', *Sydney Morning Herald*, 6 August 2022. See also Jonathan Chancellor, 'The schools that ate Sydney: no stopping prestige school expansion as they buy up the neighbourhoods', 7 December 2020, https://tinyurl.com/2p96y64v. Cranbrook School occupies 4.34 hectares in Bellevue Hill, Sydney's most expensive real estate in the eastern suburbs (Cranbrook School Redevelopment, July 2020, https://tinyurl.com/9vvhba65). Sydney Church of England Grammar School (Shore) has grand views across Sydney Harbour and boasts 9 hectares of playing fields near the North Sydney business district. In 2022, its girls' counterpart in Darlinghurst, SCEGGS, paid almost $3 million for a terrace house next to the school to be used as a 'wellbeing hub' for students.

12 An exception is Aidan Davison, 'The luxury of nature: the environmental consequences of super-rich lives', in I. Hay and J. Beaverstock (eds), *International Handbook of Wealth and the Super-Rich*. Cheltenham: Edward Elgar, 2016, pp. 339–59.

13 Elisa Savelli et al., 'Urban water crises driven by elites' unsustainable consumption', *Nature Sustainability*, 10 April 2023.

14 'Australia's super-rich exposed among world's worst climate emitters', *New Daily*, 7 November 2022, https://tinyurl.com/4h4vyutv; Beatriz Barros and Richard Wilk, 'The outsized carbon footprints of the super-rich', *Sustainability: Science, Practice and Policy*, 17/1 (2021): 316–22. Estimates of the 2022 emissions from the private jets owned by billionaires and celebrities can be found at https://climatejets.org/. The most profligate have emissions 200 or even 300 times higher than the average American from their private jets alone.

15 Rowland Atkinson, Simon Parker, and Roger Burrows, 'Elite formation, power and space in

contemporary London', *Theory, Culture & Society*, 34/5–6 (2017): 179–200. See also Rowland Atkinson et al., 'Minimum city? The deeper impacts of the "super-rich" on urban life', in Ray Forrest, Sin Yee Koh and Bart Wissink (eds), *Cities and the Super-Rich: Real Estate, Elite Practices and Urban Political Economies*. New York: Palgrave Macmillan, 2017, pp. 253–71.

16 See, for example, the books by Oliver Bullough, *Moneyland: Why Thieves and Crooks Now Rule the World and How to Take it Back* (London: Profile Books, 2018) and *Butler to the World: How Britain Became the Servant of Tycoons, Tax Dodgers, Kleptocrats and Criminals* (London: Profile Books, 2022).

17 Ilan Wiesel, *Power, Glamour and Angst: Inside Australia's Elite Neighbourhoods*. Singapore: Palgrave Macmillan, 2019, p. 2. (The rich *reside* in a suburb while others live in them, at least in the language of estate agents.)

18 Ibid., pp. 29–30.

19 Mikael Holmqvist, *Leader Communities: The Consecration of Elites in Djursholm*. New York: Columbia University Press, 2017, p. xviii.

20 Wiesel, *Power, Glamour and Angst*, p. 18.

21 Holmqvist, *Leader Communities*, ch. 3.

22 Personal communication. One of the authors was once speaking with a newly arrived British diplomat. The author pointed out that the Canberra street in which the diplomat's residence was located is the most expensive in the city, to which the diplomat replied, 'Good'.

23 Property particulars: https://tinyurl.com/2p9ek93w; https://tinyurl.com/296dr4fb. 'This is a rare opportunity to acquire a one-of-a-kind classic contemporary residence ready to enjoy by one of Toorak's most celebrated architects in this desirable enclave.' 'The botanic beauty of the grounds and the grandeur of the external aesthetics create a stunning introduction to a series of unforgettable spaces.'

24 Holmqvist, *Leader Communities*, p. 5.

25 Ibid., p. 3.

26 Wiesel, *Power, Glamour and Angst*, pp. 118–19.

27 Ibid., p. 88.

28 Ibid., p. 83.

29 Holmqvist, *Leader Communities*, pp. 4–5, 7–8.

30 Ibid., p. 9.

31 Wiesel, *Power, Glamour and Angst*, p. 114.

32 Interestingly, Wiesel noticed a widespread feeling of 'angst' among residents of the elite suburbs he interviewed. Despite their privileged positions and the opportunities their neighbourhoods provide for the further accumulation of capital of various kinds, he often heard a 'narrative of paradise lost'. They may have triumphed in the political and economic spheres yet, 'in the realm of everyday life in the Australian city, elites experience themselves as almost powerless victims of congestion, noise, and pollution.' Wiesel interprets this as a 'blindness to their own objective privilege'. Ibid., pp. 167, 172.

33 Ibid., p. 116.

34 Ibid., pp. 51–2.

35 Ibid., pp. 48–9.

36 Ibid., p. 20.

37 Ibid., p. 103.

38 Holmqvist, *Leader Communities*, p. 5.

39 Wiesel, *Power, Glamour and Angst*, pp. 54–5.

40 Ibid., pp. 47–8.

41 Ibid., pp. 53–4.

42 More generally, Laura Weinrib wrote: 'Disgust plays a role in structuring social relationships

across class lines.' Laura Weinrib, 'Class and classification: the role of disgust in regulating social status', in Zoya Hasan et al. (eds), *The Empire of Disgust: Prejudice, Discrimination, and Policy in India and the US*. Delhi: Oxford Academic, 2018.

43 Benita Kolovos, 'Victorian Liberal MP Wendy Lovell chastised for saying children in social housing "cannot mix" in wealthy areas', *The Guardian*, 24 March 2022. Ironically, two months after Lovell made her comments, Anthony Albanese, a man brought up by a single mother in public housing in a rundown suburb, became prime minister.

44 Stephanie Lawler, 'Disgusted subjects: the making of middle-class identities', *Sociological Review*, 53/3 (2005).

45 Kolovos, 'Victorian Liberal MP Wendy Lovell ...' (emphasis added).

46 William Reilly, 'On the state of waiting.' Online notes (undated), Faculty of History, University of Cambridge.

47 Javier Auyero, 'Patients of the state: an ethnographic account of poor people's waiting', *Latin American Research Review*, 46/1 (2011): 5–29, at p. 6.

48 Barry Schwartz, 'Waiting, exchange, and power: the distribution of time in social systems', *American Journal of Sociology*, 79/4 (1974): 841–70, at p. 841.

49 Ibid., p. 849.

50 Pierre Bourdieu, *Pascalian Meditations*. Stanford, CA: Stanford University Press, 2000, p. 228.

51 Danièle Bélanger and Guillermo Candiz, 'The politics of "waiting" for care: immigration policy and family reunification in Canada', *Journal of Ethnic and Migration Studies*, 46/16 (2020): 3472–90.

52 Brendan O'Shannassy, *Superyacht Captain*. London: Adlard Coles, 2022, p. 178.

Chapter 5 Replicating Privilege

1 The conclusion too of Francis Green and David Kynaston in *Engines of Privilege: Britain's Private School Problem* (London: Bloomsbury, 2019).

2 Pierre Bourdieu, *Distinction: A Social Critique of the Judgement of Taste*. London: Routledge & Kegan Paul, [1979] 1984, p. 72.

3 Mikael Holmqvist, *Leader Communities: The Consecration of Elites in Djursholm*. New York: Columbia University Press, 2017, p. 171.

4 Sutton Trust and Social Mobility Commission, *Elitist Britain 2019: The Educational Backgrounds of Britain's Leading People*. London: Sutton Trust and Social Mobility Commission, 2019, p. 12. See also Independent Schools Council, *ISC Census and Annual Report 2022*. London: Independent Schools Council, 2022; and Sally Weale, 'Britain's top jobs still in hands of private school elite, study finds', *The Guardian*, 25 June 2019.

5 Green and Kynaston, *Engines of Privilege*, pp. 20, 15.

6 See 'How much does private school cost in the UK? Guide for 2023', https://tinyurl.com /3ru9tpet.

7 'England school fees by grade (2023)', www.edarabia.com/england-school-fees/. Note: Elite private schools in England are referred to as 'public schools' because, historically, they opened themselves to students from beyond the local area or a certain profession.

8 See Council for American Private Education, 'The voice of America's private schools', https:// tinyurl.com/3yu3mb53.

9 Shamus Rahman Khan, *Privilege: The Making of an Adolescent Elite at St. Paul's School*. Princeton, NJ: Princeton University Press, 2011, p. 4.

10 Raj Chetty, David Deming and John Friedman, *Diversifying Society's Leaders? The Determinants and Causal Effects of Admission to Highly Selective Private Colleges*, Working Paper 31492, National Bureau of Economic Research, July 2023 (https://tinyurl.com/yj54yhbx). See also

Aatish Bhatia, Claire Cain Miller and Josh Katz, 'Study of elite college admission data suggests being very rich is its own qualification', *New York Times*, 24 July 2023.

11 One beneficiary told the *New York Times* that legacy admissions are 'affirmative action for the rich' (https://tinyurl.com/fxnz42a9).

12 Emma Rowe, 'Counting national school enrolment shares in Australia: the political arithmetic of declining public school enrolment', *Australian Educational Researcher*, 47 (2020): 517–35, table 2, p. 527.

13 Rachel Brown, 'Means test selective parents', *Sydney Morning Herald*, 4 March 2012.

14 Futurity Investment Group, 'The top ten most expensive schools in Australia', blog post, undated, but data for 2022, see https://tinyurl.com/4t9tns8h.

15 Reply to John Broomfield, see 'The public cost of private schools', *The Conversation*, 27 June 2022 (https://tinyurl.com/3ahb4cbr). Elsewhere, after a close study of the history of English and Welsh tax and charity law pertaining to schools, Boden and her colleagues conclude that, in the nineteenth century, granting of tax deductibility of donations to elite schools 'involved the purposive intervention of ruling elites in defence of class privilege' and that reform has been blocked by the power of those linked to the schools. Rebecca Boden, Jane Kenway and Malcolm James, 'Private schools and tax advantage in England and Wales – the *longue durée*', *Critical Studies in Education*, 63/3 (2022): 291–306. On the contemporary politics of tax benefits for private schools in Britain, see Sean Coughlan, 'Labour has backed plans for private schools to lose tax benefits and be "integrated" into the state sector', *BBC News* online, 30 September 2019. A Labour Party spokesman said: 'Of course the establishment will try to defend its privileges.'

16 Susan Ostrander, *Women of the Upper Class*. Philadelphia: Temple University Press, 1984, p. 85.

17 Ilan Wiesel, *Power, Glamour and Angst: Inside Australia's Elite Neighbourhoods*. Singapore: Palgrave Macmillan, 2019, p. 86.

18 Ostrander, *Women of the Upper Class*, p. 85.

19 Jane Kenway, Johannah Fahey, Debbie Epstein, Aaron Koh, Cameron McCarthy and Fazal Rizvi, *Class Choreographies: Elite Schools and Globalization*. London: Palgrave Macmillan, 2017, p. 5.

20 Ibid., p. 244.

21 Quoted by Mike Donaldson and Scott Poynting, *Ruling Class Men: Money, Sex, Power*. Oxford: Peter Lang, 2007, pp. 85, 209.

22 Fahey, Prosser and Shaw consider for elite schools the 'relationship between their "complex sensory and aesthetic environments" and the construction of privilege within and beyond the school gates.' Johannah Fahey, Howard Prosser and Matthew Shaw (eds), *In the Realm of the Senses: Social Aesthetics and the Sensory Dynamics of Privilege*. Singapore: Springer, 2015.

23 Quoted by Jasmine Andersson, 'When my best friends went to private school, our relationship changed forever', *Refinery29*, 4 November 2019.

24 Holmqvist, *Leader Communities*, p. xvii.

25 Kenway et al., *Class Choreographies*, p. 81. After conducting a sexual consent course in a joint class of boys from a low-fee private school from the western suburbs and from one of the Sydney's most elite schools, the teacher observed that the boys from the low-fee school looked upon those from the elite school 'in awe' (personal communication).

26 Green and Kynaston, *Engines of Privilege*, p. 117.

27 Christopher Harris, '"Most schools would be quite scared": inside Sydney's competitive debating scene', *Sydney Morning Herald*, 14 August 2023.

28 Sue Saltmarsh, 'Elite education in the Australian context', in Claire Maxwell and Peter Aggleton (eds), *Elite Education: International Perspectives*. Abingdon: Routledge, 2016.

29 Erving Goffman, 'Symbols of class status', *British Journal of Sociology*, 2/4 (1951): 294–304, at p. 302.

30 Kenway et al., *Class Choreographies*, pp. 14, 80.

31 See https://scots.college/about-scots/our-heritage-and-faith/.

32 See, for example, Old Geelong Grammarians, 'OGG mentoring', https://tinyurl.com/yu7pzs99.

33 Donaldson and Poynting, *Ruling Class Men*, pp. 85–6. Speaking in the school's chapel in 1999, Hawkes told the story of a boy who had 'thumped' a girl because of her greater verbal acuity. He described the frustrated boy as 'an extraordinary victim' because he had been sacrificed on 'the altar of gender equality'. Ibid., p. 88.

33 See 'Tim Fairfax receives medal for service to society', https://tinyurl.com/2p89vadu.

35 '2022 independent schools guide', *Sydney Morning Herald*, advertorial insert, undated. The children themselves are uniformly depicted as attractive, smooth-faced and happy. They are often shown focused contentedly on a scientific experiment or interacting in sociable and collaborative ways. Older boys may be shown on the water in a rowing eight or leaping high on a well-tended rugby field. Outdoor shots depict expansive playing fields, large shady trees and well-tended gardens framing monumental buildings. Wherever possible, the Sydney Harbour Bridge appears in the background. Drew and his colleagues 'consider how the promotional texts of elite private schools in Australia draw upon and contribute to the discursive constitution of childhood happiness as a commodified feature of ideal studenthood.' Christopher Drew et al., 'The joy of privilege: elite private school online promotions and the promise of happiness', in Aaron Koh and Jane Kenway (eds), *Elite Schools: Multiple Geographies of Privilege*. London: Routledge, 2016.

36 Alexandra Allan and Claire Charles, 'Cosmo girls: configurations of class and femininity in elite educational settings,' *British Journal of Sociology of Education*, 35/3 (2014): 333–52, at p. 348,

37 Kenway et al., *Class Choreographies*, p. 84.

38 Ibid., p. 91.

39 Petter Sandgren, *Globalising Eton: A Transnational History of Elite Boarding Schools since 1799*. Thesis, European University Institute, 2017, p. 214.

40 A point made by Wiesel, *Power, Glamour and Angst*, p. 118.

41 Warilla High School, *Parent Newsletter*, May 2007, https://tinyurl.com/2tzwnbce.

42 Old Wesley Collegians (www.owca.net/) hold black-tie dinners in the school's grand dining hall modelled on those of Oxbridge colleges. 'With more than 22,000 members, the OWCA is one huge network. Doors open when OWs reconnect, or meet for the first time. *OWConnect* is the new OW Directory App for your phone and an historic change in OWCA thinking. A brand-new way to connect with all online Alumni. *OWConnect* is the best way to access your OWCA community, to maximise its benefits, to network, or to search for an OW business or service. It's free and with geo positioning, it's global.'

43 Wiesel, *Power, Glamour and Angst*, p. 86.

44 Quoted by Tom Ball, 'Online (old boy) networks just the job for top private schools', *The Times*, 5 October 2019. Tidmarsh added: 'I myself have done property deals in the past where all concerned have been OMs [Old Marlburians]. The common denominator is trust.' The article refers to 'the 30 elite public schools'.

45 Wiesel, *Power, Glamour and Angst*, p. 119.

46 See https://scots.college/about-scots/our-heritage-and-faith/.

47 Jackie Camilleri, 'Young minds, but a global outlook', Independent Schools Guide, *Sydney Morning Herald*, 29 July 2023. 'The internationally minded student of today', she added, 'will lead the world of tomorrow.'

48 Watchable (or perhaps unwatchable) at www.youtube.com/watch?v=lg6QwH5xSHU.

49 Jane Kenway, Diana Langmead and Debbie Epstein, 'Globalizing femininity in elite schools for girls: some paradoxical failures of success', in Agnès van Zanten et al. (eds), *World Yearbook of Education 2015: Elites, Privilege and Excellence: The National and Global Redefinition of Educational Advantage*. Abingdon: Routledge, 2015, pp. 153–66, at p. 155 passim.

50 Ibid., pp. 163–4.

51 Allan and Charles, 'Cosmo girls', p. 346.

52 Kenway, Langmead and Epstein, 'Globalizing femininity in elite schools for girls', p. 160.

53 Jane Kenway, 'Travelling with Bourdieu: elite schools and the cultural logics and limits of global mobility', in L. Adkins, C. Brosnan and S. Threadgold (eds), *Bourdieusian Prospects*. London: Routledge, 2017, pp. 31–48, at p. 40.

54 For a discussion of this complex question, see Kenway et al., *Class Choreographies*, pp. 174–8.

55 Kenway, 'Travelling with Bourdieu', p. 33.

56 Sally Rawsthorne and Jenny Noyes, 'From Sydney Grammar to Silverwater: the criminal life and lonely death of Bennet Schwartz', *Sydney Morning Herald*, 25 March 2022. Note: the 'long fall' expression was used in the headline of the printed version of the paper.

57 Lucy Carroll and Jordan Baker, 'Boys and girls at other schools "involved" in Knox Grammar scandal', *Sydney Morning Herald*, 6 September 2022.

58 Josh Hanrahan and Louise Ayling, 'Boys at $33k-a-year Sydney school mock "poor" suburbs full of "druggos" in another TikTok atrocity', *Daily Mail*, 23 September 2020. Among the Shore boys there was one dissenter who nominated Mosman, because 'all the rich kids live there.'

59 'Lad-speak includes words like "shank" (stabbing) and "eshays" (Pig Latin for a pot-smoking "sesh"), and thus lads as a subculture are associated with criminality.' Stephen Pham, 'Mundane glories', *Going Down Swinging*, 40 (2019): 31–40, at p. 32. See also Rachel Fenner, 'What is an eshay and why would a Perth nightclub ban them?' *Perth Now*, 9 January 2023.

60 Although Pham writes of the effect of these lads or eshays: 'It reminded me of the private school boys who started dressing like lads in the late 2000s, recognising that lads' reputation of being hard gave rich boys licence to behave recklessly in public.' Pham, 'Mundane glories,' p. 32.

61 Alexis Carey, 'Shore School's disgusting past revealed amid muck-up day list scandal', News. com.au, 28 September 2020.

62 Fergus Hunter, '"Spit on homeless man": Shore School year 12s plan crime-filled muck-up day', *Sydney Morning Herald*, 22 September 2020,

63 The full list of dares can be found at www.mamamia.com.au/shore-school-muck-up-day/.

64 See Sue Saltmarsh, 'Disrupting dominant discourses of private schooling', paper presented to the AARE annual conference, Parramatta, 2015.

65 Shore's previous headmaster pushed back against the view that wealth is a character flaw. 'The boys are privileged, and it's not their fault. It's what you do with your opportunities in life that I think you are responsible for.' Jordan Baker, 'Shore headmaster: "The boys are privileged, and it's not their fault"', *Sydney Morning Herald*, 18 August 2019.

66 Jessie Stephens, '"Spit on homeless man": buried in that vile muck up day checklist is a sad grain of truth', www.mamamia.com.au/shore-school-muck-up-day-checklist/.

67 Jane Kenway, 'Rolling in it: the rules of entitlement at wealthy schools for boys', *Gender and Education*, submitted 2023.

68 'For the students who go to Shore,' wrote Jessie Stephens, '... getting arrested as part of muck up day is a joke. A funny story to tell a group of mates around a boardroom table in 25 years.' Stephens, '"Spit on homeless man"'.

69 Holmqvist, *Leader Communities*, p. 51.

70 Hunter, 'Spit on homeless man'.

71 Hanrahan and Ayling, 'Boys at $33k-a-year Sydney school mock "poor" suburbs', comments.

72 Hunter, 'Spit on homeless man'.

73 Raveen Hunjan, 'Child abuse royal commission: Trinity Grammar School students raped other students, inquiry hears', *Sydney Morning Herald*, 20 October 2016.

74 Royal Commission into Institutional Responses to Child Sexual Abuse, *Final Report: Volume 13, Schools* (Commonwealth of Australia, 2017), pp. 137, 139.

75 See also Donaldson and Poynting, *Ruling Class Men*, p. 228.

76 The Royal Commission into Child Sexual Abuse found that sexual abuse has been far more prevalent in private schools, both Catholic and 'independent' (Protestant), attributing the high share to certain institutional factors. 'Factors include concern for a school's reputation and financial interests; hyper-masculine or hierarchical cultures; a sense of being part of a superior and privileged institution; the selection of ex-students for employment; and long-serving principals in governance structures with little or no accountability in the area of student wellbeing and safety' (Royal Commission, p. 11). It added that Trinity Grammar School 'has a culture of breeding its own teachers, which means there is a loyalty to the school among the staff that is beyond normal. This loyalty … promotes a culture of covering up' (p. 151; see also p. 153).

77 Barbara Preston, 'State school kids do better at uni', *The Conversation*, 17 July 2014. Preston writes: 'High pressure, close supervision and narrowly defined learning leave little room for independent, self-motivated learning, and developing the personal and social skills required for success at university.' British researchers have suggested that private school students may do less well at university because they have lower incentives to perform; they are confident these other assets are enough to guarantee them success. See Richard Adams, 'Top state school pupils "get better degrees than those from private schools"', *The Guardian*, 5 November 2015. For the United States, see Chetty, Deming and Friedman, *Diversifying Society's Leaders?*.

78 Sally Larsen and Alexander Forbes, 'Going to private school won't make a difference to your kid's academic scores', *The Conversation*, 21 February 2022.

79 Holmqvist, *Leader Communities*, pp. 217, 222.

80 Ibid., pp. 227–31.

81 Jordan Baker and Nigel Gladstone, '"A complex problem": richest schools claim most HSC disability provisions', *Sydney Morning Herald*, 23 November 2021; Linda Graham, Helen Proctor and Roselyn Dixon, 'How schools avoid enrolling children with disabilities', *The Conversation*, 28 January 2016.

82 Green and Kynaston, *Engines of Privilege*, p. 106.

83 Tom Bateman, 'Independent school students gain extra time for exams', *BBC News online*, 10 February 2017.

84 There is good evidence that private schools gamed the GCSE and A-level marking system during Britain's Covid restrictions in 2021, when teachers were called on to assess students' grades. When exams resumed, the performance of private school students fell sharply. The Conservative chair of the education select committee, Robert Halfon, said: 'It seems the independent sector milked the school-assessed grade system for all it was worth.' Julie Henry, 'Private schools in England accused of "gaming the system" on lockdown exam results', *The Guardian*, 28 August 2022.

85 Jordan Baker, 'NSW uni bosses order review of perfect ATARs after IB students beat James Ruse', *Sydney Morning Herald*, 13 February 2022. MLC School in Sydney boasted that twelve of its forty-nine IB students in 2021 achieved the perfect score of 45, converting to 99.95.

One can only agree with the school's boast that the result was a 'simply staggering outcome'. MLC School, 'IB diploma programme', https://tinyurl.com/2ezpcebh.

86 Scotch College in Perth emphasises its acceptance of and attention to students with dyslexia and channels those students into the IB. 'The International Baccalaureate is more generous than the state-based system, which offers between 25% and 50% additional working time depending on the severity of the disability. In contrast, the state-based system offers an additional 10 minutes for every assessment hour, regardless.' See www.scotch.wa.edu.au /articles/dyslexia-a-long-history-in-education.

87 The public perception that elite schools are cheating was not allayed when the IB scoring system was adjusted to reduce the number of IB students receiving the top grade. Gross distortions persisted. For example, of the twenty-four students opting for the IB at the exclusive Cranbrook School, twenty-one achieved a university entrance score of 98 or higher, and at Redlands school nearly one-third received a score of 99 or higher. Christopher Harris, '"Perfect" scores of 99.95 given to IB students drops by half after conversion process overhaul', *Sydney Morning Herald*, 5 January 2023.

88 Adam Howard and Claire Maxwell, 'Conferred cosmopolitanism: class-making strategies of elite schools across the world', *British Journal of Sociology of Education*, 42/2 (2021): 164–78, at pp. 165, 169.

89 See www.scotch.wa.edu.au/.

90 Newington College (Year 12 fee $39,000) declares: 'It is hoped the Service Learning program will play an important role in the development of our leaders in the College, establishing a very clear link between service and leadership. We believe our Newington graduates will ... be more aware of the responsibility that we all have to look after those less fortunate than ourselves.' Newington College, *Annual Report 2019*, https://tinyurl.com/yuhh9yvr

91 See www.scotch.vic.edu.au/media/229673/Scotch%20College%20Prospectus.pdf.

92 World Expeditions Schools, 'Himalaya school trips & projects'. https://worldexpeditionsschools .com/where-we-go/himalaya. 'Over the next 5 days there'll be plenty of opportunities to engage with the lifestyles of the small Sherpa villages and to interact with local Nepali school students. You will get your hands dirty working side by side with the locals to improve the local school. This will be a real highlight where you will be fully immersed in village life and gain a real sense of personal achievement. Building Khmer house, learning outcome: "Taken outside of their comfort zone to build resilience and independence."'

93 For MLC Year 10 girls, 'the students are ready to go global, travelling to Chiang Mai, Thailand. Girls labour intensively and assist in building roads, playgrounds and classrooms for remote, impoverished communities. Teamwork and collaboration are engendered as girls teach in a Thai orphanage and gain a strong understanding of the people and culture of Thailand' (https://tinyurl.com/3vz34ue3).

94 Allan and Charles, 'Cosmo girls', p. 346.

95 Ibid., p. 343.

96 Joel Windle and Greg Stratton, 'Equity for sale: ethical consumption in a school-choice regime', *Discourse: Studies in the Cultural Politics of Education*, 34/2 (2013): 202–13, at p. 211.

97 Kenway et al., *Class Choreographies*, p. 174.

98 Allan and Charles, 'Cosmo girls', p. 346.

99 Jane Godfrey et al., 'The "volunteer tourist gaze": commercial volunteer tourists' interactions with, and perceptions of, the host community in Cusco, Peru', *Current Issues in Tourism*, 23/20 (2020): 2555–71.

100 Kenway et al., *Class Choreographies*, p. 222.

101 Allan and Charles, 'Cosmo girls', p. 343.

102 See www.wesleycollege.edu.au/.

103 See www.ggs.vic.edu.au/explore/our-anglican-tradition/.

104 SCEGGS, 'Prospectus', https://tinyurl.com/y4h5jtr7. Against the grain, Scots College appears to cleave resolutely to its original mission, believing that 'young men discover true wisdom through reverence for God and faith in Jesus Christ' (https://scots.college/about -scots/).

105 Kenway et al., *Class Choreographies*, p. 163.

106 Ibid., p. 168.

107 See www.ibo.org/programmes/diploma-programme/curriculum/.

108 Paul Tarc, 'International Baccalaureate: meanings, uses and tensions in a globalizing world', *Elsevier International Encyclopedia of Education*, 4th edn, Oxford: Elsevier, 2022, pp. 344–54.

109 Catherine Doherty, Mu Li and Paul Shield, 'Planning mobile futures: the border artistry of IB diploma choosers', *British Journal of Sociology of Education*, 3/6 (2009): 757–71.

110 MLC School, 'IB diploma programme'.

111 Kenway et al., *Class Choreographies*, p. 185.

112 Sandgren, *Globalising Eton*, p. 217.

113 Kenway et al., *Class Choreographies*, p. 229.

114 See www.roundsquare.org/.

115 See www.roundsquare.org/membership/what-is-expected/.

116 Sandgren, *Globalising Eton*, p. 185.

117 Clive Hamilton, 'Active voices: fighting for a change in climate', *Meanjin*, December 2021.

118 Kenway et al., *Class Choreographies*, pp. 242–3.

119 Newington College, 'A message from the head of Lindfield', *Prep Talk Bulletin*, 29 June 2018, https://tinyurl.com/spzvzv4j. Privilege, he says, is a problem only when it becomes entitlement, the difference being gratitude.

120 Pierre Bourdieu, 'Symbolic capital and social classes', *Journal of Classical Sociology*, 13/2 (2013): 292–303, at p. 299. The hollowness of elite schools' claim to the high ground of virtue has been forcefully expressed by the *Sydney Morning Herald*'s education reporter Jordan Baker, who alludes to political blackmail as one of their vices. 'The chasm between the social justice of the schools' religious faith and the opulence of their facilities grows ever wider, while political leaders are too worried about a backlash to act on the obvious moral travesty.' Jordan Baker, 'Private school funding exposes the nation's lack of heart', *Sydney Morning Herald*, 2 July 2022.

121 Jane Kenway and Michael Lazarus, 'Elite schools, class disavowal and the mystification of virtues', *Social Semiotics*, 27/3 (2017): 265–75.

122 There is one association in each state, and they are brought together in the federal independent schools lobby group.

123 Helen Davidson, '"You're almost instantly disadvantaged": Indigenous students on their schools away from home', *The Guardian*, 4 August 2017. See also Adam Carey, 'Off country: private schools' tough lessons on Indigenous education', *The Age*, 10 July 2022.

124 Marnie O'Bryan, *Boarding and Australia's First Peoples: Understanding How Residential Schooling Shapes Lives*, Singapore: Springer, 2021.

125 Ibid., pp. 77, 73.

126 Ibid., p. 74. A boarding house master at an elite school recounted the pressure from the headmaster on an Indigenous student to take on a leadership position in the school, so that he could 'get around and shake everyone's hand'. The boy resisted, and when he (the master) met with the boy, 'he was just "I don't want to do it", and he sat in this meeting shaking, crying' (ibid.).

127 Ibid., p. 77.

128 The quoted phrase is from Kenway et al., *Class Choreographies*, pp. 242–3.

129 SCEGGS, 'Prospectus'. Jane Kenway has pointed out that, in the UK, in return for their charitable status, private schools are expected to make their facilities available for public use.

130 Lucy Carroll, 'Cranbrook unveils $125m revamp as private schools compete in building boom', *Sydney Morning Herald*, 15 October 2022.

131 'These buildings', the school declared in a flourish of elite globalist rhetoric, 'connect us to place and to people, and reflecting the global outlook of Cranbrook, face the Heads [of Sydney Harbour], creating and empowering our students as global citizens of tomorrow' ('Cranbrook School official opening', 25 October 2022, https://tinyurl.com/3tmbt7fm).

132 On the destructive effects of neoliberalism in universities, see Jane Kenway, Rebecca Boden and Johannah Fahey, 'Seeking the necessary "resources of hope" in the neoliberal university', in Margaret Thornton (ed.), *Through a Glass Darkly: The Social Sciences Look at the Neoliberal University*. Canberra: ANU Press, 2015.

133 Katy Swalwell, '"With great power comes great responsibility": privileged students' conception of social justice-oriented citizenship', *Democracy & Education*, 21/1 (2013): 1–11, at p. 2.

134 Kenway et al., *Class Choreographies*, pp. 200–1, 208, 213.

135 Goffman, 'Symbols of class status', p. 303.

136 A teacher at an expensive private school in Sydney's eastern suburbs said: '… what does the majority of an eastern suburbs population of students want to do? Train for uni … probably medicine or law … even non-academic white kids at [that school] are a bit of an underclass. If you were to say … in Year 9 or Year 10 I'm thinking of doing an apprenticeship – you'd probably be politely recommended to try elsewhere.' O'Bryan, *Boarding and Australia's First Peoples*, p. 72.

137 Jane Kenway, 'The work of desire: elite schools' multi-scalar markets', in Claire Maxwell et al. (eds), *Elite Education and Internationalism*. London: Palgrave, 2018.

138 George Variyan, 'Missionaries or mercenaries? How teachers in elite private schools embrace privilege', *British Journal of Sociology of Education*, 40/8 (2019): 1204–18.

139 Ibid., p. 1215.

Chapter 6 Sites of Privilege

1 The movements for women's rights, Black rights and other minority rights have had many victories. In the United States, an authoritative study of 'multiple indicators of gender inequality for the period of 1970 to 2018' shows 'dramatic progress in movement toward gender equality'. However, it adds, 'there was still substantial gender inequality favoring men' (Paula England, Andrew Levine and Emma Mishel, 'Progress toward gender equality in the United States has slowed or stalled', *PNAS* [Proceedings of the National Academy of Sciences], 117/13 (2020): 6990–7). On racial equality, the US Congress Joint Economic Committee provided a helpful overview in 2020. 'Over the past half-century, Black Americans have made substantial social and economic progress, gaining political rights that long had been denied to them, entering professions from which they had been blocked and largely overcoming centuries of overt racism and oppression. … However, these very visible signs of improvement mask deep inequities that relegate tens of millions of Black Americans to second-class status' ('The economic state of black America in 2020', https://tinyurl.com/334362r3).

2 On billionaires buying sporting clubs, see Frank Chaparro, 'Billionaires are buying sports teams for different reasons than they used to', *Insider*, 26 October 2017, https://tinyurl.com/4axbnbwp.

3 James Bloodworth, *The Myth of Meritocracy*. London: Biteback, 2016, pp. 53–4.

4 Cate Blanchett attended Ivanhoe Girls' Grammar School and then Methodist Ladies' College; Hugh Jackman attended Knox Grammar; Heath Ledger attended Guildford Grammar School in Perth; Rebel Wilson went to Tara Anglican School for Girls; Eric Bana

attended Penleigh and Essendon Grammar School; Hugo Weaving attended Knox Grammar; Joel Edgerton attended The Hills Grammar School; Simon Baker attended Trinity Catholic College in Lismore.

5 Paul Garvey, 'AFL coach pilloried for "elitist" remarks', *The Australian*, 24–5 July 2021.

6 Of the 300, 170 are public schools and 130 are non-government (Legislative Assembly of Western Australia, Public Accounts Committee, *Report 17: More than Just a Game*, November 2020, https://tinyurl.com/2uvak9nh).

7 Disconcertingly, the top ten 'most liked' comments by readers under the news story all defended the coach and his argument that the club is better off choosing recruits from elite schools and stable families.

8 Stefan Szymanski and Tim Wigmore, *Crickonomics: The Anatomy of Modern Cricket*. London: Bloomsbury, 2022, pp. 5–9.

9 In England, more bowlers come from state schools because bowling is less dependent on coaching and more on genetics (height and the ability to bowl fast), which may not be apparent until boys are eighteen or so and have left school. Australia's current crop of fast bowlers – Pat Cummins, Scott Boland, Josh Hazelwood and Mitchell Starc – are all well over 6 foot. Cummins attended the expensive St Paul's Grammar School in Sydney (year 12 fees around $20,000) and Boland attended a private school with modest fees, while Hazelwood and Starc attended public schools.

10 Tom Heyden and Alice McConnell, 'Private or state: where do professional sportspeople go to school?', *BBC News Magazine*, 14 February 2013.

11 See www.harrowschool.org.uk/learning-2/sport.

12 Sutton Trust and Social Mobility Commission, *Elitist Britain 2019: The Educational Backgrounds of Britain's Leading People*, 2019.

13 Ibid., p. 6.

14 Bloodworth, *The Myth of Meritocracy*, pp. 53–4.

15 Szymanski and Wigmore, *Crickonomics*, p. 51.

16 Jake Niall, 'How private schools have taken over the AFL', *The Age*, 23 November 2019.

17 'Pathways for elite athletes at Knox', https://tinyurl.com/27yhdhnv. The BBL cricket star Chris Green attended Knox Grammar (https://tinyurl.com/cu5eyva5).

18 Jacob Saulwick, 'With another pool closed, Sydney's councils struggle to keep city cool', *Sydney Morning Herald*, 6 January 2019. Several swimming champions attended expensive private schools. Kieran Perkins attended Brisbane Boys School and Mack Horton attended Caulfield Grammar.

19 James Tompsett and Chris Knoester, 'The making of a college athlete: high school experiences, socioeconomic advantages, and the likelihood of playing college sports', *Sociology of Sport Journal*, 39/2 (2021): 129–40.

20 Jeff Grabmeier, 'Want to play college sports? A wealthy family helps', *Ohio State News*, 30 August 2021, https://news.osu.edu/want-to-play-college-sports-a-wealthy-family-helps/.

21 Lamiat Sabin, 'CPS passed file on alleged cash-for-honours scandal involving King Charles's charity', *The Independent*, 20 November 2022.

22 Jacqueline Maley and Nigel Gladstone, 'Want an Order of Australia? It helps to be rich, powerful and male', *Good Weekend* [*Sydney Morning Herald* magazine], 23 January 2021.

23 Emma Connors, 'What an Order of Australia means and how to get one', *Australian Financial Review*, 25 January 2019.

24 Maley and Gladstone, 'Want an Order of Australia?'

25 Connors, 'What an Order of Australia means and how to get one'.

26 Maley and Gladstone, 'Want an Order of Australia?'

27 Ibid.

28 Ibid.

29 We consulted *Who's Who* and searched the internet for biographical information.

30 An analysis in 2010 of the 435 people who have received the top awards since 1975 showed that alumni of elite private schools have a huge advantage. Victoria's two most expensive schools, Scotch College and Geelong Grammar, boast of nineteen and seventeen alumni respectively receiving top awards. In Sydney it is a similar story, although academically selective state schools performed well. Jewel Topsfield, 'Ties that bind prove a private education has its awards', *The Age*, 4 December 2010.

31 The names of the schools attended by all but two of the sixty-four recipients for the earlier period could be established. In the more recent period, we were able to determine only forty-eight of the schools attended by the sixty-three recipients. Some recipients have become shy about naming their schools.

32 Alison Branley and Eliza Borrello, 'Dyson Heydon on panel that awarded PM Tony Abbott Rhodes scholarship, documents show', *ABC Online*, 17 August 2015.

33 McKinsey is said to have recruited three of the seven Australian Rhodes scholars in 1986 (Lisa Pryor, 'Rhodes a luxury brand bogans can't buy', *Sydney Morning Herald*, 25 August 2007). Peter Fray, 'The Rhodes scholarship, its birthday and an academic row', *The Age*, 2 July 2003. See also Justine Landis-Hanley, 'Sydney law student one of 10 women in NSW history to become Rhodes scholar', *Sydney Morning Herald*, 4 December 2017.

34 'The stereotype is a male who plays rugby and wants to be PM', said Marnie Hughes-Warrington, who oversaw the Australian selection system, in 2018. Aaron Patrick, 'The new Rhodes Scholarship doesn't require sport or a private school', *Australian Financial Review*, 21 May 2018. 'When Prime Minister Malcolm Turnbull was selected in 1978, his school, Sydney Grammar, had produced 25 per cent of the state's Rhodes Scholars, according to his biography, *Born to Rule*. … Today, more than half of all applicants for the scholarship in Australia are from non-Catholic private schools, even though independent schools only have 14.5 per cent of the student population.'

35 Michael T. Nietzel, 'The U.S. Rhodes scholars for 2023 have been announced', *Forbes*, 13 November 2022, https://tinyurl.com/5n8v694v.

36 In summary, 'Candidates are selected on the basis of outstanding intellect, character, leadership, and commitment to service. The Rhodes Scholarships support students who demonstrate strong propensity to emerge as leaders for the world's future' (www.miragenews .com/rhodes-scholar-on-mission-to-curb-domestic-violence/).

37 See www.quadeducationgroup.com/blog/how-to-become-a-rhodes-scholar.

38 Ibid.

39 Aaron Patrick, 'The new Rhodes scholarship doesn't require sport or a private school', *Australian Financial Review*, 21 May 2018.

40 In the United States, attempts have been made to open the application process to students from disadvantaged backgrounds. They are asked to recount an instance of overcoming obstacles in their lives, providing an opportunity for such students to recount the challenges they faced in order to star academically, a process that invites biographical fabrication. Jerry Oppenheimer and Isabel Vincent, 'Uni student loses scholarship after allegedly lying on her application', News.com.au and *New York Post*, 13 January 2022.

41 Data for Tasmania and Western Australia are available online; the data for Queensland have been kindly provided by Professor Peter Kanowski, the secretary of the Australia Rhodes Trust. The Tasmanian data do not include the schools attended by the Rhodes scholars, so they had to be found by other means. In three cases, they could not be found.

42 Over the last decade, 2013–22, it remained 41 per cent. Among Tasmanian recipients, 38 per cent were women in both the first two and the second two decades.

43 We classified those with 2022 Year 12 day-school fees in excess of $20,000 per annum as high, those with fees of $10,000 to $20,000 as medium and those with fees less than $10,000 as low. Elsewhere in this study, Sydney and Melbourne schools were considered high fee if their fees exceeded $30,000 per annum.

44 This change over the two periods was heavily influenced by Tasmania, which saw a sharp reduction in state school recipients (from 67 to 37 per cent) and a sharp rise in high-fee school recipients (up from 22 to 63 per cent). This fact points to a strong need for this analysis to be performed for all states and the ACT.

45 Data on enrolments in private secondary schools by fee level are not available. However, a rough approximation is possible using numbers of schools rather than enrolments. High-fee schools (almost all non-Catholic) account for around 10 per cent of all secondary private schools, using our classification of high fee. In Melbourne they account for around 12 per cent of all private secondary schools (see the online Private School News list for Melbourne). In Sydney, the figure is around 8 per cent, in Brisbane around 5 per cent, and in Perth around 11 per cent (see the online Private School News lists for Sydney, Brisbane and Perth). Non-government secondary schools accounted for 45 per cent of all secondary schools in 2022 (up from 42 per cent in 2004). See www.abs.gov.au/statistics/people/education/schools /2022, table 33a (Lucy Carroll and Christopher Harris, 'Parents flock to private schools amid public system exodus', *Sydney Morning Herald*, 15 February 2023, https://tinyurl.com /2xa89rec).

46 Julia Baird, 'Privilege still protects the violent from the consequences of their behaviour', *Sydney Morning Herald*, 2 October 2021.

47 Boulten has been described in the media thus: 'When Sydney's wealthy and powerful wind up in court there are a select few legal minds they turn to. These are the 12 brightest legal eagles gracing the courts in 2021' (https://tinyurl.com/6326hf86).

48 The judgement can be read at https://tinyurl.com/4we72czp. A year later, twenty students from Knox Grammar were disciplined for using a chat room to 'share racist and homophobic videos, messages and rantings on violent misogyny.' Lucy Carroll and Jordan Baker, 'Boys and girls at other schools "involved" in Knox Grammar scandal', *Sydney Morning Herald*, 6 September 2022.

49 Sutton Trust and Social Mobility Commission, *Elitist Britain 2019*, p. 6.

50 Susan Navarro Smelcer, *Supreme Court Justices: Demographic Characteristics, Professional Experience, and Legal Education, 1789–2010*. Washington, DC: Congressional Research Service, 2010.

51 Authors' calculations.

52 Michele Benedetto Neitz, 'Socioeconomic bias in the judiciary', *61 Cleveland State Law Review*, 137 (2013).

53 Ibid., p. 3.

54 Quoted by Rosemary Hunter, 'More than just a different face? Judicial diversity and decision-making', *Current Legal Problems*, 68/1 (2015): 119–41.

55 Ruth Frankenberg, 'Growing up white: feminism, racism and the social geography of childhood', *Feminist Review*, 45 (1993): 51–84.

56 For a perceptive analysis, see Lucille A. Jewel, 'Bourdieu and American legal education: how law schools reproduce social stratification and class hierarchy', *56 Buffalo Law Review*, 1155 (2008). The quote is from p. 1205.

57 Louise Ashley and Laura Empson, 'Differentiation and discrimination: understanding social class and social exclusion in leading law firms', *Human Relations*, 66/2 (2013): 219–44.

58 Andrew Leigh, 'Behind the bench: associates in the High Court of Australia', *Alternative Law Journal 291*, 25/6 (2000).

59 Katharine Young, 'Open chambers: High Court associates and Supreme Court clerks compared', *Melbourne University Law Review 646*, 31/2 (2007).

60 See https://justinian.com.au/bloggers/moulds-remain-unbroken.html; see also Marianna Papadakis, 'The depressing truth for law graduates: you may have to be a secretary', *Australian Financial Review*, 27 November 2015.

61 Pierre Bourdieu and Jean-Claude Passeron, *Reproduction in Education, Society and Culture*. London: Sage, 1990, p. 162.

62 Melissa Coade, 'Elite have "overwhelming" advantage in legal recruitment, data shows', *Lawyers Weekly*, 1 March 2017.

63 Mark Peel and Janet McCalman, *Who Went Where in Who's Who 1988: The Schooling of the Australian Elite*. Parkville, Vic.: University of Melbourne, 1992.

64 Geoff Maslin, 'Schooling the elite of the land', *The Age*, 31 July 1992.

65 Although this might be nuanced by noting Piketty's case for the dominance in Western democracies of two rival elites, the wealthy 'Merchants' on the neoliberal right and the highly educated 'Brahmins' on the left. The latter have lost faith in serious redistributive policies (especially progressive taxation) and concentrate on advancing cultural diversity. As we see it, both elites have won; there are fewer constraints on wealth accumulation and there is greater cultural diversity. What has been lost is social justice.

66 On the first claim, see chapter 6, note 1.

Chapter 7 The Power of Giving

1 Hayley Dixon, 'Extinction Rebellion funded by charity set up by one of Britain's richest men', *The Telegraph*, 10 October 2019; Megan Agnew and Laith Al-Khalaf, 'Just Stop Oil bankrolled by fossil fuel heiress whose cash pays activists to protest', *The Times*, 22 October 2022. Hohn is a complex character. A vegetarian with a modest lifestyle, he is a major donor to progressive causes, donations funded from his hedge fund, owned by a company registered in a tax haven.

2 One of the authors, Clive Hamilton, was a beneficiary of Kantor family giving when he was executive director of the Australia Institute.

3 Judging 'progressive' giving against system-sustaining giving is, of course, a grey area. Much elite philanthropy in the United States that is described as progressive or similar (see https://tinyurl.com/yyubdf6k) does not challenge the politico-economic system but aims to reform it to make it stronger.

4 They are the Paul Ramsay Foundation, Andrew Forrest's Minderoo Foundation, the Lowy Foundation and the Yajilarra Foundation set up by conservative Christians Craig and Di Winkler; Danielle Kutchel, 'Australia's mega-rich don't give enough', *Pro Bono Australia*, 29 August 2022, https://tinyurl.com/3fv72j3h). The Winklers support the Family First Party and the Australian Christian Lobby (John Stensholt, 'True leaders 2016: Di and Craig Winkler are "not your traditional power couple"', *Financial Review*, 8 August 2016, https://tinyurl.com/28mbnvzj).

5 Mairi Maclean, Charles Harvey, Ruomei Yang and Frank Mueller, 'Elite philanthropy in the United States and United Kingdom in the new age of inequalities', *International Journal of Management Reviews*, 23 (2021): 330–52, at p. 343.

6 Paul Schervish, 'Major donors, major motives: the people and purposes behind major gifts', *New Directions for Philanthropic Fundraising*, 47 (2005): 59–87, at p. 60.

7 Ibid., pp. 62–3.

8 Ibid., p. 61. Earlier, Schervish defined hyper-agency this way: the 'admixture of self-confident disposition and material capacity to be founders of the world in which they reside, from businesses to government, and from personal homes to social philanthropy.' Paul Schervish,

'The modern Medici: patterns, motivations, and giving strategies of the wealthy', paper presented at the University of Southern California, 2000, p. 2.

9 Ibid., pp. 8–9.

10 Schervish, 'Major donors, major motives', pp. 66, 64.

11 Maclean et al., 'Elite philanthropy in the United States and United Kingdom in the new age of inequalities', p. 343.

12 Julia Crawford, 'Does Bill Gates have too much influence in the WHO?', *Swissinfo*, 10 May 2021.

13 Megan Twohey and Nicholas Kulish, 'Bill Gates, the virus and the quest to vaccinate the world', *New York Times*, 23 November 2020.

14 Quoted by Crawford, 'Does Bill Gates have too much influence in the WHO?'.

15 Lindsey McGoey, *No Such Thing as a Free Gift: The Gates Foundation and the Price of Philanthropy*. London: Verso, 2015.

16 Twohey and Kulish, 'Bill Gates, the virus and the quest to vaccinate the world'.

17 Ibid.

18 Ibid.

19 Mairi Maclean, Charles Harvey and Gerhard Kling, 'Pathways to power: class, hyper-agency and the French corporate elite', *Organization Studies*, 35/6 (2014): 825–55.

20 Jane Cadzow, 'Just a country boy', *Good Weekend* [*Sydney Morning Herald* magazine], 2 July 2022.

21 Ibid.

22 https://www.walkfree.org/who-we-are/. For a puff piece on Grace, 'a 25-year-old firebrand who is blazing a humanitarian trail', see Gail Williams, 'Grace Forrest's fight for a better world', *PerthNow*, 4 December 2018.

23 In 2017, a prominent politician, Kristina Keneally, congratulated Forrest for making the biggest philanthropic donation ever in Australia but suggested 'perhaps Andrew Forrest's companies could have just paid more tax.' Kristina Keneally, 'Twiggy Forrest's philanthropy is great: but he could have just paid more tax', *The Guardian*, 24 May 2017.

24 Mindaroo Foundation, quoted by Zurina Simm, *Philanthropy and Social Justice: Examining the Social Impact of Grant-Making by Philanthropic Institutions in Australia*, PhD thesis, University of Adelaide, 2020, p. 30.

25 'Vatican accuses Andrew "Twiggy" Forrest of exploiting Pope Francis over anti-slavery campaign', *ABC News online*, 5 August 2015.

26 Janie A. Chuang, 'Giving as governance? Philanthrocapitalism and modern-day slavery abolitionism', *UCLA Law Review*, 62/6 (2015): 1516–56.

27 Walk Free Foundation, *The Global Slavery Index 2018*. In his preface, Andrew Forrest declares: '"Over there" doesn't exist in this fight – we must all work as one to end slavery for good.'

28 Anne T. Gallagher, 'What's wrong with the Global Slavery Index?', *Anti-Trafficking Review*, 8 (2017): 90–112.

29 The Walk Free Foundation declares, 'we fight for the silenced to regain their voices' (www.walkfree.org).

30 Andy Beckett, '*No Such Thing as a Free Gift: The Gates Foundation and the Price of Philanthropy* by Linsey McGoey – review', *The Guardian*, 24 October 2015. TED talks have also been criticised along these lines, as 'a networking event for the rich and powerful' behind a veneer of progressivism (Dylan Matthews, 'Meet the folk hero of Davos: the writer who told the rich to stop dodging taxes', *Vox*, 30 January 2019, https://tinyurl.com/2p9jr9v4).

31 Rutger Bregman, in Matthews, 'Meet the folk hero of Davos'. Bregman told the Davos gathering: 'just pay your taxes.'

32 Matthew Bishop and Michael Green, 'Philanthrocapitalism rising', *Society*, 52/6 (2015): 541–8, at p. 541.

33 Ibid., pp. 542–3.

34 It should be noted that some among the super-rich, such as Bill Gates, Warren Buffett and George Soros, have publicly supported higher taxes on the rich (Taylor Nicole Rogers and Juliana Kaplan, 'Democrats are set to unveil a new billionaire's tax and some of the wealthiest Americans are glad', *Insider*, 26 October 2021, https://tinyurl.com/5n7btsvv). Elon Musk strongly opposed a mooted wealth tax, saying that entrepreneurs like him, and not the government, were best placed to reallocate wealth (Joseph Zeballos-Roig, 'Elon Musk rips Democrats' billionaire-tax plan that could slap him with a $10 billion annual bill', *Insider*, 26 October 2021, https://tinyurl.com/4mhr8wup). Against the trend among the American ultra-rich to make huge donations, Musk gives nothing (Niall McCarthy, '2020's biggest charitable donations', *Forbes*, 7 January 2021, https://tinyurl.com/yufhdwuj).

35 McGoey, *No Such Thing as a Free Gift*, p. 20.

36 Larissa Dubecki, 'The national sport that's not very sporting', *The Age*, 9 February 2007. 'You can do bad things in the billions and wipe it out with gifts in the millions' (Paul Constant, 'Ultrawealthy Americans want you to think their philanthropy will change the world', *Insider*, 9 October 2021, https://tinyurl.com/4793d5sa).

37 McGoey, *No Such Thing as a Free Gift*, p. 20.

38 David Rieff, *The Reproach of Hunger: Food, Justice and Money in the Twenty-First Century*. London: Verso, 2015, p. 229.

39 Jeanine Cunningham and Michael Dreiling, 'Elite networks for environmental philanthropy: shaping environmental agendas in the twenty-first century', *Environmental Sociology*, 7 (2021): 351–67.

40 Simm, *Philanthropy and Social Justice*.

41 Ibid., p. 31.

42 For example, Laurie Bennett, 'Billionaires channel millions to think tanks', *Forbes*, 4 February 2012; Sharita Forrest, 'Wealthy donors, think tanks major influences on education policy, study says', *Illinois News Bureau*, 11 March 2016. Conservative American trusts have donated substantial funds to right-wing think tanks in Britain, especially the Centre for Policy Exchange, the Institute of Economic Affairs and the Adam Smith Institute. See Rob Evans et al., 'The US donors who gave generously to rightwing UK groups', *The Guardian*, 29 November 2019.

43 Mike Seccombe, 'IPA has lost all funding from ASX 100', *Saturday Paper*, 1–7 October 2022.

44 See https://grattan.edu.au/about/supporters/.

45 In 2017, the conservative Turnbull government came up with a novel way of putting pressure on charities and NGOs with more radical agendas by appointing Gary Johns to head the charities regulator. As an employee of the right-wing Institute for Public Affairs, Johns for years led a vigorous campaign to shut down the advocacy work of charities and silence non-profits that challenged the conservative government's policies. His resignation in 2022 was greeted as an end on the 'war on charities' (Christopher Knaus, 'Resignation of Gary Johns from Australian charities regulator ends Liberals' war on sector, Labor says', *The Guardian*, 3 June 2022).

46 Danielle Faber and Debbie McCarthy, 'Breaking the funding barriers: philanthropic activism in support of the environmental justice movement', in Faber and McCarthy (eds), *Foundations for Social Change: Critical Perspectives on Philanthropy and Popular Movements*. Lanham, MD: Rowman & Littlefield, 2005, pp. 175–209, at p. 177.

47 J. Craig Jenkins, Jason T. Carmichael, Robert J. Brulle and Heather Boughton, 'Foundation funding of the environmental movement', *American Behavioral Scientist*, 61/13 (2018): 1640–57, at p. 1654.

48 See Robert J. Brulle, Galen Hall, Loredana Loy and Kennedy Schell-Smith, 'Obstructing

action: foundation funding and US climate change counter-movement organizations', *Climatic Change*, 166/17 (2021).

49 Cunningham and Dreiling, 'Elite networks for environmental philanthropy', p. 14. Nonetheless, alternative discourses, especially environmental justice, received over 5 per cent of grants in 2000 (Jenkins, Carmichael, Brulle and Boughton, 'Foundation funding of the environmental movement').

50 Tim Bartley, 'How foundations shape social movements: the construction of an organizational field and the rise of forest certification', *Social Problems*, 54/3 (2007): 229–55.

51 Robert Winnett and James Kirkup, 'George Osborne: I'm going after the wealthy tax dodgers', *The Telegraph*, 9 April 2012; 'Wealthy abuse charity donations to cut tax, says No. 10', 10 April 2012, www.bbc.com/news/uk-politics-17664893.

52 Mairi Maclean and Charles Harvey, '"Give it back, George": network dynamics in the philanthropic field', *Organization Studies*, 37/3 (2016): 399–423. See also Maclean et al., 'Elite philanthropy in the United States and United Kingdom'.

53 'Wealthy abuse charity donations to cut tax, says No. 10'.

54 Maclean and Harvey, 'Give it back, George', p. 416,

55 Elizabeth Cham, *Trustee Companies: Their Role in Australian Philanthropy*, PhD thesis, University of Technology Sydney, 2016.

56 Australian Government, The Treasury, *Improving the integrity of Prescribed Private Funds*, discussion paper, November 2008, https://tinyurl.com/5x83utxv.

57 Philanthropy Australia, *Giving Trends and Opportunities*, 2022.

58 This secrecy in part explains why elite philanthropy in Australia has received so little scholarly attention compared to that in the United States.

59 Australian Government, The Treasury, *Improving the integrity of Prescribed Private Funds*.

60 Ibid., pp. 5, 6.

61 Quoted by Cham, *Trustee Companies*, p. 140.

62 Ibid., pp. 148–9.

63 Maclean et al., 'Elite philanthropy in the United States and United Kingdom', p. 342.

64 Brock Colyar et al., 'Who was Jeffrey Epstein calling?' *Intelligencer*, 22 July 2019.

65 Ibid. Stephen Hawking visited Epstein's private island (nicknamed 'Paedophile Island'). Summers's tenure at Harvard overlapped with what the magazine has called 'Harvard's love affair with Epstein'. Epstein is believed to have donated $6.5 million to the university.

66 Ibid. Whatever their public statements about Epstein now, and many have insisted their contact with him was minimal and that they did not like him, they did not call out his money-for-credibility schemes or his intellectual pretensions; they played the game and took the rewards.

67 He added, 'I don't feel tarnished in any way by my relationship with Jeffrey; I feel raised by it.' Krauss was later dismissed from his job after sexual misconduct allegations. See Alexandra Wolfe, 'Jeffrey Epstein's society friends close ranks', *Daily Beast*, 1 April 2011.

68 Colyar et al., 'Who was Jeffrey Epstein calling?'.

69 Leland Nally, 'I called everyone in Jeffrey Epstein's little black book', *Mother Jones*, 9 October 2020.

70 Adam Rogers, 'Jeffrey Epstein and the power of networks', *Wired*, 27 August 2019.

71 Ibid.

72 On the black book, see Nally, 'I called everyone in Jeffrey Epstein's little black book'.

73 Emily Flitter and James Stewart, 'Bill Gates met with Jeffrey Epstein many times, despite his past', *New York Times*, 12 October 2019. Gates later said that he 'didn't realise that by having those meetings it would be seen as giving [Epstein] credibility', which seems astonishingly naive for someone in his position. See also 'The links between Jeffrey Epstein and Bill Gates explained', *The Week*, 3 May 2022.

74 Colyar et al., 'Who was Jeffrey Epstein calling?'.

75 Colleen Flaherty, 'Pinker, Epstein, Soldier, Spy', *Inside Higher Education*, 16 July 2019.

76 Kylar Loussikian, 'Arts companies are recruiting corporate gurus', *The Australian*, 1 May 2021.

77 Gwen Moore et al., 'Elite interlocks in three U.S. sectors: nonprofit, corporate, and government', *Social Science Quarterly*, 83/3 (2002): 726–44.

78 Luna Glucksberg, *Gendering the Elites: An Ethnographic Approach to Elite Women's Lives and the Re-production of Inequality*, LSE International Inequalities Institute Working paper 7, October 2016.

79 Linda Morris, 'Secrets of giving: meet the philanthropists helping revive Sydney's arts and culture institutions', *Sydney Morning Herald*, Spectrum, 9 April 2022.

80 Carrie Cousins, 'What is a giving circle and why should nonprofits care?', *Give*, 20 January 2021, https://tinyurl.com/4chthj25.

81 The late Neil Belnaves 'wanted to be in the driver's seat with you', recalls the NGA director Nick Mitzevich. 'He was the one who wrote the cheques but was happy to contribute to strategy and game plans …' (Morris, 'Secrets of giving').

82 Anna Schlia, 'Five questions to uncover donor motivations', 15 September 2021, https://grahampelton.com/insights/donor-motivations. In the UK, one business, named Awards Intelligence, offers bespoke advice on how to get a knighthood or damehood (see https://tinyurl.com/3my2cyw6).

83 See https://www.mca.com.au/get-involved/mca-next/; Morris, 'Secrets of giving'.

84 Morris, 'Secrets of giving'. Brian Sherman died in 2022.

85 Mairi Maclean and Charles Harvey, 'Crafting philanthropic identities', in Andrew D. Brown (ed.), *The Oxford Handbook of Identities in Organizations*. Oxford: Oxford University Press, 2020.

86 Ian Birrell, 'He's taken millions from dictators and cosied up to warlords', *Daily Mail*, 12 January 2013.

87 Maclean et al., 'Elite philanthropy in the United States and United Kingdom', p. 342.

88 Maclean and Harvey, 'Crafting philanthropic identities'.

89 Cadzow, 'Just a country boy'.

90 See https://tinyurl.com/4kpnce74.

91 Mario Christodoulou and Stephen Long, 'Fortescue helped fund Wirlu-Murra Yindjibarndi Aboriginal elders' campaign against mine land owners', *ABC Four Corners* online, 28 July 2015.

92 'Pilbara native title case: the fight to decide if Fortescue pays compensation to Indigenous owners', *The Guardian*, 27 August 2023.

93 Julie-Anne Sprague, 'Andrew Forrest applies business know-how to philanthropic causes', *AFR Magazine*, 27 April 2018.

94 In the United States, Smith & Wesson, manufacturer of an AR-15 style semi-automatic rifle used in a number of school massacres, contributes to children's charities. According to the NRA, gun companies 'often find ways to give back and donate generously to all types of causes.' See www.nrablog.com/articles/2015/7/firearms-companies-who-give-back/.

95 John Heathershaw et al., *The UK's Kleptocracy Problem*. London: Chatham House, 2021, https://tinyurl.com/mvm7pyb9

96 In Australia, a billionaire accused of serious wrongdoing has been following the playbook. He has been a prodigious donor to political parties, with senior politicians publicly defending his good character. And he has become a generous donor to prestigious institutions and venerated charities, winning praise from respected public figures. He has sued news organisations that published articles exploring his background, with a chilling effect, not least on us.

97 Owen Jones, 'We don't want billionaires' charity. We want them to pay their taxes', *The*

Guardian, 27 October 2018. For Bono's net worth, see Garrett Parker, 'How Bono achieved a net worth of $700 million', 10 April 2023, https://moneyinc.com/how-bono-net-worth/.

98 Mark Sweney, 'Jeff Bezos vows to give away most of fortune – and hands Dolly Parton $100m', *The Guardian*, 15 November 2022.

99 Rubén Gaztambide-Fernández and Adam Howard, 'Social justice, deferred complicity and the moral plight of the wealthy', *Democracy & Education*, 21/1 (2013): 1–4.

100 A study of the CEO Sleepout found: 'Besides affecting CEOs on an emotional level, many reported taking practical measures to change things in their companies to prevent homelessness.' Jacki Montgomery and Alla Khan, 'Take heart, charity stunts can make CEOs better people', *The Conversation*, 21 June 2018.

101 Jason Blaiklock, 'I'm a CEO sleeping out for Vinnies, but 30 years ago I really was sleeping rough', *Sydney Morning Herald*, 17 June 2021.

102 Cameron Parsell and Beth Watts, 'Charity and justice: a reflection on new forms of homelessness provision in Australia', *European Journal of Homelessness*, 11/2 (2017): 65–76.

103 See www.ceosleepout.org.au/the-australian.

104 Aaron Patrick, 'There's nothing like a CEO humblebragger', *Australian Financial Review*, 17 June 2021. Hugh Marks is CEO of Nine Entertainment, which owns the *Australian Financial Review* and the *Sydney Morning Herald*.

105 'BankSA's chief executive, Nick Reade, joins business leaders sleeping rough in the city', *The Advertiser*, 18 June 2019, https://tinyurl.com/d98k429r.

Chapter 8 The Privilege Blender

1 Pierre Bourdieu, 'The forms of capital', in J. Richardson (ed.), *Handbook of Theory and Research for the Sociology of Education*. Westport, CT: Greenwood Press, 1986, pp. 1–29, at p. 22.

2 Bourdieu warned against a 'naively Machiavellian view' (ibid., p. 28, n.18).

3 Ibid., p. 24.

4 Brendan O'Shannassy, *Superyacht Captain*. London: Adlard Coles, 2022, p. 158. O'Shannassy is far from being a critic of these men, confessing to being in awe of them and, in an uncanny echo of *Remains of the Day*, regards himself as blessed to have worked in service to their greatness.

5 Ibid., pp. 51, 160.

6 Mairi Maclean, Charles Harvey and Gerhard Kling, 'Elite business networks and the field of power: a matter of class?', *Theory, Culture & Society*, 34/5–6 (2017): 127–51, at p. 127.

7 Ibid., p. 129.

8 Claire Wright, 'Board games: antecedents of Australia's interlocking directorates, 1910–2018', *Enterprise & Society*, 24/2 (2022): 1–28, at p. 9.

9 Maclean et al., 'Elite business networks and the field of power', p. 130.

10 Ibid., p. 131.

11 Michael Evans, 'Sydney bigwig to head Future Fund', *Sydney Morning Herald*, 13 March 2012. See also 'David Gonski', Australian Government, *Boardlinks*, https://tinyurl.com/5n8z8zkx; 'David Gonski: Australia's "chairman of everything" talks life, big business and education', *ABC News*, 25 June 2015, https://tinyurl.com/yukhcz78.

12 Michael Smith, 'Corporate power 2016: David Gonski leads list of 15 most powerful business-people in Australia', *Australian Financial Review*, 28 September 2016, https://tinyurl.com/ycxh9c37.

13 Ibid.

14 Ithai Stern and James D. Westphal, 'Stealthy footsteps to the boardroom: executives' backgrounds, sophisticated interpersonal influence behavior, and board appointments', *Administrative Science Quarterly*, 55/2 (2010): 278–319.

15 Maclean et al., 'Elite business networks and the field of power', p. 131.

16 For a discussion of these ideas, see Charles Harvey and Mairi Maclean, 'Capital theory and the dynamics of elite business networks in Britain and France', *Sociological Review*, 56/1 (2008): 105–20, at p. 110 passim.

17 Ibid., p. 113.

18 Yoni Bashan and John Stensholt, 'VIP guests make their mark at AFL grand', *The Australian*, 26 September 2022.

19 Rob Pegley, 'How Atlassian co-founder Mike Cannon-Brookes became an accidental billionaire', *CEO Magazine*, 25 November 2021; Twitter (now 'X'): https://tinyurl.com /292s7exc.

20 Joanne Gray, 'Michael Cannon-Brookes snr: how I raised a son who became Atlassian billionaire', *Australian Financial Review*, 9 June 2016.

21 Kishor Napier-Raman, 'Mansion moguls: the $523m property portfolio of Sydney's Atlassian founders', *Sydney Morning Herald*, 29 December 2022.

22 The study itself does not appear to be available but is summarised here: Zev Stub, 'Parents' income, not smarts, key to entrepreneurship – study', *Jerusalem Post*, 28 January 2021.

23 Nicole Kobie, 'The UK's startup founders are way too posh. Here's how to fix that', *Wired*, 5 August 2019.

24 'If the tech founder went to Oxbridge, worked at a tech giant like Google, or at a consultancy like McKinsey, they'll have had the opportunity to meet a business partner; if not, how do you find one?' Ibid.

25 Luna Glucksberg, *Gendering the Elites: An Ethnographic Approach to Elite Women's Lives and the Re-production of Inequality*, LSE International Inequalities Institute Working paper 7, October 2016.

26 Ibid., p. 7. Bourdieu also wrote about this theme.

27 Ashley Mears reached a similar conclusion in 'Girls as elite distinction: the appropriation of bodily capital', *Poetics*, 53 (December 2015): 22–37.

28 Miller McPherson, Lynn Smith-Lovin and James M. Cook, 'Birds of a feather: homophily in social networks', *Annual Review of Sociology*, 27/1 (2001): 415–44.

29 Lauren Rivera, 'Hiring as cultural matching: the case of elite professional service firms', *American Sociological Review*, 77/6 (2012): 999–1022.

30 Isabelle Allemand, Jean Bédard, Bénédict Brullebaut and Jérôme Deschênes, 'Role of old boys' networks and regulatory approaches in selection processes for female directors', *British Journal of Management*, 33 (2022): 784–805.

31 Ibid., p. 801.

32 Elena Greguletz, Marjo-Riitta Diehl and Karin Kreutzer, 'Why women build less effective networks than men: the role of structural exclusion and personal hesitation', *Human Relations*, 72/7 (2019): 1234–61.

33 Ibid., p. 1256.

34 Deb Verhoeven et al., 'Net effects: examining strategies for women's inclusion and influence in ASX200 company boards', *Applied Network Science*, 7 (2022).

35 Harvey and Maclean, 'Capital theory', p. 116.

36 Here we draw particularly on Allemand et al., 'Role of old boys' networks and regulatory approaches in selection processes for female directors'. However, it is a complex question. Studies indicate that, while women and people of colour are recruited into the global elite, white men dominate in the 'core' while others find themselves on the 'periphery'. Kevin Young, Seth Goldman, Brendan O'Connor and Tuugi Chuluun, 'How white is the global elite? An analysis of race, gender and network structure', *Global Networks*, 21/2 (2021): 365–92. On the other hand, evidence suggests that firms that appoint more female senior

executives become more socially responsible (as well as more risk averse and profitable). See Corinne Post, Boris Lokshin, and Christophe Boone, 'Adding women to the C-suite changes how companies think', *Harvard Business Review*, 6 April 2021.

37 Maria Adamson and Marjana Johansson, 'Writing class in and out: constructions of class in elite businesswomen's autobiographies', *Sociology*, 55/3 (2021): 487–504.

38 Two of this genre in Australia are: Gail Kelly, *Live, Lead, Learn*. Melbourne: Viking, 2017, and Colleen Callander, *Leader by Design: Be Empowered to Lead with Confidence in Business and in Life*. Elsternwick: Major Street, 2021. Elsewhere Callander writes, in a log cabin story once removed: 'My father left Italy for Australia when he was just four years old, with his parents, a couple of suitcases and little money. They went in search of a better life and my father worked very hard all his life. My mum's life was very different … She was one of 12 children and lost her own mother when she was just 21.'

39 Peter Bloom and Carl Rhodes, *CEO Society: The Corporate Takeover of Everyday Life*. London: Zed Books, 2018 (blurb).

40 Adamson and Johansson, 'Writing class in and out', p. 494.

41 Ibid., p. 495.

42 Chanel Contos, 'Do they even know they did this to us? Why I launched the school sexual assault petition', *The Guardian*, 15 March 2021.

43 In their study of how young femininities intersect with class difference in elite private girls' schools, Alexandra Allan and Claire Charles show how 'embracing diversity' has become part of the construction of the middle-class self ('Cosmo girls: configurations of class and femininity in elite educational settings', *British Journal of Sociology of Education*, 35/3 (2014): 333–52). Although elite girls' schools today deploy a 'strong rhetoric of female empowerment' and gender equality, Jane Kenway and others argue that the feminism of elite girls' schools is individualistic, 'centred on successful careers rather than social change' (Jane Kenway et al., *Class Choreographies: Elite Schools and Globalization*. London: Palgrave Macmillan, 2017, p. 240).

44 Lisa Murray, 'Chanel Contos intended to get only three schools to teach consent', *Australian Financial Review*, 25 February 2022. (A journalist who met her for lunch wrote: 'Contos' favourite dish, kingfish sashimi with yuzu dressing, is on only the dinner menu, but she convinces the waiter to make a special request.') See also Peter FitzSimons, 'What Chanel Contos uncovered about school-age sex abuse, we all need to know', *Sydney Morning Herald*, 21 August 2022.

45 'Students from Scots College, Cranbrook, Sydney Grammar, Waverley College, Kambala, Kincoppal-Rose Bay, Monte Sant Angelo and Pymble Ladies' College are repeatedly mentioned in the testimonies.' Ben Graham, 'Sexual assault: dark secret at some of Sydney's most elite schools', *News.com*, 25 February 2021.

46 Jane Kenway, 'Rolling in it: the rules of entitlement at wealthy schools for boys', *Gender and Education*, submitted 2023.

47 Caitlin Fitzsimmons, 'Parents at private boys' schools back more teaching of sexual consent', *Sydney Morning Herald*, 28 February 2021.

48 Elsewhere, Kenway acknowledges that economic capital is the 'root' form of capital ('Travelling with Bourdieu: elite schools and the cultural logics and limits of global mobility', in L. Adkins, C. Brosnan, and S. Threadgold (eds), *Bourdieusian Prospects*. London: Routledge, 2017, pp. 31–48, at p. 33).

49 Nina Funnell, Anna Hush and Sharna Bremner, *The Red Zone: An Investigation into Sexual Violence and Hazing in Australian University Residential Colleges*. End Rape on Campus Australia, 2018, p. 101. Note: one of the authors, Myra Hamilton, lived for six months at a University of Sydney residential college.

50 'Broderick report on cultural renewal at colleges received', 29 November 2017, https://tinyurl.com/52dhuhd8.

51 Nina Funnell, 'How the Broderick report on university colleges glossed over rape culture', *Sydney Morning Herald*, 19 December 2017.

52 Elizabeth Broderick & Co., *Report to St Andrew's College on Cultural Renewal*, 2017, https://tinyurl.com/2p8tacyu.

53 She became a partner in a top law firm and was appointed Sex Discrimination Commissioner by the conservative prime minister John Howard.

54 Jasmine Andersson, 'When my best friends went to private school, our relationship changed forever', *Refinery29*, 4 November 2019.

55 Ben Ellery, Katy Amos and Nicola Woolcock, 'Former pupils compile dossier of "rape culture" at Westminster School', *The Times*, 20 March 2021. See also Olivia Petter, 'Anyone who went to a private school shouldn't be shocked by the allegations – rape culture was everywhere', *The Independent*, 25 March 2021.

56 Fiona Scolding, *A Review into Harmful Sexual Behaviours at Westminster School and Recommendations for the Future*, 2022, https://tinyurl.com/hwyfrddr. It also reported that 'Female pupils from an ethnic minority spoke of being at a double disadvantage since they were treated differently, and assumptions were made about them on the basis both of their sex and ethnicity.'

57 Emily Jane Fox, '"I was ashamed": after Ford's accusation, Holton-Arms alumnae wrestle with their own truths – together', *Vanity Fair*, 26 September 2018.

58 Xanthe Scharff, 'I went to an elite prep school like Christine Blasey Ford's', *Time*, 28 September 2018.

59 Brendan Kiely, 'The girls who live in an all-boys world', *The Atlantic*, 25 September 2018.

60 Nancy Fraser and Axel Honneth, *Redistribution or Recognition? A Political-Philosophical Exchange*. London: Verso, 2003.

61 Bob Pease, *Undoing Privilege: Unearned Advantage in a Divided World*. London: Zed Books, 2022.

62 Recognising, of course, that gender at birth may not remain fixed.

63 Pease, *Undoing Privilege*, p. 23. And see Pease's helpful section on 'internalised domination', pp. 23ff.

64 Ibid., p. 23.

65 See chapter 6, note 1.

66 'Number of billionaires worldwide in 2022, by region', https://tinyurl.com/2p9tsnds; 'Distribution of billionaires around the world in 2022, by gender', https://tinyurl.com/txysfetc.

Chapter 9 Hiding and Justifying Privilege

1 The phrase is from Dylan Riley, 'Bourdieu's class theory', *Catalyst*, 1/2 (2017), p. 37.

2 Rahm Emmanuel, 'It's time to hold American elites accountable for their abuses', *The Atlantic*, 21 May 2019.

3 The words are a paraphrase of Bourdieu by Mara Loveman, 'The modern state and the primitive accumulation of symbolic power', *American Journal of Sociology*, 110/6 (2005): 1651–83, at p. 1655. Bourdieu was writing of state power.

4 Candace West and Don Zimmerman, 'Accounting for doing gender', *Gender & Society*, 23/1 (2009): 112–22, at p. 117; Pierre Bourdieu, 'Symbolic capital and social classes', *Journal of Classical Sociology*, 13/2 (2013): 292–303, at p. 300.

5 Christina Starmans, Mark Sheskin and Paul Bloom, 'Why people prefer unequal societies', *Nature Human Behaviour*, 1 (2017).

6 See Adam Jaworski and Crispin Thurlow, 'Mediatizing the "super-rich," normalizing privilege', *Social Semiotics*, 27/3 (2017): 276–87.

7 Daniel Markovits, *The Meritocracy Trap*. London: Penguin, 2019, p. x.

8 'Susan Kiefel: worthy and inspirational chief justice', *Sydney Morning Herald*, 29 November 2016.

9 For Bourdieu, the status quo is bolstered, as Wacquant put it, by the 'subtle imposition of systems of meaning that legitimize and thus solidify structures of inequality.' Loïc Wacquant, 'Pierre Bourdieu', in Rob Stones (ed.), *Key Contemporary Thinkers*. London: Macmillan, 2006, p. 264. Bourdieu was writing of the 'symbolic violence' of the state.

10 Zoe Samios, 'My job is just a job. It doesn't define who I am or what I am', *Sydney Morning Herald*, 20 August 2022, pp. 24–5.

11 Anne Hyland, 'In the driver's seat', *Good Weekend* [*Sydney Morning Herald* magazine], 5 February 2022.

12 Kadhim Shubber and Michael O'Dwyer, 'Boston Consulting in nepotism claims after London jaunt for kids of top staff', *Financial Times*, 30 July 2022.

13 Jim Waterson, 'FT's How To Spend It magazine rebrands as big spenders go out of style', *The Guardian*, 30 May 2022; Shawn McCreesh, 'Why is the *Financial Times* trying to hide the wealth porn?', *Intelligencer*, 3 June 2022. FT contributor Henry Porter views the new name as merely 'camouflage for consumer porn'.

14 Amplifying the ham-fistedness of the new branding, the editor was keen to repudiate any ambiguity in the new name: 'We make optimism, pleasure and beauty a focus in a world where such things can be hard to find.' Waterson, 'FT's How To Spend It magazine rebrands as big spenders go out of style'.

15 Erving Goffman, 'Symbols of class status', *British Journal of Sociology*, 2/4 (1951): 294–304, at p. 295.

16 See 'Australian values', https://tinyurl.com/34c6sudm.

17 See www.youtube.com/watch?v=NTNgzcUnLas.

18 David Browne, 'The real yacht rock: inside the lavish, top-secret world of private gigs', *Rolling Stone*, 2 April 2022.

19 Bourdieu's observation that economic power 'universally asserts itself as the destruction of riches, conspicuous consumption, squandering, and every form of *gratuitous* luxury' sounds dated today. Pierre Bourdieu, *Distinction: A Social Critique of the Judgement of Taste*. London: Routledge & Kegan Paul, [1979] 1984, p. 55.

20 Brendan O'Shannassy, *Superyacht Captain*. London: Adlard Coles, 2022, p. 155.

21 Candace West and Don Zimmerman, 'Doing gender', *Gender & Society*, 1/2 (1987): 125–51, at p. 135.

22 Emma Spence, 'Eye-spy wealth: cultural capital and "knowing luxury" in the identification of and engagement with the superrich', *Annals of Leisure Research*, 19/3 (2015): 1–15.

23 Jane Cadzow, 'Just a country boy', *Good Weekend* [*Sydney Morning Herald* magazine], 2 July 2022.

24 Clive Hamilton, *Provocateur: A Life of Ideas in Action*. Melbourne: Hardie Grant Books, 2022, p. 182.

25 Sam Friedman, Dave O'Brien and Ian McDonald, 'Deflecting privilege: class identity and the intergenerational self', *Sociology*, 55/4 (2021): 716–33.

26 Ibid., p. 725.

27 Ibid., pp. 717, 727, 718. While identifying class as lying in one's immediate family upbringing may be a sociologists' construct, it is nevertheless used to obscure or deny the structural advantages that one relied on to be successful.

28 Jill Sheppard and Nicholas Biddle, *Social Class in Australia: Beyond the 'Working' and 'Middle' Classes*, ANU Centre for Social Research and Methods, report no. 19, September 2015.

29 'The deal that made Australian prime minister Malcolm Turnbull his millions', news.com.au, 26 June 2018.

30 Paddy Manning, 'The lonely childhood of Prime Minister Malcolm Turnbull', *Sydney Morning Herald*, 23 October 2015.

31 Ibid.

32 A point made by Rubén Gaztambide-Fernández and Adam Howard, 'Social justice, deferred complicity and the moral plight of the wealthy', *Democracy & Education*, 21/1 (2013): 1–4, at p. 3.

33 Katy Swalwell, '"With great power comes great responsibility": privileged students' conceptions of justice-oriented citizenship', *Democracy and Education*, 21/1 (2013): 1–11.

34 Adam Howard and Jane Kenway, 'Canvassing conversations: obstinate issues in studies of elites and elite education', *International Journal of Qualitative Studies in Education*, 28/9 (2015): 1005–32, at p. 1013.

35 Gaztambide-Fernández and Howard, 'Social justice, deferred complicity and the moral plight of the wealthy'.

36 Raymond Gill, 'Mr Gantner, take a bow', *The Age*, 3 July 2007.

37 Gaztambide-Fernández and Howard, 'Social justice, deferred complicity and the moral plight of the wealthy', p. 2.

38 Rachel Sherman, '"A very expensive ordinary life": consumption, symbolic boundaries and moral legitimacy among New York elites', *Socio-Economic Review*, 18/2 (2018): 411–33, at p. 412.

39 Anu Kantola and Hanna Kuusela, 'Wealth elite moralities: wealthy entrepreneurs' moral boundaries', *Sociology*, 53/2 (2019): 368–84.

40 Ibid., p. 376.

Chapter 10 Psychic Harms

1 Andrew Sayer, *The Moral Significance of Class*. Cambridge: Cambridge University Press, 2005, p. 1.

2 A similar point was made by Bourdieu and quoted by J. Daniel Schubert, 'Suffering/symbolic violence', in Michael Grenfell (ed.), *Pierre Bourdieu: Key Concepts*. 2nd edn, Abingdon: Routledge, 2014, p. 180.

3 Eduardo Bericat, 'The sociology of emotions: four decades of progress', *Current Sociology*, 64/3 (2015): 491–513, at p. 499.

4 Ibid., p. 501.

5 Diane Reay, 'Beyond consciousness? The psychic landscape of social class', *Sociology*, 39/5 (2005): 911–28, at p. 912.

6 Ibid. Reay argues that each class is the other's 'Other'. This may be true, although being 'othered' is not such a big deal when, standing above those othering you, one has resources and access to powerful institutions.

7 The phrase is borrowed from Derald Wing Sue who uses it to describe the indignities inflicted on people of colour, women, LGBT populations or other marginalised groups. Quoted by Jenée Desmond-Harris, 'What exactly is a microaggression?', *Vox*, 16 February 2016.

8 Lesley Branagan, 'Class act: no longer failures', ABC Radio National, 2 October 2005.

9 Matthew Benns, 'Being labelled worst still causes pain', *Sydney Morning Herald*, 31 January 2010.

10 Ibid.

11 In November 2000, the *Daily Telegraph* published an apology to the students, their parents and their friends 'for all the hurt, harm and suffering it has caused them.' 'Students'

defamation action against Daily Telegraph successful', *Alternative Law Journal*, 12 (2001), https://tinyurl.com/25fp5sdk.

12 A 2015 SBS documentary, 'Struggle Street', further damaged the suburb's reputation. In more recent times, Mount Druitt has experienced a real-estate boom. See Brett Thomas, 'The notorious Sydney suburb that's gone viral thanks to its booming property market', Realestate. com.au, 21 December 2021.

13 Alicia Wood, 'Sydney's suburbs of shame named', *Daily Telegraph*, 14 June 2013.

14 Diego Zavaleta Reyles, *The Ability to Go About Without Shame: A Proposal for Internationally Comparable Indicators of Shame and Humiliation*. OPHI Working Paper no. 3, Oxford Poverty & Human Development Initiative, May 2007. Also, Annette Kämmerer, 'The scientific underpinnings and impacts of shame', *Scientific American* online, 9 August 2019. Reyles writes, 'while shame is the result of a personal judgment of failure (and thus involves the belief that one deserves to feel shame), humiliation tends to involve the belief by the target that he or she does not deserve this treatment.'

15 Mary Lamia, 'Shame: a concealed, contagious, and dangerous emotion', *Psychology Today*, 4 April 2011.

16 The figure was more or less the same irrespective of household income or type of school, although levels of shame among those who attended low-fee private schools are substantially higher (48 per cent).

17 Kämmerer, 'The scientific underpinnings and impacts of shame'.

18 Or the focus group conversations may overstate it, although a plausible hypothesis as to why this should be so is not obvious.

19 Reay, 'Beyond consciousness?', p. 913. Reay is drawing on Andrew Sayers here.

20 Stephanie Lawler, 'Disgusted subjects: the making of middle-class identities', *Sociological Review*, 53/3 (2005): 429–46, at p. 443.

21 Reay, 'Beyond consciousness?', p. 914.

22 Ibid., p. 915. Reay focuses on fear and shame among working-class children. For middle-class children, their 'resources of cultural, social and economic capital helped to alleviate feelings of risk, fear, shame and guilt' (pp. 921–2).

23 Personal communication

24 Jordan Baker, 'Two of Sydney's highest-fee private schools collected more than $15 million in JobKeeper', *Sydney Morning Herald*, 25 June 2021.

25 Lucy Carrol, 'Cranbrook unveils $125m revamp as private schools compete in building boom', *Sydney Morning Herald*, 15 October 2022.

Chapter 11 Economic and Social Harms

1 One answer is to note that there are elites other than the wealthy who enjoy exclusive privileges, although that poses the same kind of question: how are the harms arising from *inequalities* of power and influence as such to be separated from the harms due to the *privileges exercised* by the powerful and influential?

2 Sydney P. Freedberg, Spencer Woodman, Scilla Alecci and Margot Gibbs, 'Lawmakers and regulators around the world take action in the wake of Pandora Papers', International Consortium of Investigative Journalists, 6 October 2021, https://tinyurl.com/mb5tjsn4.

3 Neil Chenoweth and Liam Walsh, 'US response leaves Australia exposed', *Australian Financial Review*, 9–10 October 2021.

4 In practice, it is the super-rich like Packer who are more susceptible to mental illness and need their heads read. Psychiatrists report that, among super-rich clients, 'Money is seen as dirty and secret. ... Money is wrapped up in guilt, shame, and fear.' Clay Cockrell, 'I'm a therapist to the super-rich: they are as miserable as Succession makes out', *The Guardian*, 23 November 2021.

5 Although, for comparison, the relationship between productivity and cultural diversity in workplaces is not clear cut. Günter Stahl and Martha Maznevski, 'Unraveling the effects of cultural diversity in teams: a retrospective of research on multicultural work groups and an agenda for future research', *Journal of International Business Studies*, 52/1 (2021): 4–22.

6 Jack Barbalet, *Emotion, Social Theory, and Social Structure: A Macrosociological Approach*. Cambridge: Cambridge University Press, 2001, p. 63.

7 Jack Barbalet, 'A macro sociology of emotion: class resentment', *Sociological Theory*, 10/2 (1992): 150–63.

8 Richard Sennett and Jonathan Cobb, *The Hidden Injuries of Class*. New York: Knopf, 1972.

9 For example, Gary Gerstle, *The Rise and Fall of the Neoliberal Order: America and the World in the Free Market Era*. New York: Oxford University Press, 2022.

10 George Monbiot, 'How the neoliberals stitched up the wealth of nations for themselves', *The Guardian*, 28 August 2007.

11 Anu Kantola and Hanna Kuusela, 'Wealth elite moralities: wealthy entrepreneurs' moral boundaries', *Sociology*, 53/2 (2019): 368–84, at p. 380.

12 Ibid.

13 Ibid., p. 381.

14 Nous Group, *Schooling Challenges and Opportunities: A Report for the Review of Funding for Schooling Panel*, Melbourne Graduate School of Education, 2011, p. 30.

15 At a time of a severe teacher shortage, some offer salaries tens of thousands of dollars higher to talented teachers in the public system (Gabriella Marchant, 'Private schools are poaching teachers from the public sector with better salaries, principals say', *ABC News* online, 5 February 2023). With well-heeled parents paying closer attention to university entrance league tables, elite schools in Sydney are now competing for talented students at state primary schools by offering scholarships to nine- and ten-year-olds (Lucy Carroll, 'Private schools lock in high achievers as demand for scholarships rise', *Sydney Morning Herald*, 29 January 29, 2023).

16 Although conscious of the rank unfairness of public funding of elite schools, governments have been too afraid to end funding of high-fee private schools. Scare campaigns led by elite schools have roped in parents at low-fee private schools to oppose any radical remaking of the funding system. In effect, low- and medium-income voters are backing an education funding system that reduces the chances that their children will have a more equal opportunity in life. Once again, the privileged have mobilised the less advantaged to do their work for them.

17 Pierre Bourdieu, *Distinction: A Social Critique of the Judgement of Taste*. London: Routledge & Kegan Paul, [1979] 1984, p. 24.

18 Paul Schervish, 'Major donors, major motives: the people and purposes behind major gifts', *New Directions for Philanthropic Fundraising*, 47 (spring 2005): 59–87, at p. 70.

19 Ilan Wiesel, *Power, Glamour and Angst: Inside Australia's Elite Neighbourhoods*. Singapore: Palgrave Macmillan, 2019, p. 20.

20 Caletrío reviewed four books on the topic in 2012. Javier Caletrío, 'Global elites, privilege and mobilities in post-organized capitalism', *Theory, Culture & Society*, 29/2 (2012): 135–49.

21 Dominic-Madori Davis, 'Billionaires are chartering superyachts for months at a time to ride out the coronavirus pandemic', *Business Insider*, 28 March 2020.

22 Evan Osnos, 'The haves and the have-yachts', *New Yorker*, 25 July 2022.

Chapter 12 Contesting Privilege

1 Thomas Piketty, *Capital in the Twenty-First Century*. Cambridge, MA: Belknap Press, 2014. See especially figures 14.1 and 14.2 (pp. 499, 503). Although the falls have been less elsewhere, in the United States the top marginal income tax rate fell from 70 per cent in 1980 to 28 per cent in 1988. In Britain it fell from 90 per cent in 1970 to 40 per cent in 1990.

2 Ibid., figure 14.2, p. 503.

3 Anthony J. Cordato, 'Death and Taxes: Part 1 – What were inheritance taxes in Australia?', *Legalwise*, 6 June 2022, https://tinyurl.com/m2fmc784.

4 Anthony Atkinson, *Inequality: What Can Be Done?* Cambridge, MA: Harvard University Press, 2015. With thanks to Peter Saunders for suggesting the Atkinson model to us.

5 OECD, *Inheritance Taxation in OECD Countries*. Paris: OECD, 2021, 'Summary and recommendations', https://tinyurl.com/yppj448r.

6 Many studies show this to be the case for students of law and medicine.

7 Challenge panels for gender diversity in universities have been proposed by Myra Hamilton, Alison Williams and Marian Baird, *Gender Equity and Inclusion by Design: A Toolkit for the Australian University Sector*. Canberra: Universities Australia Women, 2022, p. 23.

8 Nicola Ingram and Kim Allen, '"Talent-spotting" or "social magic"? Inequality, cultural sorting and constructions of the ideal graduate in elite professions', *Sociological Review*, 67/3 (2019).

9 See www.ipso.co.uk/editors-code-of-practice/.

Appendix 2

1 Shamus Khan and Colin Jerolmack, 'Saying meritocracy and doing privilege', *Sociological Quarterly*, 54 (2013): 9–19, at p. 11.

Appendix 3

1 Thomas Piketty, *Capital in the Twenty-First Century*. Cambridge, MA: Belknap Press, 2014.

2 Ibid., p. 361.

3 Ibid., pp. 333, 305.

4 Robert Blanton and Dursun Peksen, 'Economic liberalisation, market institutions and labour rights', *European Journal of Political Research*, 55/3 (2016): 474–91.

5 Piketty, *Capital*, pp. 308, 315; see also pp. 302, 290.

6 Ibid., pp. 334, 416.

7 Ibid., pp. 333–5.

8 Ibid., p. 351.

9 Ibid., p. 355. In Australia, state and federal taxes on inheritances, which could reduce large bequests by half, were abolished in the early 1980s. See Anthony J. Cordato, 'Death and Taxes: Part 1 – What were inheritance taxes in Australia?', *Legalwise*, 6 June 2022.

10 Piketty, *Capital*, p. 402.

11 Sandra Black, Paul Devereux, Petter Lundborg and Kaveh Majlesi, 'Poor little rich kids? The role of nature versus nurture in wealth and other economic outcomes and behaviours', *Review of Economic Studies*, 87/4 (2020): 1683–725.

12 Productivity Commission, *Wealth Transfers and their Economic Effects*, Research paper, Australian Government, November 2021, pp. 57–60. In the media release announcing the report, one of the authors was quoted. 'About one third of this observed persistence is due to inherited wealth. The rest comes from all the other things parents give to their children – education, networks, values and other opportunities,' Commissioner Gropp said.

13 Black et al., 'Poor little rich kids?', p. 1683. They also find that genetics matter little for wealth transfer. 'We conclude that biology is important for skill transfers but less important for wealth, as dynasties can transfer wealth across generations regardless of their skills and abilities' (p. 1714).

Index